"With *Affect Regulation Theory*, Daniel Hill makes an invaluable contribution to the growing field of psychotherapy that is reflective of a psychobiological perspective. The book is well-written, well-researched, and comprehensive. For any therapist seeking to broaden his or her theoretical knowledge base, with the ultimate goal of incorporating that information into clinical practice, I recommend reading this book first and foremost." — **Stan Tatkin, PsyD, MFT,** clinician, researcher, teacher, and developer of A Psychobiological Approach To Couples Therapy® (PACT)

"Affect regulation theory is the surprising meeting ground of neurobiology, developmental psychology, and psychoanalysis. In this important book, Daniel Hill captures its relevance to each of these realms. His book not only enhances our understanding of the physiological basis of emotions but also illuminates how emotional trauma in childhood emerges from prolonged states of dysregulation. Wonderfully comprehensive and engagingly written, this book will be a boon to students. But it will also captivate those of us whose education preceded these exciting cross-disciplinary developments." **—Robert B. Karen, PhD,** author of *Becoming Attached: First Relationships and How They Shape Our Capacity to Love* and *The Forgiving Self: The Road from Resentment to Connection*

"Daniel Hill's *Affect Regulation Theory* is a superb synthesis of cutting-edge developments in attachment theory and research, mother-infant research, research on mentalization, affect regulation theory, neurobiology, and psychoanalytic theory. Clinically astute and gracefully written, it will be of great interest to clinicians coming from a wide range of theoretical orientations." **—Jeremy D. Safran, PhD,** Chair & Professor of Psychology, The New School for Social Research, author of *Negotiating the Therapeutic Alliance: A Relational Treatment Guide* and *Psychoanalysis and Psychoanalytic Therapies*

The Norton Series on Interpersonal Neurobiology
Louis Cozolino, PhD, Series Editor
Allan N. Schore, PhD, Series Editor, 2007–2014
Daniel J. Siegel, MD, Founding Editor

The field of mental health is in a tremendously exciting period of growth and conceptual reorganization. Independent findings from a variety of scientific endeavors are converging in an interdisciplinary view of the mind and mental well-being. An interpersonal neurobiology of human development enables us to understand that the structure and function of the mind and brain are shaped by experiences, especially those involving emotional relationships.

The Norton Series on Interpersonal Neurobiology provides cutting-edge, multidisciplinary views that further our understanding of the complex neurobiology of the human mind. By drawing on a wide range of traditionally independent fields of research—such as neurobiology, genetics, memory, attachment, complex systems, anthropology, and evolutionary psychology—these texts offer mental health professionals a review and synthesis of scientific findings often inaccessible to clinicians. The books advance our understanding of human experience by finding the unity of knowledge, or consilience, that emerges with the translation of findings from numerous domains of study into a common language and conceptual framework. The series integrates the best of modern science with the healing art of psychotherapy.

A Norton Professional Book

Affect Regulation Theory

A CLINICAL MODEL

Daniel Hill

Foreword by
Allan N. Schore

W. W. NORTON & COMPANY
New York • London

Note to Readers: Standards of clinical practice and protocol change over time, and no technique or recommendation is guaranteed to be safe or effective in all circumstances. This volume is intended as a general information resource for professionals practicing in the field of psychotherapy and mental health; it is not a substitute for appropriate training, peer review, and/or clinical supervision. Neither the publisher nor the author(s) can guarantee the complete accuracy, efficacy, or appropriateness of any particular recommendation in every respect.

For information about permission to reproduce selections from this book, write to Permissions, W. W. Norton & Company, Inc., 500 Fifth Avenue, New York, NY 10110

For information about special discounts for bulk purchases, please contact W. W. Norton Special Sales at specialsales@wwnorton.com or 800-233-4830

Manufacturing by LSC Communications Harrisonburg
Production manager: Christine Critelli

Library of Congress Cataloging-in-Publication Data

Hill, Daniel (Psychologist)
Affect regulation theory : a clinical model / Daniel Hill ; foreword by Allan N. Schore. — First edition.
pages cm. — (The Norton series on interpersonal neurobiology)
Includes bibliographical references and index.
ISBN 978-0-393-70726-7 (hardcover : alk. paper)
1. Affect (Psychology) 2. Affective disorders. 3. Affective neuroscience.
I. Title.
BF175.5.A35.H55 2015
152.4—dc23
2015017865

ISBN: 978-0-393-70726-7

W. W. Norton & Company, Inc.,
500 Fifth Avenue, New York, N.Y. 10110
www.wwnorton.com

W. W. Norton & Company Ltd.
15 Carlisle Street, London W1D 3BS

3 4 5 6 7 8 9 0

To Thing 1 and Thing 2

and to Nina . . . a noue'

Contents

Preface and Acknowledgments   ix

Foreword by Allan N. Schore   xiii

INTRODUCTION Affect and Its Regulation   1

PART I   **Theory of Bodymind:** Regulated-Integrated
Versus Dysregulated-Dissociated   13

CHAPTER 1 Affect Regulation and the Attachment
Relationship   15

CHAPTER 2 Self-States: Regulated-Integrated Versus Dysregulated-
Dissociated   27

CHAPTER 3 The Neurobiology of the Primary Affect-Regulating
System   49

CHAPTER 4 The Right Brain, Implicit Processes, and the
Implicit Self   68

PART II   **Theory of Development:** Secure Attachment
and the Development of Affect Regulation   83

CHAPTER 5 Classical Attachment Theory   85

CHAPTER 6 Mentalization: The Secondary Affect-Regulating
System   98

CHAPTER 7 Modern Attachment Theory: The Development of the
Primary Affect-Regulating System   112

PART III **Theory of Pathogenesis:** Relational Traumas
and Their Sequelae   133

CHAPTER 8 Relational Traumas: Developmental Origins of
Disordered Affect Regulation   135

CHAPTER 9 Chronic Dissociation: A Sequela of Relational
Trauma   154

CHAPTER 10 Personality Disorders: A Second Sequela
of Relational Trauma   168

CHAPTER 11 Pervasive Dissociated Shame: A Third Sequela
of Relational Trauma   183

PART IV **Theory of Therapeutic Actions:** Therapeutic
Processes and the Emergence of the Self   193

CHAPTER 12 Therapeutic Aims: Restoration of Self-
Development   195

CHAPTER 13 Therapeutic Actions: Explicit and Implicit   206

CHAPTER 14 Interactive Regulation and Vitalizing Attunement   219

Bibliography   237

Index   257

Preface and Acknowledgments

AFFECT REGULATION THEORY is a dream fulfilled for me professionally and personally. During my entire career I have been distressed by the fragmentation of the field. I have searched for a model that integrates psychoanalysis and its schools of thought with other approaches.

Affect regulation theory, as I'm using the term, derives from Allan Schore's work and my integration of it with mentalization theory developed by Peter Fonagy and his collaborators. It is an integration of attachment theory, developmental affective neurobiology, developmental social-cognitive neurobiology, emotional studies, mother-infant studies, and developmental psychoanalysis. It is thus a developmentally based approach to psychobiology in the tradition of Piaget and Freud (my early professional enthusiasms) whose work is based in an understanding of how the mind emerges from the body into a bodymind. John M. Bowlby and Allan N. Schore are of this tradition—integrating psychology and biology.

Affect regulation theory is also a dream fulfilled for my work with patients. Psychotherapy has suffered from being either comprehensive and inefficient (too inefficient for our times), or efficient but failing to appreciate and treat problems as they extend throughout the bodymind and into the whole person. It has also suffered from being overly focused on either the mind or the body, with resulting application of top-down or bottom-up approaches. Affect regulation theory and the therapeutic techniques that are being developed from it bring efficiency and the body to psychodynamic psychotherapies. More than ever, I feel that I am working with the core of my patients and from the core of myself.

I now understand patients with developmental disorders to be suffering from the sequelae of relational trauma. Along with the focus on affect, nothing has changed the way I work more than the understanding of the effects of early attachment trauma on self experience, relational life, and vulnerability to psychiatric disorders. It puts a malformed nervous system, shame and dissociation at the center of clinical work.

This book is my attempt to make affect regulation theory more accessible to practitioners. Learning enough of the disciplines that provide the theoretical underpinning for affect regulation theory is a daunting task. Learning the language and concepts of a new, paradigm-shifting theory is only slightly less daunting. I have provided the necessary understanding of affective neurobiology and classical and modern attachment theories. The book is organized around Allan Schore's regulation theory, and my contributions are additions to it.

There are many friends, colleagues, and students to whom I am indebted. Allan Schore has been a generous mentor, guiding my reading and discussing his theory. Along the way he has become a valued colleague, friend, and occasional partner in crime. I am extremely grateful to the staff at Norton. Deborah Malmud, Andrea Costella Dawson, Kevin Olsen, Kathryn Moyer, Trish Watson, and Ben Yarling were attentive, helpful, and, above all, patient throughout the process.

The book was written with my study groups in mind. I spoke to them as my study of affect regulation therapy deepened, and they provided a secure exploratory haven for my developing understandings and ideas. I shared early drafts of the book with them, and their reactions have been invaluable. They are Beverly Brisk, Amy Gladstone, Ann Rasmussen, Debby Russ, Kitty Cullina-Bessey, Janice Rosenman, Susan Markowitz, and Susan Parente; Clair Goldberg, Deborah Kaplan, Harriet Power, Hea-Kyung Kwon, Naomi Fox, Rosemarie Ciccarello, Sarah Karl, and Susan Levine; and Alice Rosenman, Carol Antler, Claire Haimon, Emily Nash, Kenneth Greenwald, Maria Rosen, and Satya Lauren. Friends and colleagues Barbara Gerson, Laura Kogel, Marty Rock, Peter Deri, Sharon Kozberg, and Terry Marks-Tarlow offered important feedback on early chapters, and Bob Karen offered invaluable help with my writing style.

Beyond everything, I am grateful to my partner, Nina, my other half, without whom this book would not be what it is. Imagine the ideal editor, attuned emotionally and intellectually, reading closely and rereading every chapter, whom you feel loved by and whom you love. Imagine that.

Foreword

by Allan N. Schore

IN THE FOLLOWING chapters, Daniel Hill clearly articulates the specific, dual purposes of this book: to formulate a coherent clinical model of affect regulation theory and to offer numerous concrete clinical examples of affect regulation therapy. In light of the fact that the theory has substantially developed over the last three decades, this is no easy task. It involves synthesizing the essential principles of the theory and translating these principles into not only an overarching clinical model but also one that describes the subtleties and uniqueness of any individual psychotherapy. This ambitious goal calls for the efforts of an author who is simultaneously a writer, able to bridge and integrate a number of scientific literatures, and a master clinician familiar with the complexities of the clinical encounter. Let me say up front that this remarkable book succeeds on both counts, and then goes even further. Much more than presenting a concise, coherent formulation of regulation theory, it expands the affect regulation model with a significant number of creative clinical contributions. But before I speak directly about Hill's exposition and expansion of regulation theory, let me give some background to what he is building upon.

The central tenets of affect regulation theory were set out in 1994, in my first book, *Affect Regulation and the Origin of the Self: The*

Neurobiology of Emotional Development. The volume offered for the first time an overarching psychoneurobiological model of early emotional development. In parallel, various clinical literatures including clinical psychology, psychiatry, and psychoanalysis were presented, interwoven with extant research data from neuroscience and infant studies. The early chapters integrated psychology and biology in order to model normal development. The latter chapters offered clinically relevant heuristic models of the interpersonal neurobiological origins of a spectrum of psychopathologies, as well as a model of psychotherapeutic change that focused on emotion, especially affective processes that operate beneath levels of conscious awareness. The 37 chapters described developmental changes in not only emerging psychological function but also biological structure, addressing both critical early periods and later psychotherapeutic contexts.

This first articulation of regulation theory thus presented an interdisciplinary theoretical perspective that attempted to integrate both the scientific and the clinical domains. That said, the book on the early beginnings of the human experience was written as a scientific treatise, covering a wide range of disciplines, including amongst others developmental neuroscience, developmental psychology, developmental biology, and developmental neurochemistry. At the time, the volume offered challenges to both clinicians unfamiliar with the science and researchers unfamiliar with the complexities of psychotherapy. No easy read. Indeed, some readers suggested that the work was groundbreaking but "dense" (I can't imagine how they came to that!).

Over the last three decades, three ensuing Norton volumes, *Affect Regulation and Disorders of the Self, Affect Regulation and the Repair of the Self,* and most recently *The Science of the Art of Psychotherapy,* as well as every article and chapter that followed them, represent the continual growth of the original theory. At the most basic level, regulation theory's contributions to the field of interpersonal neurobiology attempt to explain precisely how early emotional experiences indelibly influence later experience (via the social maturation of the early developing right brain), and to understand the underlying mechanisms by which brains align their neural activities in social interactions (via right brain-to-right brain communications).

In *The Science of the Art of Psychotherapy* I assert that the term regulation theory is used in order to explicitly denote that what I am offering is a theory, a systematic exposition of the general principles of a science. Specifically, it is a formulation of an explanatory conception of the processes of development, which I have asserted is one of the fundamental objectives of science. Over the course of the last three decades, what were originally presented as theoretical hypotheses have now been validated by numerous methodologies across a number of research and clinical disciplines (see the above volumes).

As of this writing, regulation theory has been cited more than 12-13,000 times in Google Scholar. A large number of researchers in various fields are now not only validating the principles of the theory but also using it to generate heuristic hypotheses. Over the course of what has been called "the emotional revolution" in the mental health field many psychotherapists are adopting the theory as a basis for treating a number of psychiatric disorders, and a multitude of clinical writers have translated the model into novel "evidence-based" formulations of psychotherapeutic treatment grounded in the interpersonal neurobiology of regulation theory. It is a great personal pleasure to find, on a daily basis, new clinical books, articles, and chapters that integrate and build upon the principles of regulation theory. Indeed, it has been particularly gratifying to see how so many authors in the *Norton Series on Interpersonal Neurobiology* have incorporated the theory into a deeper explication of a variety of specific clinical problems and thereby advanced the field's understanding of the basic processes that lie at the core of a number of psychological phenomena and psychiatric disorders.

That said, this volume represents the first attempt to offer a general overview of the basic foundational tenets of the theory, especially as applied to the implicit nonconscious change processes that lie at the core of the psychotherapeutic relationship. Over the years, I've been asked many times for a comprehensive and clinically explicit expression of how, specifically, nonconscious right brain processes are expressed in therapy. This book does exactly that. In addition to offering a concise synopsis of the essential clinically relevant basic principles of the theory, Hill, a gifted clinician and teacher, also characterizes in some detail the rapid, nonconscious hidden mechanisms that lie beneath the words. Along the way he repeatedly demonstrates pragmatic applications of the theory by providing the reader with numerous evocative clinical vignettes, which directly reflect how right brain implicit nonverbal processes become explicit within the therapeutic relationship. These case examples demonstrate the way he works with affect on a moment-to-moment basis, which is also the way I work in real time with a patient.

It is no coincidence that our clinical approaches are so similar. Hill has steeped himself in regulation theory for many years. When we first met in the early 2000's he informed me of his intention of delivering affect regulation to New York City, no small task. Beginning in 2006 he and I co-produced a series of affect regulation conferences in Manhattan, for which we invited a large number of leaders in neuroscience, psychotherapy, psychoanalysis, early development, and psychiatry to discuss how the ongoing explosion of scientific knowledge was changing the practice of psychotherapy. Many of the presenters were already, or soon became, Norton authors. These affect regulation conferences, which are ongoing, continue to be intellectually stimulating and creative contexts for both audiences and presenters. Such occasions have also provided numerous opportunities for discussion between Hill and I about the evolution of regulation theory. Indeed, they are a central element in the present book, in which he uses a fresh eye to offer a panoramic view of the affect regulation model. I now turn my attention to what is in store for the reader over the following chapters.

Consonant with the utilization of regulation theory as an overarching model of development, psychopathogenesis, and treatment of the right brain implicit subjective self, the book is divided into four sections: Theory of Bodymind, Theory of Development, Theory of Pathogenesis, and Theory of Therapeutic Action. In each, Hill deftly translates theory into practical applications, especially in regard to a host of complex yet subtle, affectively driven therapeutic phenomena well-known to clinicians. Throughout, he offers numerous examples of the essential role of background unconscious process in both early right brain social-emotional development and later right brain therapeutic social-emotional development. There are smooth, almost effortless transitions, not only between biology and psychology, but also between the conscious and unconscious realms of psychotherapy.

The first two parts (about two-thirds of the volume) represent at the same time a wide-angle lens of overview and a zoomed lens of in-depth detail on the affect regulation model of emotion and development. These chapters offer not only succinct definitions of the primary theoretical constructs of the theory but also an integration of these constructs into the basic organizing principles of the theory. Those who have read any of my writings will be familiar with this material. The basic tenets are presented with a clarity that is reflective of the precision of the author's scientific and clinical mind. The book is extremely well-written, with an intrinsic fluidity, and thus represents a surprisingly easy read of very complex material.

More specifically, the first section, Part I, "Theory of Bodymind," contains four chapters describing the psychology and neurobiology of affect and affect regulation, including discussions of functional self-states and structural right brain implicit processes. A central construct of regulation theory, the self-state, is defined as an assemblage of the affect-regulating system and a set of discrete coordinated cognitive, attentional, perceptual, representational, memory, and reflective systems. In a succinct statement of the centrality of this construct, Hill observes that the "unitary self" is in actuality fundamentally composed of a multiplicity of self-states. Each of these discrete self-states represents a different mode of feeling, thinking, and acting, and thereby different ways of being in different relational contexts. In this manner, each self-state is its own personality system, what Hill calls a "context-dependent assemblage of the affective and cognitive processes that assemble into versions of us." He then extensively discusses the clinically important distinction between regulated-integrated and dysregulated-dissociated self-states, a central theme in the later chapters on therapeutic actions.

In the three chapters of Part II, "Theory of Development," the author outlines the different perspectives of modern attachment theory and its focus on the primary affect regulating system and classical attachment theory and its emphasis on mentalization. Indeed, he offers one of the best clinical explications of attachment theory in terms of therapeutic psychodynamics that I've seen. Even more, utilizing a developmental and interpersonal neurobiological perspective he bridges these two theories and begins to hint at what this will look like in the type of clinical work the patient is engaged in at different stages of the therapy. At later points in the book he also differentiates the perspectives of these theories as they relate to both nonverbal primary (affective-relational) and verbal secondary (insight) mechanisms of therapeutic actions. Throughout, Hill offers numerous developmental and clinical examples of subtle, covert, yet essential nonverbal right brain-to-right brain communications of attachment dynamic in the therapeutic alliance.

With this foundation firmly laid, Hill's last eight chapters reflect more than an overview of the theory. They offer a number of very important and unique contributions that represent significant expansions of the theory, all with very specific clinical implications. Indeed, the latter chapters represent a crescendo of the book, albeit written in a low-key manner, and of its author's creativity. In the following I offer the reader some hints and glimpses of surprising things to come. I direct attention to these chapters because of their importance and clinical relevance as novel contributions to regulation theory.

In Part III, "Theory of Pathogenesis," Hill elaborates another essential construct of regulation theory, relational trauma. In the lead chapter of that section he presents a clear and accurate explication of not only psychobiological and neurobiological formulations of disorganized relational trauma but also new ideas on preoccupied and avoidant relational trauma. This leads to another chapter on chronic dissociation wherein, after discussing the familiar conception of severe dissociation and disorganized attachment associated with the extreme levels of arousal of overt early abuse and neglect, Hill suggests that moderate forms of dissociation originate in the organized structured insecure attachment patterns. He further argues that insecure preoccupied trauma results in proneness to moderate hyperaroused dissociation, while insecure avoidant trauma (what I would call "benign neglect") results in proneness to moderate hypoaroused dissociation.

Furthermore, Hill puts forth clinical evidence demonstrating that moderate dissociation is distinguished by mid-level intensities of hypo- or hyperarousal and a concomitant moderate degree of dysfunctionality. There is some modulation of the intensity of affect but not enough to stay regulated. When there is a breakdown in subjectivity it is partial, without complete collapse. Whereas severe detachment fully disrupts the sense of going-on-being, moderate detachment generates experiences of "sort-of-going-on-being." He concludes that moderate dissociation, although more common and critically important in clinical work, has been relatively overlooked. This "subclinical" or "subsyndromal" dissociation is debilitating but not necessarily disabling, and often passes unobserved.

In the ensuing chapter, Hill proposes that internal working models are manifest in the clinical presentations of various adult personality disorders. Specifically, a preoccupied bias toward hyperarousal supports disorders of underregulation that are symptomatically expressed as agitated depression, hypomania, overt anxiety, and chronic hyperaroused dissociation. On the other hand, an avoidant bias towards hypoarousal supports disorders of overregulation manifesting as overt depression, covert/underlying anxiety, and chronic hypoaroused dissociation. In a parallel neurobiological model, he suggests that these autonomic biases are associated with different patterns of hemispheric dominance, and therefore central to different personality organizations. In contrast to preoccupied personalities who, under relational stress, show enhanced fast, holistic processing of the right brain and a diminution of analytic processes, left brain-dominant avoidant personalities, typically maladapted in understanding and navigating the socioemotional environment, are hindered by an underdeveloped right brain and overreliance on the slow linear processing of the left brain.

Building upon this Hill then examines how the sympathetic bias of preoccupied attachment supports a disinhibited, extroverted narcissism, whereas the parasympathetic bias of avoidant attachment supports an inhibited, introverted type. Expanding regulation theory he proposes that the hyperaroused narcissistic personality disorder specifically derives from preoccupied attachment. This type has been variously termed grandiose, overt, fragmented, excited, and inflated narcissism, all reflecting the core state of hyperarousal. Hill prefers the terms "preoccupied" or "hyperaroused narcissism." The second, often overlooked type of narcissistic personality disorder derives from avoidant attachment. Variously called deflated, covert, and depressed narcissism, it is a parasympathetic-dominant, inhibited form that he refers to as "avoidant" or "hypoaroused narcissism." After discussing these narcissistic personality organizations based on organized insecure attachment histories, Hill ends the chapter with a discussion of borderline personality disorder and its relationship to disorganized internal working models of attachment.

In the final chapter of this section, Hill expands another central tenet of regulation theory, shame, specifically offering novel ideas on manifestations of pervasive dissociated shame in the patient's character structure, and the central role of dissociated shame (and dissociated pride) in the treatment of disordered affect regulation. My own earliest writings on shame appeared in 1991, and I strongly agree with Hill's assertion that even now the psychological and physiological differences between shame and guilt are still not appreciated by most clinicians, nor is the adaptive role of moderate regulated shame. Hill further argues that attention must also be paid to pride's place in our emotional economy. Importantly, he observes, utilizing modern attachment theory, that the shame born of early relational trauma is dissociated during the traumatic interaction, and that it remains dissociated when reactivated, thereby making it an elusive therapeutic target. Dissociated shame and dissociated pride thus permeate insecure personalities, yet despite the ubiquity of these covert clinical phenomena they are often hidden to those who suffer from and those who treat the distress associated with characterological dysregulations of shame and pride.

In the final section of the volume, Part IV, "Theory of Therapeutic Actions," Hill articulates the critical differences between the two major classes of change mechanism in psychotherapy. Citing the clinical literature, he differentiates "second-order" therapeutic changes in self-reflective capacity (i.e., insight, self-awareness, and self-knowledge) from "first-order" changes in the very tendencies, states, and affects that one is reflecting on. This is expressed in the distinction between one's implicit and "automatic" expectation (as well as accompanying feelings) of rejection and, on the other hand, one's reflection on that implicit and "automatic" expectation. I agree with his assertion that initial changes in primary affect regulation in the midst of a live affective experience must occur for there to later be effective secondary, left-brain mentalizing.

With regard to implicit primary affect regulation, over the years much of my own work in neuropsychoanalysis has explored structure-function relationships of the human unconscious system, which is located in the right brain. My intent has been to shine a scientific and clinical searchlight on the deepest strata of the human mind, what I call "the deep unconscious" that underlies the "hidden realm of therapy." Towards that end I have focused on the early development of this system, as well as its later appearance in certain affective moments of treatment when this background essential system comes into the foreground. Thus the bulk of my studies has attended to the role of this right brain unconscious system in the rapid implicit dynamics of affectively charged therapeutic moments, much more so than on the role of explicit insight-oriented verbal narratives over a different time frame, the longer course of the treatment. This psychobiological unconscious system responds to both threat and interpersonal novelty with changes in attention and, ultimately, energetic-arousal.

In this book Hill ties together implicit and explicit processes in both early and late stages of the treatment. Furthermore, he asserts, utilizing an interpersonal neurobiological perspective, that left brain, secondary processing (linear, conscious, verbal functions) are dominant during moderate levels of arousal. This left hemispheric mode is used for processing known and familiar information and navigating predictable events. In contrast, right brain holistic, nonconscious, nonverbal primary processing is dominant at intense heightened or reduced levels of arousal, and activated when processing novel events and stressful emotional information. Furthermore, the neuropsychodynamics of the "emotional," "social" right brain are overtly expressed in transference and countertransference expressions in the therapeutic alliance. Integrating extant formulations of regulation theory and astute clinical observations, Hill proposes that an avoidant transference involves moving away from attachment to the therapist and being in an emotionally distanced, hypoaroused-dissociated state of bodymind. On the other hand, a preoccupied transference manifests as a hyperaroused-dissociated state, ambivalently preoccupied, with subjective movement towards an emotional attachment to the therapist.

At the end and, indeed, climax of the book, Hill addresses an overarching theme of regulation theory's models of therapeutic action, and thus of the relationship between interactive regulation, vitalizing attunement, and the emergence of self. In line with the dual change mechanisms described above, he confidently asserts that therapeutic change can occur dramatically, as a result of powerful therapeutic events, or quietly and incrementally, as a result of ongoing, run-of-the-mill therapeutic actions. As an example of the former he offers a dynamic interpersonal neurobiological model of clinical enactments, a central theme of the theory that integrates modern attachment theory, developmental neuroscience, and updated relational models of psychotherapy. Enactments, he notes, have come to be understood as a playing out of dissociated parts of the patient and therapist. Such overt, dyadic expressions of transference-countertransference dynamics are co-created by events that resonate with some unresolved aspect of the past of each member of the therapeutic alliance. And so Hill asks the reader to ponder the essential questions: "What is at stake in an enactment? Is the therapist able to tolerate the expressed affect and regulate the patient? What are the effects of such transactions on the therapeutic relationship? What are the effects of such experiences on the internal working model and on the primary affect-regulating system at its core?"

To date, regulation theory has mostly focused on clinical re-enactments of attachment trauma in insecure disorganized attachments. But here Hill shines a spotlight on the clinical terrain of working with re-enactments of insecure organized histories of vacillating states of dysregulated hyperarousal and hypoarousal. Harkening back to the earlier chapters, he suggests in this final section that it is crucial to keep in mind that intersubjectively shared states of hyperaroused dissociation represent reenactments of preoccupied insecure attachment, while states of hypoaroused dissociation are reenactments of avoidant developmental trauma. In a hyperaroused enactment, the dyad must downregulate; in a hypoaroused enactment (what he calls a deenactment), the emotional energy of life must be infused into the intersubjective field. In an extremely creative clinical contribution, Hill offers a case example of a hyperaroused enactment and describes three different therapeutic approaches, each associated with a different therapeutic outcome: one de-evolving into an iatrogenic pathological enactment, another working at the level of second-order therapeutic change, and one an interactive regulatory approach that effects first-order change in the affect regulating system.

This book makes a perfect bookshelf companion for my four volumes. I look forward to not only its pragmatic impact on current clinical practice but also its stimulation of other clinicians (and researchers) to creatively apply regulation theory to a deeper understanding and more effective treatment of the variety of clinical problems that are encountered and addressed in infant, child, adolescent, and adult psychotherapy. I'm sure that your reading the following pages will be accompanied by evocative images of a number of your patients.

As I hand you off to Daniel Hill, get ready for a rich and stimulating amalgam of the science of the art of psychotherapy. What lies ahead is illuminating clinical material and neuroscience that will enhance our understanding and treatment of even our most difficult cases. So pull up an easy chair and enjoy.

AFFECT REGULATION
THEORY

Affect and Its Regulation

AFFECT IS AT the core of our being, a measure of our heart. It excites and deflates us, connects and distances our relations with others. It organizes us and undoes us.

When affect is regulated, we are at our most adaptive, our most self-possessed, our most engaged, our best. We are alert and all our psychological resources are available. Relevant memories are accessible to guide our actions based on prior experience. Our attention goes where it needs to go, and, when the situation calls for it, we can concentrate it where we wish. Our ability to reflect on our mental life is available as needed. We have a background sense of self-mastery. Our self-experience is infused with feelings of presence, agency, authenticity, and well-being. We are available for interpersonal connection, for play and exploration. We feel good.

Regulated affect optimizes flexibility and the capacity for adaptive responses to the changing demands of the environment and the needs of the self. When regulated, we are in a homeostatic state, functioning optimally. Regulated affect states occur when we feel safe.

In a dysregulated state, we do not feel safe. Our sense of agency, authenticity, and well-being is diminished, as is our availability for intersubjective relating. We are detached, in varying degrees, from self-experience and from the experiencing of others. Our sense of reality is "off." Our reflective capacity is diminished or inaccessible. Perceptions are narrowly filtered. Representational accuracy is compromised, replaced by scripted versions of self and others. Response flexibility is replaced by automatisms. Spontaneity is replaced by reactivity.

We can see from this that the regulation of the organism is fundamental to survival.[1] Remaining regulated in the midst of strong affect and efficient return from a dysregulated to a homeostatic state are crucial for adaptive functioning. Affect tolerance and resiliency are the hallmarks of an adaptive emotional system.

Regulation theory (Schore 1994, 2003a, 2003b, 2012) posits that the regulation of affect is foundational for optimal functioning. Mental states are organized by and around affect. Regulatory deficits are fundamental to all developmental psychological disorders, and the mechanisms of affect regulation are primary targets for therapeutic action.

A visual representation depicting zones of regulation and dysregulation helps us to understand the regulation of affect (see Figure I.1). The self thrives in and attempts to maintain homeostasis. The illustration represents the range of arousal levels—hyperaroused and hypoaroused—that we can tolerate without becoming dysregulated and losing functionality. The "windows of tolerance" (Ogden, P. & Minton, K., 2000; Siegel, 1999; Schore, 2012) represent the boundaries of affect tolerance. Affect regulation therapy aims to extend the tolerance for affect by working at its edges.

Adaptive functioning is affect state dependent. Tolerance for affect is crucial and is linked to the capacity to modulate the intensity of

---

1 Allan Schore begins *Affect Regulation and the Origin of the Self* (1994), his seminal work on regulation theory, with the statement that "there is nothing more basic to survival than the regulation of the organism" and asserts that there is agreement about this across all disciplines studying living systems, from microbiology to sociology.

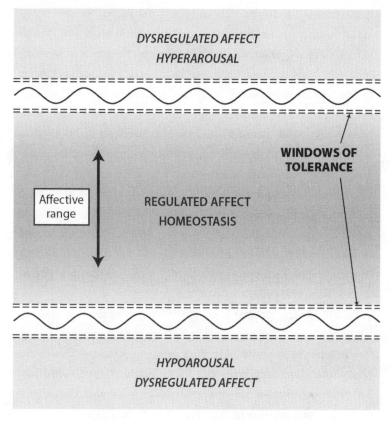

Figure 1–1. Affect regulation-dysregulation
Adapted from Ogden & Minton, 2000.

affect. We can enter states of high and low arousal without becoming dysregulated. We can be angry (hyperarousal), for example, without losing our temper. We can experience sadness (hypoarousal) without becoming depressed. However, if our affect state exceeds our tolerance for hyper- or hypoarousal, our adaptive capacities are diminished. Thinking, for example, may become scrambled in dysregulated states of hyperarousal, sluggish in dysregulated states of hypoarousal.

Affective resilience is another key dimension of regulatory capacity.

Resilience is defined as the capacity for individuals to recover functioning after exposure to stress-induced dysregulation (Cicchetti, 2010).[2] Becoming dysregulated is part of everyday life. The capacity to return efficiently to a regulated state maximizes adaptive functioning. Parents must be able to maintain regulated states to regulate their infants competently and maximize their time spent in growth-facilitating states. The same is true for psychotherapists and their patients.

Deficiencies in affect tolerance, modulation, and resilience manifest as psychiatric symptomatology, such as anxiety states or depressive states. Borderline personality disorder is marked by chaotic vacillations from one affective extreme to the other and by remaining in dysregulated affect states for prolonged periods. Deficiencies in regulation underlying narcissistic personality disorders are less obvious, but as we will see, they too suffer from frequent and prolonged dysregulation.

Capacities for affect regulation tend to be passed down from caretaker to infant in attachment relationships. The caretaker's regulatory deficits are internalized by their infants. Like the mother-infant relationship,[3] the therapeutic relationship requires a stable, regulating, and vitalizing emotional connection in order to establish the psychological and neurobiological conditions for development. As with the mother-infant relationship, the affect-regulating experiences of psychotherapy are imprinted onto the neurobiological structures responsible for the regulation of our patients.

---

2 Cicchetti (2010) also discusses other factors contributing to resiliency, such as culture, genetics, and gene-environment interaction.

3 By *mother* I mean the mothering one, nurturing one, or loving one. Throughout the book I use the terms *mother, caretaker, parent,* and *attachment figure* interchangeably to refer to the person who regulates the infant's affect.

Affect

What is affect? A key distinction is between primary and categorical affect (aka discrete affect). *Primary affect* is the somatic representation of the state of the organism—a sensorimotor, physiological representation that generates a felt sense. It has two dimensions: level of arousal and hedonic tone. These are represented as negative or positive states of hyper- or hypoarousal that generate a felt sense of inflation or deflation and pleasure or displeasure. Primary affect is fundamental: the nonverbal representation of the state of the body.

Categorical affects are what we typically think of when talking about emotions. Darwin (1872/1965) delineated seven categorical affects: shame, sadness, joy, anger, surprise, fear, and disgust.[4] He found that they are displayed as distinct facial expressions that are uniform across cultures. This suggests that their importance for survival is so crucial that they evolved into an inherited neurological substrate.

Categorical affects may be hyperaroused, such as joy, pride, and anger, or hypoaroused, such as sadness, disgust, and shame. They have names (categories) and families of names designating their intensity. For example, degrees of anger are captured by miffed, irritated, angered, furious, and enraged.

Categorical affects may be ready-made evaluations of primary affects in particular contexts. For example, if I am in a negative hypoaroused state and I have lost someone of value to me, I automatically become organized into a sad state. Primary affect in the context of loss is trans-

---

4 Paul Ekman (see, e.g., Ekman & Friesend, 1975) continued Darwin's study of the categorical affects. He reduces the array of categorical affects to six: anger, disgust, fear, happiness, sadness, and surprise. (There is still controversy about which affects should be designated as categorical affects.) It was Ekman who demonstrated that if one, for example, intentionally puts on a smile, one begins to feel happy. The two-way street between the mind and body has never been more clearly demonstrated.

formed into a secondary and more differentiated categorical affect. A somatic experience has become a cognitive-affective experience. Our concern in this book is mostly with primary affect. I will refer to it simply as *affect.*

Primary and secondary (categorical) affect make up an experiential-cognitive appraisal system that alerts us to the importance of stimuli—what things mean to us and what our motives, needs, and desires are. Observed affect informs us of others' inner states: of their intentions and what things mean to them.

Affect is the conscious or nonconscious registration of the ebbs and flows of energy infusing the organism—*an expression of the body read by the mind.* Damasio (1994) provides a neurobiological understanding.[5] The brain is an information-processing machine, with modules performing specialized functions that are organized into systems. The limbic system is continuously mapping the state of our vital organs—registering the status of the heart (especially important for affect), lungs, and digestive organs. When the heart is racing, we register hyperaroused affect; when it is slowed, we experience hypoaroused affect. So, *affect is somatic-based information signaling the arousal level of the vital organs. To regulate affect is to regulate the body.*

Autonomic and Limbic Nervous Systems

Our vital organs are regulated by the autonomic (involuntary) nervous system (ANS). Arousal level is determined either by activation of the sympathetic, upregulating aspect of the ANS or by the activation of its parasympathetic, downregulating aspect. The sympathetic and parasympathetic components of the ANS are the accelerator and brake of the organism. They determine heart and lung rate and,

---

5 Antonio Damasio, along with Jaak Panksepp and Joseph LeDoux, is credited with originating affective neuroscience, the subfield of the neurosciences from which regulation theory draws many of its basic ideas.

ultimately, metabolic rate and the associated experience of vitality. Along with the ANS, there is an associated neuroendocrine system called the hypothalamic-pituitary-adrenal (HPA) axis. This "stress system" is a series of glands that set off neurochemical reactions that up- and downregulate the organism and are experienced positively or negatively.

The ANS is regulated by the limbic system. Its function is to integrate information coming up from the body with information coming in from the senses, to assess it, and to regulate the organism accordingly. It is the executive center of the organism. Indeed, the limbic system is anatomically at the center of the brain—ideally located for functioning as control central for the regulation of the organism.

To summarize, the limbic system processes information about our internal and external environments and regulates the ANS and the HPA axis. They, in turn, regulate our vital organs. Affect represents the arousal level of our vital organs and provides a reading of the state of the self.

Implicit Communication of Affect

Affect is contagious. One baby in the nursery cries, and all the babies start crying. Laughter is contagious, as is depression. It is as if there is an emotional current conducted between brains. But how? And how is it that mothers and infants have complex emotional relationships before there is language?

Body-based affect is expressed automatically through implicit communications: facial displays (which can last only 30 milliseconds), the rhythm, intonations, and stresses of speech (prosody), and our posture and gestures. We are wired to match one another's affect states. Involuntary neurobiological matching is the fundamental way that we know and experience the subjective experience of others. Implicit communication is the medium of felt connection between us and the basis for reading what is going on in others. Implicit exchanges of affect—the expression and matching/reception—are the physiological basis of intersubjectivity.

The interpersonal transmission of affect is often processed too quickly for consciousness, which requires from a quarter to half a second of focused attention. Affect is conducted nonconsciously from brain to brain—neuroceptively[6]—in, for example, an ever so slight pause or a barely perceptible change in pitch, or a split-second, subliminal facial expression. Such implicit transfers of affect transmit meaning. If we are defended against its reception or read it wrong, we suffer a costly social disadvantage. Affect tells us about another's subjective state—crucial information for cooperation and competition.

Imagine, for example, that while I am listening to you my eyes widen for a fraction of a second. Other muscles in my face will have contracted as well. You would receive this neuroceptively and match it. The matching unavoidably upregulates you: it gives you a little charge that may or may not get your focal attention at that moment. If it did become conscious, it would inform you that I had become alert in reaction to something you said. We have had a nonconscious, brain-to-brain communication mediated by the face. You perceived my affect state nonconsciously, matched it, and received information about me in relationship to you—about what you said meant to me. We have communicated psychologically and biologically. Such psychobiological, implicit communications of affect are foundational for the communication of meaning.

The exchange of affect is the fundamental way we know what we mean to one another—whether we care and the nature of our intentions. We sense our own subjectivity and the subjectivity of others

---

6 I borrow this term from Porges (2012) who uses it specifically to refer to detection of danger. I will be using it more broadly to refer to the nonconscious detection of affect in general.

through the ebbs and flows of arousal that course through our bodies and theirs. Such moment-to-moment reciprocal exchanges of positively and negatively toned surges and retreats of arousal can be thought of as "primary intersubjectivity" (Trevarthen, 1993).

Attunement

Schore (1994, 2012) describes attunement as a synchronicity of affect states. The synchrony generates a shared affective resonance that amplifies the experience. The attuned therapist is psychobiologically in sync with the positively or negatively toned, up and down flows of affect that represent a patient's subjective experience. When the shared affect states are regulated, the resonance is pleasurable and energizing. Even when shared affects are negatively toned, there is something positive about regulated attunement. Such viscerally experienced empathy offers a reassuring and vitalizing connectedness. One feels felt, known, and accepted—nurtured.

Growth-enhancing experience relies heavily on affect attunement established via implicit communications exchanged between mother and infant. Schore (1994) argues that attunement is crucial to regulating the infant; that it sets up the ideal metabolic conditions for neural development. Siegel (1999) emphasizes that attunement allows the parent to help the infant organize its own mind. A chronic lack of attunement—chronic misattunement—is neurologically and psychologically pathogenic. Attunement is at the heart of the attachment bond and of the positive therapeutic relationship.

Dyadic Regulation

At birth the infant is crucially dependent on caregiving for affect regulation. Although rudimentary forms of self-soothing are wired in, the developed capacity to autoregulate affect begins when the limbic system enters its critical period of development. This pre- and postnatal wiring up of the brain involves both an epigenetic unfolding and experience-dependent development that occurs within the mother-infant relationship.

Regulation theory and interpersonal neurobiology (Schore, 1994, 2003a, 2003b, 2012; Siegel, 1999) are focused on the limbic, socio-emotional brain shaped by experiences in attachment relationships. Neurological growth-enhancing conditions depend on the emotional capacities of our caretakers. The socioemotional brain remains plastic throughout the life span. The effectiveness of psychotherapy relies on this experience-dependent plasticity of the brain and setting optimal emotional conditions for neural and psychic growth.

The regulation of the infant's affect is a primary task of the care-taker. It occurs at first largely via the visceral effects of touch and then increasingly through distal, nonverbal, implicit communications of affect that also have visceral effects. Implicit communication, the medium for the transmission of affect, is touch-at-a-distance.

The caregiver regulates the infant's distress by receiving his or her implicit communications and responding via implicit communica-tions. Imagine that during a period of quiet and focused watching, the baby's face begins to tense up, her attention turns inward, her arms start to flap a bit, and she utters sounds of increasing distress. The caretaker moves in to help before the dysregulation goes too far. She reflexively displays a matched negative state on her face that mirrors and captures the baby's attention. Her face quickly transforms into a slightly exaggerated facial expression of negative affect followed imme-diately by relaxing into an expression of confidence that things will be made right. She gives off a soothing "OOOooo . . ." that corresponds to the crescendo and decrescendo of arousal shown in her face. The baby matches the mother's return from momentary hyperarousal to regulated affect. Through such nonverbal exchanges the mother brings the baby back to a more organized, regulated state, and together they go about finding why the baby began to fuss.

This dyadic regulation of affect involves the processing of emotional information communicated nonverbally. With sufficient repetition, these experiences of dyadic regulation become neurologically engrained—internalized. They become the automatic, psychobiological processes and relational moves by which the child is able to self-regulate.

The development of the capacity for affect regulation is optimal when we can alternate, as necessary, between auto- and dyadic regulation. Deficits in affect regulation involve problems with autoregulation, with dyadic regulation, or both. Patterns of efficient and deficient auto- and dyadic regulation are established in the attachment relationship.

Primary and Secondary Affect-Regulating Systems

Two distinct theories of affect regulation have been elucidated during the past twenty years. *Regulation theory* (Schore, 1994, 2012; Schore & Schore, 2008) explicates what I will call the primary affect regulation system. It consists of early-forming, automatic, fast, nonconscious, psychoneurobiological processes. *Mentalization theory* (Fonagy et al., 2000; Allen & Fonagy, 2006) illuminates the secondary affect regulation system. It consists of later-forming, verbal-reflective, slow, deliberate, conscious cognitive processes.

My focus in what follows is on the primary affect-regulating system (Schore, 1994, 2003a, 2003b). Chapter 6 provides an overview of mentalization-based therapy sufficient to illustrate how it fits with clinical work aimed at the primary affect-regulating system. Clinical work with the primary affect-regulating system goes hand in glove with, and is fundamental for building up, the secondary system.

The Aims of This Book

To a large extent this text is a didactic effort. Part I provides necessary background material in summaries of attachment theory and interpersonal neurobiology. Parts II and III summarize and discuss Schore's ideas about optimal and pathological development. Part IV discusses Schore's ideas about therapeutic aims and actions and how I have been applying theories of affect regulation in my practice. I present Fonagy and his collaborators' ideas about mentalization in Chapter 6. The model of bodymind presented in Chapter 2 is my own invention. The ideas about moderate dissociation in Chapter 8 are also original.

My overarching aim is to lay out a clinical model for affect regulation therapy. I have divided the book into the four parts, representing the four domains of a clinical model: a theory of bodymind in which self-states are understood to be integrated when affect is regulated and to be dissociated when affect is dysregulated (Part I); a theory of optimal development of affect regulation in secure attachment relationships (Part II); a theory of pathogenesis in which disordered affect regulation originates in relational trauma that marks insecure attachment relationships (Part III); and a theory of therapeutic actions suggesting that efficient repair of the primary affect-regulating system marshals adult versions of the nonverbal affect-regulating processes by which it was originally formed (Part IV).

Key themes include how and why different patterns of affect regulation develop; how such regulatory patterns are transmitted from caretakers to infants; what adaptive and maladaptive regulatory patterns look like neurobiologically, psychologically, and relationally; how deficits in affect regulation manifest as psychiatric symptoms and personality disorders; and ultimately, the means by which regulatory deficits can be repaired.

Part I

Theory of Bodymind

Regulated-Integrated
Versus
Dysregulated-Dissociated

CHAPTER 1

Affect Regulation and the Attachment Relationship

THE CAPACITY TO regulate affect emerges from the early attachment relationship, before words, while children are still crucially dependent on their caretakers for self-regulation. Different regulatory capacities and patterns can be observed by one year of age.

In this chapter I introduce four 18-month-old children who typify different ways of being and acting when afraid. We can already see in them emotional patterns at the core of personality and ways of relating that function to regulate affect. I pay particular attention to their capacity to return from dysregulated back to regulated affect states. We will be concerned with the type, intensity, and duration of their dysregulation, with their expectations of how their caretaker will engage them when they are distressed, with their use of dyadic or autoregulation, and with how they adapt to caretakers who themselves have difficulty self-regulating.

In Baltimore in the mid-1960s Mary Ainsworth conducted a study that shed extraordinary light on ways that mothers and infants relate when the infant is afraid. She was a student of John Bowlby, who was developing attachment theory to understand the effects on children of separation from their caretakers.

Ainsworth's work ignited the field of attachment studies. Thousands of empirical studies throughout the world have replicated and extended her findings and Bowlby's theory. These include longitudinal studies that have followed people for more than forty years (Sroufe, Egeland, & Carlson, 2005; Grossmann et al., 2005a). Attachment theory now provides fundamental constructs for understanding the development of how the brain and the mind are organized, the origins of fundamental personality characteristics, the capacity to regulate affect, and the etiology of developmental disorders.

Ainsworth's study of human attachment relationships can be thought of as an examination of the mother-infant relationship when the infant is afraid. When an infant is frightened, its attachment system is activated. The mother's function is to deactivate it by helping the infant feel safe. Ainsworth looked at different ways mothers responded to their infants' dysregulation and how their infants adapted these maternal responses.

She called the test the Strange Situation Procedure.[7] It consisted of two parts. The first involved eighteen home visits, four hours each, during the first year of the baby's life.[8] During home visits Ainsworth's graduate students observed how the mother related to her child. The second part was conducted when the baby was 18 months of age. Mothers brought their infants to Ainsworth's lab at the University of Virginia, where they were observed in "strange" situations.

The test comprised a series of episodes. Each episode provided an opportunity to observe how mother and infant managed fear: that is, how they responded when the infant's attachment system was activated. In the first episode mothers and infants were introduced

---

7 You can see videos of the experiment by searching for "strange situation" on YouTube.

8 We can see in the research design the influence of ethology, which studies animals in their natural environment.

to a pleasant room with an adult chair and toys for the infant. The mother was encouraged to have her baby play with the toys, and they were then left alone. Once mother and baby had settled in, a friendly stranger entered the room. After the stranger stayed for a while, the mother left the baby alone with the stranger. In the next episode, the mother returned to the room and the stranger left. After a period of hanging out with her baby, the mother left the child completely alone. Three minutes later (unless this was too much for the baby) the mother returned to the room.

As you may imagine, most babies tended to be moderately frightened when the stranger entered, considerably more distressed when left alone with the stranger, and consumed by fear when left completely alone. Each time the mother reentered the room, the reunion involved a period of soothing before the baby returned to play with the toys. Ainsworth was particularly interested in the reunion—in the way the mother and infant interacted while the infant was dysregulated, and in the time required for the infant to return to a regulated affect state and resume play.

Ainsworth distinguished three patterns of mother-infant relating at reunion. One she called secure attachment. The others were classified as two different types of insecure attachment: avoidant and anxious/ambivalent. In the 1990s two additional categories of insecure attachment were added: disorganized/disoriented and cannot classify (Hesse, 1996). Let's look at each of the patterns. I begin with a securely attached infant named Frances.

Frances and her mother settle into the room quickly. Frances readily takes a "let's play" cue from her mother and moves to fully engaged play with the toys. When the stranger enters, Frances stops playing and focuses on her mother. She crawls closer. However, she is easily reassured, even from a distance, and returns to play.

When her mother leaves her alone with the stranger, Frances

becomes upset. The stranger is unable to calm her fully. If she does return to play, it is less fully engaged than before. When her mother returns, Frances hurries to her and puts her arms out to be picked up and soothed. The stranger leaves while the mother reassures Frances, who quiets down relatively quickly and returns to play.

Once Frances is reregulated, her mother again leaves the room. Frances, now completely alone, becomes intensely distressed and stays so until her mother returns. Again, Frances goes to mother with positive expectations of soothing and is calmed without undue difficulty. The experiment is over. Ainsworth categorizes this dyad as *securely attached*. How so?

Frances shows her ability to immerse herself in play, to forget about her mother and focus on exploring the toys. She expresses normal amounts of distress upon the entrance of the stranger, upon being left with the stranger, and upon being left alone. When she rushes with arms out to greet her mother, she seems to *expect* that her mother will be available and up to the task of soothing her. And she is right—her mother responds effectively to her distress. Frances calms down and returned to play relatively quickly. Note that Frances is able to autoregulate sufficiently to play autonomously, and she also expects, seeks, and uses dyadic regulation well. Ainsworth would classify her as *secure-autonomous*.

The observations of Frances's mother in the home were what one might expect of the caretaker of a child with emotional resilience. She read Frances's distress well and responded empathically and competently. She tuned in to her baby—not every time, but sufficiently to engender positive expectations. She was observed to be sensitively responsive to the emotional states of her infant. She is Winnicott's good-enough mother (1973).

Kenneth's responses to the strange situation are very different. Like Frances, he quickly begins to play with the toys in the presence of his mother. However, the entrance of the stranger barely fazes him. When his mother leaves him with the stranger, he does not appear as frightened as Frances and is able to return to play with the toys. His play, however, is a bit listless, lacking the vitality that Frances showed. When his mother returns, he seeks her out but does not fully engage with her. For example, as he approaches her he does not look at her face but turns his gaze elsewhere. He does not mold when she holds him. In the next episode, when his mother leaves him completely alone, he is upset but is able to return to a less than fully engaged play while she is out of the room. Again, when she returns, he does not fully engage her—he quickly turns his attention to the toys and to play in his constricted manner.

Kenneth appears to be functioning well—perhaps too well. Atypically, he does not seem to be much frightened by the stranger or by being left alone. On further investigation, his seeming calm is belied by physiological measures of stress.[9] Whereas Frances seemed aware of her distress and expressed her needs directly, Kenneth seems oblivious to his fear. He does not seek much comfort from his mother, nor is he receptive to it. His expectations of caretaking seem to be minimal—perhaps negative. He has a detached quality and plays without vitality. He turns his attention away from the stranger; that is, he turns his attention away from the source of stress. He also does not look at his mother's face—which suggests that he expects a negative expression or a lack of interest. When soothing is in order, he tends not to seek dyadic regulation but, rather, relies on himself (autoregulation).

Note particularly that, in stressful episodes, not only is Kenneth's attention diverted from the sources of stress, but also his affect is

---

9 Measures of autonomic response, for example heart rate or breathing rate, showed Kenneth to be experiencing considerable stress (Fox & Hane, 2008).

downregulated. Ainsworth would classify Kenneth as *avoidant*—one of the three types of classifiable insecure attachment patterns.

In the home study Kenneth's mother was assessed as emotionally unresponsive to him—as insensitive. She might, for example, walk out of a room without anticipating that it would upset him, or ignore his distress in its early stages. Compared with Frances, Kenneth was seen as more often angry and noncompliant. Although Ainsworth did not think in these terms, Kenneth's mother was unresponsive to his implicit communications of affect expressing his inner states. This lack of contingent emotional responsiveness suggests the dulled affectivity and barren inner life of depression.

Kenneth's mother had an aversion to physical contact and rarely expressed emotion. When Kenneth did seek comfort she would discourage crying and minimize his distress. She might say, "Come on now. You're fine. Be a big boy." She would often become irritated and reject Kenneth's appeals for soothing, or become impatient and stop comforting before Kenneth had fully calmed down. Kenneth developed a strategy of avoidance to minimize the experience of being rejected. Ainsworth would classify her as *dismissive*, reflecting her rejection of Kenneth's appeals for comfort. The relationship is classified as *avoidant-dismissive*. One can already see a fit between Kenneth and his mother. Kenneth has coped adaptively with his caretaking environment.

Barbara represents a second type of insecure attachment pattern. When she first enters the observation room with her mother, she takes a long time before playing with the toys. When she does play, she keeps an eye on her mother. She has a strong reaction to the arrival of the stranger and does not return to play. Rather, Barbara engages with her mother in a manner that compels the latter's attention. When left alone with the stranger she cannot be soothed and is unable to play. When her mother returns Barbara reacts by clinging, interspersed with hitting. When left completely alone, she is so intensely distressed that her mother returns early and again has difficulty calming her. Barbara is unable to play except in the presence of her mother and even then checks on her frequently. This interrupts her from fully engaging with the toys and suggests an anxious preoccupation with abandonment.

Barbara's vacillation between hitting and clinging seems to indicate that she's caught up in some kind of conflict as her mother tries to calm her. Although the mixture of anger and fear is confusing, her emotions are strongly expressed—more pronounced than those of Frances. When left alone she becomes emotionally overwhelmed. She is difficult to sooth.

Barbara can be thought of as being on the other end of a continuum from Kenneth. She compels her mother's attention. Kenneth makes few requests of his mother. Barbara is intensely and ambivalently enmeshed in their relationship. He is detached. She is hypervigilant, her attention constantly returning to her mother. Kenneth binds his attention by playing and keeps his attention focused away from sources of stress, such as his mother's absence or presence. He relies on autoregulation and suffers from prolonged states of downregulated affect. Barbara seeks but is not positively responsive to dyadic regulation, demonstrates little capacity for autoregulation, and suffers from states of prolonged and intense negative hyperarousal. When stressed she becomes hyperaroused and exhibits a mixture of fear of abandonment and anger in the attachment relationship. By contrast, Kenneth tends toward a clenched, solitary hypoarousal when stressed. Ainsworth would classify Barbara as *ambivalent-resistant*—the second type of insecure attachment.

In the home study Barbara's mother was often observed to be sensitive and responsive. However, unlike the case with Frances's mother, her own needs and emotions frequently impinged and took precedence over Barbara's. For example, she might intrude on Barbara's play, completing things for her or imposing her own agenda, or she might interrupt Barbara's play to hug her. Whereas Kenneth's mother was consistently unavailable and rejecting, Barbara's mother was inconsistently emotionally available and frequently intrusive. Ainsworth would classify Barbara's mother as *preoccupied*, reflecting her too frequent absorption in her own urgently felt needs.

For all their differences, Kenneth and Barbara have some striking similarities. In the home study, when compared with Frances, they were both seen as more frequently angry and noncompliant. Also, unlike Frances, Kenneth and Barbara did not express needs clearly and directly. Finally, they seemed to have negative expectations about their mother's availability that are based in the actualities of their upbringing. In keeping with home observations in which Kenneth's mother was seen to be insensitive and unresponsive to his affect states, Kenneth's avoidance suggests that he expects his mother to be unresponsive or negatively responsive to his distress. Barbara's hypervigilance suggests anxiety about her mother's emotional availability and fears of abandonment.

Douglas and his mother show a third insecure pattern of relating called *disorganized/disoriented*. Ainsworth's student Mary Main identified the pattern in her own groundbreaking attachment studies (Main & Solomon, 1986). Like Barbara, Douglas is unable to play and difficult to sooth. He also demonstrates ambivalent behaviors toward his mother. He checks constantly on his mother and often interrupts his play to engage her. He was often angry at her. When distressed he easily becomes overwhelmed by emotion. However, there were important differences. Unlike Barbara, Douglas displays dramatically contradictory behaviors. For example, he might fall to the floor or veer off or turn his head away as he approaches his mother. (There are even instances of disorganized children walking backward toward their mothers.) Douglas was observed to be confused and occasionally seemed frozen, with a dazed look on his face suggesting a complete collapse of behavioral and attention-orienting capacities.

The disorganized attachment pattern has been associated with severe mental disorders, including borderline personality disorder, dissociative disorders, and posttraumatic stress disorder (Dozier, Stoval, & Albus, 1999; Liotti, 1992; Lyons-Ruth, and Jacobovitz, 1999; Lyons-Ruth et al, 2003). The trance-like states suggest profound dissociation. The affective extremes, susceptibility to negative states, and ambivalent relationship with his mother conform to the emotional profile of the borderline personality disorder. Douglas's emotional lability is consistent with the chaotic quality of his behavior and attention. Like Barbara, he is hyperaroused and unable to play much of the time during the test.

There is a strong association between abuse or neglect and disorganized attachment (see, e.g., Carlson, Cicchetti, Barnett, & Braunwald, 1989; Liotti, 2004; Ogawa, Sroufe, Weinfeld, Carlson, & Egeland, 1997). The explanation may lie in the fact that mothers of disorganized children tend also to be disorganized. Like their children, they often have histories of abuse or neglect.[10] They, too, are vulnerable to unregulated affect and loss of impulse control.

Some mothers in disorganized attachment relationships with their children are overtaken by fear when their baby is frightened. Unable to regulate themselves, they lack the capacity to regulate their children. Indeed, their fear amplifies the fear of their infants and further dysregulates them.

Whether encountering a frightening or frightened attachment figure, the infant is faced with an irresolvable dilemma: the source of safety is the source of the fear. The infant is trapped.

---

10 There may also be a history of unresolved loss.

Insecurely attached infants have caretakers who too often exacerbate, rather than ameliorate, their dysregulation. The insensitivity and unresponsiveness of dismissive mothers and the frequent emotional intrusions by underregulated, preoccupied mothers worsen their infant's dysregulation. Yet the infant's survival depends on staying attached. The problem is how to stay attached without becoming catastrophically dysregulated.

For infants of dismissive and preoccupied caretakers there is a solution: Avoidant infants have learned not to ask for help when distressed and to direct their attention away from attachment concerns. Ambivalent infants, having adapted to inconsistent caretaking, have learned to be hypervigilant—focused on attachment and maintaining their mother's attention. In both these types of insecure attachment there is a solution that allows for an organized pattern to form. Avoidant and preoccupied attachment patterns are referred to as *structured insecure*. These are problematic adaptations to suboptimal caretaking environments, but at least they offer a solution to the problem of remaining attached. There is no solution to Douglas's desperate situation.

As mentioned, a fifth category for classifying attachment patterns called "cannot classify" (Hesse, 1996) was delineated. This involves instances in which no one pattern could be distinguished as most pronounced. Like the disorganized classification, this pattern has a stronger association with severe mental illness than the structured insecure patterns, but it has not gained clinical currency.

Let me summarize the major attachment categories, with an emphasis on their affect-regulating characteristics. We observed children when their attachment systems were activated and saw different patterns of relational behaviors. The *securely attached* child moved toward the attachment figure with positive expectations. The *avoidant child* moved away from or turned his or her attention away from the attachment figure. The *anxious-ambivalent* child moved against the attachment figure.[11] Finally, the *disorganized/disoriented* child was without organized relational behavior. These, then, are the regulatory object relations of secure and insecure attachment and key determinants of the transference-countertransference relationship in psychotherapy (Schore, 1994).

We also noted different patterns of attentional deployment. Attention determines consciousness and is the leading edge of affect regulation strategies. The securely attached child's attention was flexible, moving adaptively between opportunities for play and the dangers of strangers or abandonment. The anxious-ambivalent child's attention was riveted on her mother or on high alert for any possible danger. The avoidant child's attention was diverted from the source of stress and was the basis for denial of danger and of his own stress. The disorganized child's attention was disoriented.

We also saw different patterns of affect arousal. The securely attached child's affect regulation was resilient, moving from hyperarousal when afraid and returning efficiently to homeostasis when reassured. The anxious-ambivalent child suffered prolonged states of hyperarousal, and the avoidant child prolonged states of hypoarousal. The disorganized child showed no organized pattern, vacillating between states of hyper- and hypoarousal and subject to blank, deactivated states.

Lastly, we saw different procedures used for affect regulation. The secure child made flexible use of both auto- and dyadic regulation; the anxious-ambivalent child made use only of dyadic regulation, and the avoidant child, only of autoregulation. Neither of these worked optimally but did allow a workable relationship to develop. The disorganized child was unable to use either auto- or dyadic regulation successfully (see Table 1.1).

---

11 Schore (1994) points out that Karen Horney observed these three basic interpersonal modes in adults: moving toward, moving away, or moving against.

TABLE 1.1. CHARACTERISTICS OF DIFFERENT ATTACHMENT PATTERNS

CHARACTERISTIC	Attachment Pattern			
	SECURE	AVOIDANT	ANXIOUS-AMBIVALENT	DISORGANIZED/DISORIENTED
ATTENTION DEPLOYMENT	Directed toward expected solution to stress	Directed away from expected source of stress	Hypervigilant for expected source of stress	Disoriented, chaotic attention
RELATIONAL BEHAVIOR	Moves toward attachment figure	Moves Away From Attachment Figure	Moves Against Attachment Figure	Inconsistent Or Contradictory Relational Moves
AFFECT REGULATION	Resilient	Prolonged states of hypoarousal (dysregulated affect)	Prolonged states of hyperarousal (dysregulated affect)	Chaotic pattern of hyper- and hypoarousal (dysregulated affect)
MEANS OF REGULATING AFFECT	Either dyadic or autoregulation	Autoregulation	Dyadic regulation	Neither dyadic nor autoregulation

These patterns comprise observable components of the self-states of the children when their attachment systems were activated. Our focus is on the *internal* state of the self. To understand that, we need a model of bodymind that explains the organization and disorganization of the affective and cognitive components of self-states.

CHAPTER 2

Self-States

Regulated-Integrated Versus Dysregulated-Dissociated

A MODEL OF bodymind (brain-body-mind) is basic to a clinical theory of affect regulation. Freud proposed a theory of bodymind in which the regulation of body-based sexual and aggressive drives is foundational for development and mental life. With the emergence of ego psychology and object relations theory came a focus on mental representation. The idea of a bodymind diminished, and psychoanalysis became more cognitively oriented. With the introduction of attachment theory (Bowlby, 1969, 1973), psychoanalysis is returned to an integration of biology and psychology, this time founded in Darwinian principles of adaptation. Most schools of psychoanalysis now embrace the idea of an embodied mind and increasingly focus on affect.

Regulation theory (Schore 1994, 2003a, 2003b, 2012) is grounded in an understanding of the psychobiological systems that process and regulate affect. Affect is understood to represent the state of the body. The affect-regulating system monitors and regulates the state of the body—our own and others'. Regulation theory proposes that the regulation of affect is fundamental to the organization of bodymind and thus for adaptive functioning and subjective experience. This is the topic of this chapter.

When affect is regulated, the organism is integrated and able to respond flexibly to the internal and external environments. We experience a sense of self-mastery, and indeed, when regulated we are optimally functional. When affect is dysregulated, we become dissociated (disintegrated) and reduced to automated processes and isolated portions of our memory. In other words, the organization of the self is affect state dependent. We organize and disorganize depending on whether or not we are regulated.

I have conceived of self-states as assemblages of the affect-regulating system and a set of cognitive systems: attentional, perceptual, representational, memory, and reflective.[12] These are the processes that enable us to assess and adjust to our internal and external environments. Adaptation requires that our attention can spontaneously go where it needs to go; that, when necessary we can exert voluntary control over it; that we can perceive and represent ourselves and others with reasonable accuracy; that we can form, store, and access relevant memories; that we can reflect on our cognitive-affective processes in order to refine meaning and adjust perceptions and representations as necessary; and that we can monitor and adjust our affect state. Our subjective experience is an indication of how well these processes are functioning.

In what follows, I describe how each of the self-state subsystems contributes to adaptive capacities and subjective experience when affect is regulated versus dysregulated.

---

12 Note that this is a delimited understanding in that I have not fully addressed the somatic aspects of self-states. Of course, affect represents somatic experience. However, there is more to say about how the body contributes to self-states that is of clinical relevance (see, e.g., Levine, 1997; Ogden et al., 2006; Ogden & Fischer, 2014; see also, 2007, esp. chap. 13).

Self-States: Adaptive Capacity and Subjective Experience

Regulation theory supports a self-state perspective (Bromberg, 1998, 2006, 2011; Howell, 2005; Stern, 1997). I discuss self-states with regard to subjective experience and adaptive capacity. They vary according to whether the state of the bodymind is regulated-integrated or dysregulated-dissociated.

What we think of as a unitary self actually consists of a set of self-states. Each self-state comprises different ways each of us has of thinking, feeling, and acting—different ways of being in different contexts. Each self-state can be thought of as its own personality system: a context-dependent assemblage of the affective and cognitive processes that assemble into versions of us. As an obvious example, we are different versions of ourselves when relaxed versus when we are stressed. Perhaps more subtly, we are different versions of ourselves in different relationships, in different roles, and in different contexts in general.

When activated, each self-state provides access to a range of memories and behaviors and involves a disposition to negative or positive perceptions and representations. Each generates a particular sense of self and others and different ways of relating.

Optimally, the overall self-state system is integrated. That is, the self-states that typify us are compatible with one another, and we can shift fluidly and comfortably between them. Optimally, memories are shared across self-states, and the varying experiences of self they generate are included in an overall, coherent sense of ourself. This is possible because the affect associated with the memories and sense of self are tolerable, and we are able to stay regulated and integrated when they are activated. Regulated affect maximizes access to the full range of our self-states and provides us with maximum response flexibility and adaptability.

Intolerable memories and appraisals of self dysregulate us and manifest in dissociated self-states. In narcissistic personalities, for example, shameful representations of self are intolerable and must be isolated from other self-states with a positive, albeit grandiose, sense of self.

Subjective experience in dysregulated-dissociated self-states contrasts with the sense of agency and self-mastery encountered in regulated-integrated states. Dissociated self-states are activated involuntarily and automatically. They come upon us. We are often unaware of being in moderately dissociated self-states. Dissociated self-states are us in a way that does not fit with our overall sense of self. The sense of coherence that accompanies regulated-integrated states is disrupted, and, if we are aware of a dissociated state we may experience a sense that something is not right.

There is increasing appreciation for the differences between partially and fully dissociated self-states (Dell, 2009a; Howell & Blizard, 2009). Howell and Blizzard (2009) note that, unlike fully dissociated self-states, "when dissociation is partial, there is usually 1) continuity of identity, 2) superficial awareness of abrupt changes in affect and behavior, 3) minimal ability to link these states in consciousness, and 4) little acknowledgment of the significance of these shifting states" (p. 408). In other words, in partially dissociated self-states we know it is us being different but have only a shallow understanding of what is happening to us.

In partially dissociated self-states, we may remember other ways of being ourselves, but they seem alien. They may be dismissed with such attitudes as "I'm not really like that." In fully dissociated self-states there may be total amnesia for the thoughts and feelings and sense of self experienced in other self-states.[13] The alters of dissociative identity disorder are fully dissociated self-states.

---

13 Patients with Dissociative Identity Disorder report that some alters are aware of other alters and some are not.

State shifting is central to a theory of multiple selves. Flexible, context-dependent state shifting supports the widest possible range of responses to changing socioemotional environments. When affect is regulated, we are able to shift self-states as needed. Secure attachment engenders affect tolerance and resiliency. This maximizes time spent in regulated states with access to the fullest range of our self-states.

The sense of self-mastery that accompanies regulated states may be due to the sense that we are able to flexibly shift states in response to environmental changes. Such confident malleability stands in stark contrast to the limitations imposed when affect is dysregulated and the self is dissociated. In hypoaroused-dissociated self-states, we are locked into passive coping. In hyperaroused-dissociated self-states, we are reduced to active coping. In both cases we have lost response flexibility.

We are shapeshifters adjusting to local conditions. Adaptation is optimal when we switch self-states flexibly and fluidly in order to respond contingently to internal and external events. Adaptation is suboptimal in dysregulated-dissociated states in which we are automated and reduced to a single way of being.

Problems with state-shifting were evident in the behaviors of the insecurely attached children in the Strange Situation Procedure described in Chapter 1. Frances (secure) returned efficiently from a dysregulated to a regulated self-state in which she could play. In contrast, Kenneth (avoidant) became mired in a prolonged, hypoaroused, negative self-state—when stressed, he automatically, inflexibly coped passively. Barbara (ambivalent-resistant) suffered the opposite fate: she was stuck in a hyperaroused, negative state—when stressed, she could only cope actively. Douglas (disorganized) had a different problem: he was subjected to abrupt, unpredictable shifts in his self-states.

The children categorized as insecure share difficulties with transitioning from dysregulated to regulated self-states. Additionally, they each became dysregulated at lower levels of stress compared with Frances. Emotional resiliency and tolerance are hallmarks of mental health. They allow us to maximize time spent in regulated-integrated states—alert, engaged, positively disposed, and able to respond contingently. Deficits in affect tolerance and resilience result in frequent and prolonged states of dysregulation-dissociation.

We have been discussing how emotional capacity affects adaptive functioning and subjective experience. Regulated-integrated self-states maximize response flexibility and a sense of agency, self-mastery, and well-being. Dysregulated-dissociated self-states are maladaptive, involuntary, and automated and generate a sense of detached self-alienation and of something gone wrong. To further understand the subjective experiences of dissociated self-states and why they are maladaptive, let's look at key characteristics of dissociative phenomena in general and of dissociated self-states in particular.

Key Characteristics of Dissociated Self-States

Dissociation is an elusive concept. Traumatologists studying dissociation are unable to agree on the meaning of the concept. In what follows, dissociated self states may be understood in terms of three characteristics that I have found particularly useful clinically: *automaticity*[14], *compartmentalization and altered states of consciousness*

Dissociation is an inborn, adaptive, automatic response to a life-threatening event from which there is no escape and which induces terror—overwhelming, painful affect consisting of fear and horror. The first response to a life threat is hyperarousal. It alerts us to the danger and supports a fight or flight response. If these are untenable, the freeze response is activated—an instantaneous, systemic state of profound hypoarousal and metabolic retardation. There is a meta-

---

14 See Dell (2009b)

bolic collapse and underlying activation of the dorsal vagal system, a neurobiological system devoted to freeze responses, which generates immobilization without loss of consciousness—feigned death. It serves adaptively as a peritraumatic survival response that conserves energy needed for physical escape. It also includes numbing of pain and a psychological detachment from self experience

Although peritraumatic dissociation has adaptive advantages in life-threatening situations, it may be predictive of posttraumatic disorders and a disposition to dissociation. Dissociation becomes pathological when it results in a hypersensitivity to trauma-related cues and endures as a characterological response to levels of stress that should be tolerable (Van der Kolk & Fisler, 1995).[15]

Dissociative phenomena may take somatic or psychological forms, may be severe or moderate and may be hyper- or hypo-aroused. Neurobiological research is just beginning to understand the underlying mechanisms accompanying different types of dissociation. (See for example Lanius et al, 2002, 2005, 2006, 2010.)

There is general agreement that pathological dissociation involves a spectrum of severity (see, e.g., Ford, 1999; Van der Kolk et al., 1996).[16] For example, the alters of dissociative identity disorder are considered

---

15 It is interesting to note an isomorphism between isolated-event trauma and the chronic relational trauma of disorganized attachment. Recall that the infant in a disorganized attachment relationship is subjected to experiences in which he or she is faced with a no-way-out situation. That is, the attachment figure, without whom the infant cannot survive and to whom the infant looks for safety, is frightening or frightened—is the source of fear. Like isolated-event trauma, there is no escape in these episodes that accumulate into the trauma of disorganized attachment. Like isolated-event trauma, disorganized attachment generates states of immobilizing dissociation.

16 There is disagreement about whether dissociative phenomena should be conceived of as a spectrum from normal to pathological, or whether pathological dissociation is a categorically different type of phenomenon (vs. dimensional approaches).

the most severe forms of dissociated self-states, whereas the partially dissociated self-states of everyday life represent a moderate form.

The *DSM-V* and *ICD-10* define dissociative disorders at the descriptive level and according to type. Symptoms may be somatoform or psychoform. The former includes dissociative phenomena such as paralysis or involuntary movements. Dell (2009a) defines somatoform dissociation as "alterations of bodily function that have no physical or medical basis" (p. 230) and includes such diverse phenomena as blindness, unexplained pain or not feeling pain, and difficulty swallowing. Psychoform symptoms include discrete phenomena, such flashbacks, and more diffuse phenomena, such as detached states of consciousness.

Dissociative phenomena may be hyper- or hypo-aroused. For example flashbacks are hyper-aroused. Freeze states are hypo-aroused. Hyper-aroused dissociative phenomena tend to generate full immersion in the experience. whereas hypo-aroused dissociative phenomena tend to generate a sense of detachment from the experience. Interestingly, both may be accompanied by numbing.

Note that I've been *describing* characteristics of dissociative phenomena. Schore (1994, 2009) argues that the field must move beyond a purely descriptive approach (see also Brown & Trimble, 2000; Spiegel et al., 2011) and proposes a specific neurobiological mechanism responsible for profound hypoaroused dissociation,[17] such as seen in the blank face that Douglas exhibited in the Strange Situation Procedure and often observed in posttraumatic stress disorder and borderline personality disorder. Lanius et al (2002, 2005, 2006, 2010) have been using brain imaging to understand the neurological correlates of both hyper- and hypo-aroused dissociative phenomena. I'll discuss

---

17 Schore (1994, 2003a, 2012) proposes that the severe, immobilizing form of dissociation is mediated by the dorsal vagal component of the parasympathetic nervous system (Porges, 2011). Again, this is the freeze part of the fight-flight-freeze survival system.

this more fully in Chapters 3 and 9. For now we examine dissociation at the descriptive level.

As stated earlier, I conceive of dissociative phenomena as sharing three features: automaticity, compartmentalization of content, and altered states of consciousness including, for example, detachment from somatic experience, self-experience, and the experience of external reality. From the point of view of adaptation, these deviations from normal functioning are problematic because they interfere with flexible responding to a changing environment. From the point of view of subjective experience, they disrupt a sense of coherence, continuity, and well-being. As we'll see in Sections 3 and 4 dissociation also impedes learning, development and therapeutic progress.

Automaticity

We are automated much of the time. Driving automatically while thinking about something else is a common example. Automaticity when one allows it, such as while driving, does not present a problem and is adaptive. In life-threatening situations automaticity is also understood to be adaptive because of its speed—making a deliberate decision would take too long.

The relational moves of everyday life are more and less automated. This, too, is adaptive. Imagine if you had to focus on walking. Normally, when walking and lost in thought, we are able to snap-to when necessary. In the case of relational moves, we are able to shift into a more deliberate, less spontaneous way of relating. When we cannot, and we are involuntarily automated, this is a sign that we have become dissociated.

Dissociated self-states are automatic in the sense both that they are activated involuntarily and that we are reduced to a scripted set of behavioral and psychological responses. For example, a dysregulating encounter with an intimidating person may activate a set of relational moves that come packaged with a delimited scope of perceptions and representations. In this state we are no longer responding voluntarily to an ongoing assessment of our own and others' inner states. Subjectivity and intersubjectivity have been replaced by automaticity.

Compartmentalization

Compartmentalization involves the involuntary isolation of content. In the case of dissociative amnesia following trauma, aspects of the event that are recorded are sectioned off—they cannot be voluntarily remembered, assessed, and integrated into one's overall functioning. Dissociated self-states may be similarly quarantined. In this case an entire personality system comprising memories, sense of self, representational and perceptual dispositions, and so forth, is segregated and may be kept from consciousness when in other self-states.

Altered States of Consciousness

Trauma-based altered states of consciousness may generate a sense of *detachment*—a hyperobjectification and sense of distance from oneself or from reality. A fully depersonalized state involves the perception of being out of one's body. In derealized states, objects may seem distanced, and sounds may seem flat or hollow or coming from far away. The more common experience of feeling out of touch with body-based feelings and emotionally distanced from others may be thought of as moderate forms of depersonalization and derealization. Like compartmentalized memories, altered perceptions are generally understood to serve protective functions. They allow us to function and even appear normal, without the disruption that would be caused by traumatic affect. In altered states of consciousness the affect is dissociated.

Whereas dissociated memories serve as a *post*traumatic defense against overwhelming affect, altered states of consciousness are thought to have evolved as a *peri*traumatic defense protecting us *during* traumatic episodes. For example, one of my patients would find herself watching from a corner of the ceiling when her brother sexually molested her. Unfortunately, when one has become dissociated during a traumatic experience, one is often vulnerable to becoming dissociated when triggered by stimuli that evoke memories of the trauma.

Automaticity, compartmentalization and detached states of consciousness tend to come as a package. For example, a patient slipped into a hypoaroused-dissociated state when I made reference to her being bullied as a child: her head dropped, and when she looked up she had lost color in her face and was dazed and silent. I was able to stay connected to her, and as she began to return to a regulated state, she said that she had been hit by the thought that I found her "repulsive." I understood this to be an automated-intrusive (dissociated) thought based in her experiences of being bullied and shamed. Still dissociated, she said that I sounded as though I was speaking to her from the waiting room and that things were happening in "slow motion". Not only was I speaking from the same room, but I regarded her as a fine young woman—in other states she knew this. Less dramatic intrusions of state-dependent, compartmentalized content and altered states of consciousness are common and may often go unnoticed.

The Affective and Cognitive Subsystems Comprising Self-States

To this point we have been discussing integrated and dissociated self-states as whole personality systems. We now turn our focus to the processes that comprise self-states. They assemble a sense of ourselves in relation to others and operate more or less flexibly.

I have conceived of self-states as assemblages of a central affect-regulating system and five cognitive systems: (1) attentional, (2) perceptual, (3) representational, (4) memory, and (5) reflective. The affect-regulating system is at the core of the assemblage. The functioning of the cognitive systems is affect state dependent.

We see here a central tenet of regulation theory. Affect is primary, and the regulation of affect is the central executive function of the organism. When affect is regulated, the bodymind is integrated. When affect is dysregulated, the bodymind is dissociated. A shift from a dissociated to an integrated self-state follows a shift from dysregulated to regulated affect. The subjective experience of self-states is also dominated by the affective experience.

In what follows I suggest examples of what may happen within each of the self-state subsystems when affect is dysregulated. My aim is to shed light on the subjective experiences of dissociation and how dysregulated-dissociated self-states deprive us of the flexibility necessary for adaptive functioning.

Attentional System

The human brain cannot process all the information available to it at a given moment—it must select salient information and filter out the rest.[18] Attention is the filter and plays a leading role in mental life. It determines what we are conscious of and what we engage with. Freud bypassed the filter by suspending focused attention and letting attention float freely to gain access to stimuli coming from his patients' and his own unconscious that would normally go unnoticed. He had to be regulated to have such mastery over his attention.

Attention comes in two basic forms. It can be contextual, in which case, like the light from a lantern, we take in the surround. Or it can

18 Perhaps this is reflected in the fact that being paid attention to generates feelings of self-worth.

be focused, like the beam of a flashlight, with which we take in a particular part of the whole. When affect is regulated, the attention system is integrated. We are able to alternate flexibly between global and focused modes as we attend to our inner and outer worlds.

Attention determines what we are conscious of and in this way plays a key role in regulating affect. It is the lead mechanism in avoidance. Putting a disturbing event outside of our attentional field downregulates the associated affect. Focusing on it intensifies the affect. Helping patients to remain regulated while focusing their attention on things that would normally dysregulate them is one of the arts of psychotherapy.

When affect is dysregulated, we lose control of attention, and attentional flexibility is lost. One mode or the other tends to dominate. If global attention dominates, we may enter an overly diffuse state, become flooded with information, overwhelmed, and confused. If attention is rigidly focused, we suffer from insufficient information and experience a narrowed, constricted state of consciousness.

In the Strange Situation Procedure described in Chapter 1, we saw Kenneth's (avoidant) attention operating to regulate his affect by keeping it focused on the toys and away from sources of stress. His global attention deactivated, Kenneth was honed in on one particular aspect of the environment at the expense of the contextual surround. His dual attentional systems were dissociated, no longer integrated and working together.

Of course, we often need to focus our attention and block out the surround. Such absorption can be thought of as a type of adaptive dissociation that operates nondefensively. Contextual attention operates in the background, alerting us to any need to attend to something else. Such volitional focused attention is a far cry from Kenneth's attention, which was narrowed involuntarily/automatically, to maintain a measure of self-regulation.

Perceptual System

Guided by attention, our perceptual system constructs the experience of the present.[19] This includes interoceptive information (body-based affective-sensorimotor experience) and exteroceptive information coming in through the senses.

When affect is regulated, interoception and exteroception coordinate to provide us with real-seeming experience. Body-based affective reactions to external stimuli are combined with the perception of those stimuli providing a sense of ourselves being in our bodies in the world. This synthesis breaks down when there is a failure of affect processing (Sierra & Berrios, 1998; Sierra et al., 2002), and we experience an altered state of consciousness in which we feel severely or moderately detached from somatic experience.

Thus, in states of depersonalization and derealization, the information coming up from the body cannot be processed and integrated with the sensory information coming in from the environment. Without the information representing somatic experience—the felt sense of our body—we do not experience ourselves in it. We also do not experience our body-based affective reactions to the external world and thus feel distanced from it.

Regulation theory proposes that when arousal levels are too high or too low, the affect-regulating system itself, responsible for processing both body-based and socioemotional information, becomes disorganized. This results in cutting off affective information and altering our perceptions of ourselves in our bodies in the world.

---

19 See Stern (2004) for an essential understanding of what our experience of the present actually is.

Representational System

The representational system enables us to think about the past and the future. "Perception presents and representation re-presents" sums up the relationship between the two systems. Representation occurs at the neurological and psychological levels—from a fundamental set of neural activations representing oneself and others, to preconscious, impressionistic, preverbal representations, and then to conscious mental images and words. For example, a set of neurological activations representing a frightening stimulus and activating a startle reaction occur before we have represented it consciously. A preconscious, fleeting, real-time impression of someone we are in a group with may barely enter awareness. If we focus on it, it may become a verbal-imagistic experience of someone we are thinking and feeling clearly about. In all cases, representations are phenomena that stand for something else.

Conscious representations are generally classified as either symbolic or presymbolic. Presymbolic representations are impressionistic. They provide a sense of things, available for further articulation, but not yet put into words (symbolic level). They are the kind of mentalese that we glimpse at the threshold of consciousness and are experienced fleetingly, perhaps as the leading edge of an intuition.[20] They may be sensed vaguely and require effort to retrieve and put into words. But mostly they are simply a preverbal thought that we then articulate into words. Symbolic representation originates in presymbolic representation developmentally and in life-as-lived. Thinking relies on both presymbolic and symbolic representation.

When affect is dysregulated, the representational system becomes

---

20 Freud referred to this as the preconscious system. It is now understood as implicit or unformulated phenomena. For an in-depth discussion, see Stern (1997).

dissociated and loses its integrative capacity. Splitting is a form of compartmentalization of content that reflects a failure of integration. For example, when we are in hyperaroused states of love or hate, we tend to regard others as part objects—idealized or demonized. We lose the ability to reconcile contradictory representations of the same person. The same is true of one's sense of self. In depressed states, we are unable to integrate positive self-representations into our sense of self. Content is segmented. Splitting of representations may be supported by state-dependent memories. That is, memories contrary to the dominant affect of the activated self-state cannot be retrieved and represented.

People suffering from borderline personality disorder, often typified by their tendency to split self- and object representations, might be better understood as frequently severely dysregulated and therefore subject to splitting due to a severely dissociated representational system. Like the other cognitive systems, the quality of representation is affect state dependent. In regulated states, we are able to access contradictory representations, construct whole objects, and tolerate the result.

Memory System

Pierre Janet (1904), the father of dissociative studies, understood trauma-based dissociation as a "phobia of memories"—actually a fear of the affective component of the memory. Dissociated memories are iconic sequelae of trauma and the poster child of compartmentalization. They cannot be processed and integrated with other autobiographical memories into an overall sense of self. When activated, traumatic memories may generate intrusive dissociative phenomena such as flashbacks and other types of reliving experiences.

Memories of traumatic events may be registered only somatically, the body reacting as it did during the trauma without a mental representation of the experience. If registered mentally, traumatic memories usually involve only fragments of the experience,[21] and these may or may not include a somatic memory of the experience of terror. It is generally accepted that memories of trauma are compartmentalized to protect us from reexperiencing the associated intolerable affect.

Flashbacks are understood to be compartmentalized memories that, when activated, intrude into normal executive functioning and take us over. They are not integrated with other autobiobraphical memories and operate independently from them. Such intrusions into consciousness come with varying degrees of intensity. For example, repetitive critical inner voices that intrude into consciousness, shaming the self (Ginot, 2012), may be comparatively moderate, but like flashbacks, they are automated and compartmentalized.

It is important to note that not all traumatic events are encoded, and if they are encoded, only fragments of the experience may be registered. In the case of unrecorded traumatic events, it is thought that the structure of the brain responsible for recording episodic memories (the hippocampus) is deactivated during the trauma. When the hippocampus is deactivated, the memory system is dissociated at the neurological level.

The effects of traumatic memories on subjective experience range from chronic, anxious hyperarousal supporting hypervigilance and action proneness, to chronic, depressive hypoarousal supporting a deactivation of mental life and social withdrawal. When memories of trauma are compartmentalized, adaptive functioning is compromised by hypoactivation and restricted functioning or hypervigilance and overreaction. Although the trauma literature focuses on acute dissociative episodes originating in isolated-event trauma, trauma based

---

21 See Van der Kolk and Fisler (1995) for how information is processed during traumatic experiences.

dissociative phenomena can be diffuse, moderate, and subtle. The latter are associated with cumulative trauma (Van der Kolk & Fisler, 1995).

Reflective System

Perhaps uniquely among species, we are capable of metacognitive processes that enable us to think about thinking and feeling. Among other functions, our reflective system is responsible for assessing our own and others' inner states. This is a developmental accomplishment (Fonagy, Gergely, Jurist, & Target, 2002).

The capacity to assess our own and others' mental states with reasonable accuracy involves a set of complex cognitive operations. Fonagy and his collaborators refer to this aspect of our reflective capacities as mentalizing (See Chapter 6).

When affect is dysregulated, reflective functioning is either severely compromised or deactivated entirely. Ideally, deliberate reflection takes into account the inherent ambiguity in reading mental states and is able to accommodate new information. When compromised, such high level reflection is replaced by the activation of scripts using forms of mentalizing that assimilate information into primitive schemas and generate certainty. Under this condition, we are vulnerable to misidentifying emotions and misinterpreting intentions. Thoughtful reflection is replaced by ready made, simplistic narratives.[22]

---

22 I discuss this further in Chapter 6, but briefly, Fonagy and collaborators (2000) identify "object equivalence" and "pretend" as primitive forms of mentalizing they call "prementalizing." They are combined in "full mentalization." Object equivalence equates the representation with the object to which it refers. Pretend mode distinguishes between the representation and its referent to a fault, stripping the representation of its meaning and connection to the object to which it refers. Object equivalence fails to take into account the inherent ambiguities of assessing one's own and others' mental states. It supports strong affects and actions. Pretend mode distances us from caring, dampens affect, and supports inaction.

Consider the counterproductive quality of reflective functioning in depressed dysregulated states. Scripted self-denigrating appraisals of oneself and despairing assessments of one's prospects are at the ready. They replace the normal analytical abilities, memories, and imagination used for balanced, integrated self- and object appraisals. Adaptive reflection is replaced by automatisms. Automated negative thinking replaces flexible assessments contingent upon the actualities. The depressed state is perpetuated, even worsened.

When affect is severely dysregulated, rather than merely compromised, the reflective system may be deactivated entirely and no longer working in conjunction with other cognitive systems. This has a direct effect on the state of consciousness.

When functioning optimally, reflective functioning includes the capacity to wonder and explore one's mental state. It provides a sense of possibility. A revised assessment and new understanding expands the state of consciousness. Without the capacity to reflect fully, the amount of information processed is constrained and contributes to a constricted state of consciousness. This is supported by the narrowing of attention and the unavailability of memories.

Flashbacks as an Example

Let's pause at this point and look at the immersive experience of flashbacks to see what happens to each of the cognitive self-state subsystems. Flashbacks are instances of severe hyperaroused affect dysregulation in which the memory system dominates. It no longer interacts with the other cognitive subsystems. It usurps the representational system, which is given over to representing a fragment of a traumatic experience. Global attention is deactivated, eliminating the current context. Only focal attention is available, and it is fixed on the memory fragment. Exteroception is deactivated, and experience is left to interoception. The reflective system, which might serve to counteract the flashback, is deactivated. This is all being driven by the affect associated with the trauma and represents a failure of the attempt to quarantine the memory.

The Primary Affect-Regulating System and Dissociated Affect

As I mentioned above, we have two affect-regulating systems. The primary one is the one you've been reading about. It is automatic, fast and functions unconsciously. The secondary one utilizes reflective functioning to reassess and refine affect after it has been processed by the primary system. It operates verbally, is deliberate, relatively slow, and conscious.

The primary affect-regulating system is foundational. It does the initial, primary processing and regulation of affect, making it available for further appraisal at the verbal reflective level—secondary processing. The body is the first place in the organism to react to salient stimuli. Affect represents that reaction and conveys the meaning to *us* of an object in a particular context. If body-based affective experience cannot be initially processed but, rather, is dissociated, it cannot be further appraised or integrated into our sense of what is happening and what it means to us. Our capacity to respond adaptively is left to automatisms.

Affect becomes dissociated and unavailable for processing when the primary affect-regulating system is itself dissociated. For now we can understand the dissociation of the primary affect-regulating system simply as a state in which neurological structures responsible for processing affective information are no longer processing information as they should. Components of the system that should be interacting are dis-associated. As a result, the state of the body is not available for higher-order processing.

Affect that cannot be regulated and processed underlies the compartmentalization of content. If the intensity of the affective component of a memory or sense of self exceeds our capacity to regulate it, it will be avoided and compartmentalized. Dissociated self-states are organized around the avoidance of dissociated affect. Narcissistic self-states, for example, are organized around the avoidance of shame.

Finally, the subjective experience of a self-state is dominated by affective experience or its absence. Saying one is sad or angry or feels nothing refers to an entire state of being. When affect is dissociated, our subjectivity is diminished or collapses entirely. Affect is at the core of self-states. Dissociated affect is at the core of dissociated self-states.

Summary and Conclusion

Regulated affect is basic to integrated, flexible self-states. It organizes us, enables us to function optimally, and is the source of a sense of self-mastery and well-being. When affect is dysregulated and dissociated, our subjective experience is altered. What we perceive, the way we represent ourselves and others, what we remember, and our ability to think and feel clearly about our own and others' internal states are compromised.

At a more granular level, when affect is dysregulated, each of the subsystems comprising self-states has itself become dissociated. These systems—affective, attentional, perceptual, representational, memory, and reflective—comprise subjective experience and support adaptation to the internal and external environments. When affect is dysregulated, the cognitive systems function suboptimally and contribute, each in its own way, to the altered states of consciousness and compartmentalization that typify dissociated self-states.

The regulation of affect is fundamental for adaptive functioning. The initial, primary processing of affect sets the stage for higher-order, secondary processing. Modifying this primary affect-regulating system is crucial to the efficiency and enduring effects of affect-regulating therapies.

CHAPTER 3

The Neurobiology of the Primary Affect-Regulating System

IN CHAPTER 2 I proposed a model of the bodymind in which the organization of the self is affect state dependent. Self-states may be regulated-integrated or dysregulated-dissociated. The regulation of affect is crucial to adaptive functioning and central to subjective experience. Understanding the neurobiological mechanisms of affect regulation is necessary for a full appreciation for what is involved and for understanding what needs to be changed when affect regulation is impaired. The neurological structures of the primary affect-regulating system are, ultimately, the targets of affect regulation therapy. This chapter summarizes Allan Schore's ideas about the neurobiological mechanisms of the primary affect-regulating system.

The primary affect-regulating system forms as an adaptation to the socioemotional environment of the early attachment relationship. The arousal patterns we observed in the Strange Situation Procedure in Chapter 1 represent imprints of recurring affect-regulating experiences that shaped the organization and functioning of the neurobiological structures of the primary affect-regulating system during their critical period of development.

As we saw with the infants, the primary affect-regulating system determines whether we can shift efficiently from dysregulated to regulated states (Frances), tend toward states of hypo- or hyperarousal when stressed (Kenneth or Barbara), or vacillate unpredictably between affective extremes (Douglas). If we wish to change patients' capacity to regulate affect, we must alter the operation of this primary affect-regulating system. It is the central organizing system of the organism and the centerpiece of regulation theory (Schore, 1994, 2003a, 2003b, 2012).

The primary affect regulating system is the biological basis for regulation theory's understanding of states of bodymind, development, pathogenesis, and therapeutic action. As we're about to see, it generates core experiences of our subjectivity and determines our capacity for intersubjectivity. It is essential to what makes us human and what makes others human to us. However, before we explore it, we need to step back and review the brain in general. How does it develop? How does it change?

The Brain as a Complex System

The brain is an information-processing machine of enormous complexity. It contains billions of neurons, perhaps hundreds of trillions of connections between neurons, and 100,000 miles of biological wiring. Neurons combine to form neural networks, which in turn combine to make up modules (e.g., a face recognition module). and these modules combine to make up modes (e.g., the visual mode) that then combine make up larger systems (e.g., the perceptual system). Systems comprise subsystems, which themselves comprise subsystems, and so on. Keeping this complexity in mind, consider the feat of integration by which the brain organizes itself to provide us with coherent experiences of our inner and outer worlds.

Complexity theory provides us with principles for understanding the dynamics and development of the brain (Thelen & Smith, 1996; Siegel, 1999; Tronick, 2007; Boston Change Process Study Group,

2010, chap. 1; Marks-Tarlow, 2012; Schore, 1994). The first principle of complexity theory is that complex systems function best in states of maximum complexity and strive toward them in order to ward off entropy. In states of maximum complexity, all the different modules of the brain are available as needed for a reciprocal exchange of information with other functionally related modules. Integrating centers operate to coordinate their functioning. The more integrated the state of the system, the more flexible and stable it is.

When a system deteriorates from a state of maximum complexity, it loses its adaptive flexibility and becomes either rigid or chaotic. Siegel (2004) notes that each of the psychiatric disorders manifest as either rigid or chaotic states: obsessive-compulsive disorder is the manifestation of a rigid state; posttraumatic stress disorder is chaotic. We saw rigid patterns of affect regulation in Kenneth and Barbara , a highly unstable pattern in Douglas, and a flexible and stable pattern in Frances.

Complex systems shift states in a nonlinear fashion. Visualize, for example, the shape-shifting of a flock of birds (a complex system) as it suddenly reorganizes into qualitatively different configurations. Change does not occur in a linear, step-by-step fashion. The new shapes (states of the system) emerge all of a piece—no prime mover or leader organizes the changes.

Complex systems self-organize into new organizations as a result of myriad small, simple changes, with each element doing its own simple thing while the whole is acquiring increasing complexity and emergent properties. At some critical point there is a qualitative shift in the organization of the system. It is a bottom-up change that first sets off a process of disorganization and then reorganization. The emergent properties are unpredictable and cannot be reduced to the operations that produce them.

Therapeutic actions perturb complex systems. Perhaps, after a period when things have been percolating, or perhaps after a single powerful experience, one may all at once feel qualitatively different about oneself. Importantly, perturbations anywhere in the organism—brain, body, or mind—can cause a qualitative state shift in the overall system.

Finally, the brain is an open system. Information is received by and transmitted from it. The openness of the system allows it to commingle with other brains. Indeed, we have evolved to develop and function in connection with others and to enter into shared states in which there is a blending of subjectivities (Schore, 1994; Trevarthen, 1993; Tronick, 2007, chap. 29). Let's say I am talking with a friend. We are in sync with one another. We are sharing thoughts and feelings about a mutually interesting topic and generating new ideas. More often than not it is hard to know who contributed what to such discussions. Ideas seem to emerge from the interaction, the product of two complex systems, greater than the sum of their parts, generating ideas that could develop only from their unique interactions.

The increased complexity derived from the interpenetration of subjectivities has implications for development and psychotherapeutic change. Attuned mothers and infants can enter into merged states that deeply penetrate each other's being. Emotionally attuned patient-therapist dyads also enter into deep states of intersubjectivity. Such shared states resonate and have emergent properties. They are a goal of psychotherapy in that they generate key therapeutic actions.

Let's now look at the neurobiological structures comprising the primary affect-regulating system—the limbic system, the autonomic nervous system (ANS), and the hypothalamic-pituitary-adrenal (HPA) axis.

The Limbic System

The limbic system performs the executive function of appraising and responding to emotional information. It is the central organizing system of the brain and the organism, and it is located where one would expect a central organizing structure to have evolved: at the center of the brain. From that location its far-reaching connections to other areas of the brain can operate most efficiently.

Siegel (1999) devised an ingenious heuristic for illustrating the basic structures of the brain with the limbic system at the center. Hold your hand up facing you and close your fingers around your thumb. Think of this as the brain. The base of your palm represents the brainstem, which extends from the spinal cord, represented by your forearm and wrist. Your thumb represents the limbic system, and your palm, above the base, and your fingers, wrapped around your thumb (limbic system), represent the cerebral cortex.

The brainstem is the most primitive and earliest developing part of the brain, both ontogenetically and phylogenetically. It mediates involuntary motor and sensory systems, as well as physiological needs and drives: temperature, hunger, sexual drives, the sleep cycle, the pulmonary and cardiac systems, and so forth. It is fully developed at birth and is located at the bottom area of the brain referred to as subcortical.

Your thumb represents the limbic system (see figure 3.1 for a more realistic sense of the limbic system's location and relative size). It has a postnatal growth spurt—a critical period of development during which it is subject to influences from the caretaking environment.[23] It

---

23 During this growth spurt, genetically programmed innervation and myelination occurs in the limbic system. In the first year the entire brain more than doubles in size, growing from 400 grams to 1,000 grams!

develops in interaction with, and as an adaptation to, the affect-regulating activities of the caretaker(s).

Your palm, above the base, and your fingers, wrapped around your thumb (limbic system), represent the cerebral cortex. This is the last part of the brain to develop. Its growth is not completed until early adulthood. Higher-order mental processes are centered in the cortex. Language, reasoning, directed attention, symbolic representation, perception, certain kinds of memory, and executive functions, including reflective functioning, are processed in the cortex.

That is the vertical organization of the brain.[24] The early-forming subcortical structures are at the bottom, the later-forming cortex is at the top, and the limbic system is in the center. The limbic system comprises both cortical and subcortical structures. Like the rest of the brain, its most primitive functions are anatomically lower and earlier developing. Its higher-order functions are responsible for inhibiting the lower, more primitive structures.

In order to regulate affect, the limbic system processes physioemotional information coming up from the body and socioemotional information coming from others.[25] That is, along with processing information about somatic states, it receives and processes implicit communications of affect coming from the relational surround. Is it important to note that the limbic system, the central organizing system of the organism, does not process words. Rather, it assesses the image of the face, the sounds of the voice, and movements of the body—"limbiquese" is nonverbal. When we facilitate affect regulation during clinical work, it is not through the words we use but through the implicit communications of affect that infuse them.

----

24 Chapter 4 discusses the laterality of the brain—the right and left sides of the brain that process different types of information and process information differently.

25 It also is responsible for the expression of affect, but that is not relevant for the present discussion.

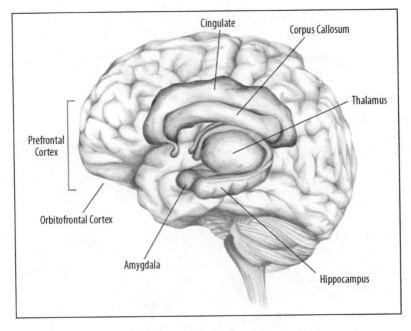

Figure 3-1. The limbic system.
From Kimberly Carraway, *Transforming Your Teaching* (Norton, 2014).
Reproduced with permission.

We can readily see that the central location of the limbic system is ideal for a three-pronged integration: (1) affective information coming up from the body is integrated with (2) information coming down from higher-order mentation generated in the cortex and (3) socioemotional information received via implicit communications of affect from others. In this way, the limbic system assembles self-states in mutually influential interaction with the self-states of others. Said differently, *the limbic system assembles a psychobiological subjectivity and a psychobiological intersubjectivity*—states of bodymind interacting with states of bodymind (see Figure 3.2). Affective dysregulation represents a disorganization of

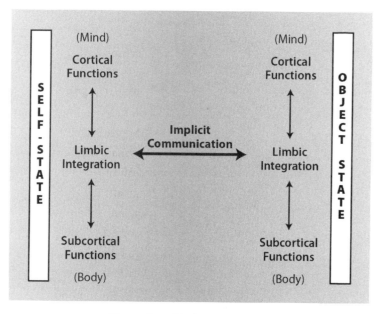

Figure 3–2. Limbic integration

the limbic system that also results in a collapse of subjectivity and intersubjectivity.

The limbic system comprises the orbitofrontal cortex and the subcortical components amygdala, anterior cingulate, insula, and hippocampus[26] (see Figure 3.1). Together they process and integrate body-based affective and socioemotional information. When optimally developed, the limbic system can flexibly regulate affect in response to changes in the internal and external environments. If the limbic system appraises stimuli as frightening, it activates the attachment system and triggers states of hyperarousal (flight and fight) or hypoarousal (freeze).

---

26 There is controversy in neurology about the boundaries of the limbic system and about which components should be included.

The Orbitofrontal Cortex

The components of the limbic system are organized hierarchically—the higher structures inhibit the lower ones. The orbitofrontal cortex, located just behind the eyes and the orbital socket of the skull, inhibits the subcortical components below it. Sometimes called the thinking part of the limbic system, the orbitofrontal cortex does the final and most complex integration of information processed by the limbic system. Referring to the hierarchical integration of the limbic system, Schore (2003) writes: "Although all components process exteroceptive and interoceptive information, the later-maturing systems in the cortex will process this information in a more complex fashion than the earlier subcortical components. The output of the lowest limbic levels have the character of automatic innate reflexes, while higher processing produces more flexible intuitive responses that allow fine adjustment to environmental circumstances" (p. 153).

The orbitofrontal cortex has a critical period of postnatal development from 10–12 to 16–18 months of age, during which time it is maximally subject to environmental influences. Subcortical structures of the limbic system come online sequentially and are thought to be fixed at the end of their critical periods, Cortical structures, however, are understood to have plasticity throughout the life span. Psychotherapy can alter the functioning of the right orbitofrontal cortex and strengthen its connections to the subcortical components of the limbic system, enabling it to have greater influence over them.

The Amygdala

Sometimes called the "red phone" of the brain, the amygdala is continuously primed and on the alert for predictors of threat. The most primitive component, located at the base of the limbic system, it is fully developed by 8 months of gestation. Memories of threatening experiences are stored in the amygdala and referenced for indications of danger from either the internal or external environment. When triggered, it puts the organism into states of hyperarousal. The hypervigilance and hyperreactivity to threat related cues seen in traumatized patients is understood to be a function of an amygdala-dominated limbic system.

Amygdala-based fear responses are activated too quickly for the perception of danger to become conscious. (Consciousness requires 250–500 milliseconds of focal attention.) Rather, the danger is detected neuroceptively (Porges, 2011). It is not hard to appreciate the adaptive qualities of neuroception and of the automatic reactions of the amygdala and motor cortex in fight-or-flight reactions. For example, while hiking one day I suddenly found myself up in the air—I had jumped. I then found myself running. It was only after taking a couple of strides that I realized that I had seen a snake. From a survival point of view, it is more adaptive to act first and think later.

Of course, misattribution of threat, due to hypersensitivities and overgeneralization of memories, can occur and be problematic for social engagement and for adaptation in general. You can also imagine the dangers of a blunted system that fails to react to relational threats or signs of impending danger in one's social environment. Both are possible sequelae of trauma.

The amygdala's neuroception of implicit communications of affect is exquisitely sensitive. It reacts to perceptions of threat in facial displays of affect that last only 30 milliseconds. It is even triggered by a constriction or expansion in another's pupil size—an indication of hypervigilance or fear.

The Anterior Cingulate

The anterior cingulate, affectionately called the "coo" of the brain, mediates maternal behaviors such as nursing and serves to regulate aggression and affect arousal. It is also involved in facial recognition and the direction of attention. It is closely linked with the orbitofrontal cortex and with it makes up the medial prefrontal cortex, which functions in an array of affect-regulating processes ranging from attuned communication to fear extinction.

The Insula

The insula, or insular cortex, is usually included among the structures of the limbic system. Like the other structures, it is involved in multiple functions having to do with affect regulation. Perhaps the most interesting clinically is that it is responsible for integrating somatosensory information with the functioning of the ANS and HPA axis and thereby provides embodied experience. It generates the visceral awareness of affect and is essential to the felt sense of subjective experience. It is deactivated in dissociative states, contributing to the numbness and emotional detachment associated with them (Schmahl, Lanius, Pain, & Vermetten, 2010).

The Hippocampus

The hippocampus mediates the recording and retrieval of memories.[27] It registers the emotional significance of an event and places a time and date stamp on it. Memories stored in the hippocampus are used to inhibit the amygdala. For example, if, on my hike, I had jumped simply because

---

27 Actually the hippocampus mediates explicit memories. We will discuss the distinction between explicit and implicit memories in Chapter 4.

I saw something long and thin with markings on it, I may have jumped needlessly. Memories that sticks with lichen on them are not dangerous, stored in the hippocampus, would have inhibited my amygdala's initial reaction. The relationship between the amygdala and the hippocampus is an example of the reciprocal partnership between neural structures. Although the hippocampus inhibits the amygdala, the amygdala's reactions alert the hippocampus to what is important to remember.

An overregulated amygdala is associated with an overly high threshold for reacting, failure to perceive threat, and insensitivity. An oversensitive (underregulated) amygdala results in hypervigilance and a lowered threshold for reacting. A system favoring either over- or underreaction has lost flexibility. Let's see how this looked in the Strange Situation Procedure.

When Barbara's (ambivalent-resistant) attachment system was activated, she became fixed in a state of hyperarousal and hypervigilant attention to her mother's potential abandonment. It is likely that her underregulated amygdala was responsible and rendered her unable to play. Kenneth (avoidant) was stuck in a hypoaroused state and seemed to use play to divert his attention from sources of stress. It is likely that his overregulated amygdala rendered him oblivious to, but not unaffected by, the age-appropriate stresses of the goings and comings of his mother.

Both Barbara and Kenneth manifested deficient complexity in their affect regulation systems. Both were incapable of reading and adjusting flexibly to the unfolding situation. Only Frances (securely attached) demonstrated emotional suppleness and response flexibility. She returned quickly to a homeostatic state through either autoregulation or dyadic regulation, depending on the social context, and adjusted to changes as they happened. Her affective, behavioral, and attentional patterns suggest a hierarchically organized, integrated limbic system in which each component is available for reciprocal interaction—a limbic system sufficiently complex to respond adaptively and recover efficiently from the stresses induced by the strange situations.

Conclusion

Let me return to the workings of the orbitofrontal cortex to see it's role in the regulation of affect. The orbitofrontal cortex is located at the apex of the limbic system. It performs the final integration of affective information coming up from the body (mediated by the subcortical limbic structires) and in through the senses receiving implicit communications representating others' affect states. It is where affect, memories of relevant events, and the evaluation of the current context are integrated. This final integration is used to regulate affect by inhibiting subcortical reactions as necessary.

Recall also that the orbitofrontal cortex is the center for the reception and expression of implicit communications of affect. It not only assembles subjective experience of the individual but also mediates intersubjective transactions and connects us to others psychobiologically. As we mutually match and resonate with one another's affect states, our subjective experiences become commingled.

The orbitofrontal cortex is the central organizing structure of the organism—the executive center of the self. It integrates the mind with the body and the bodymind with other bodyminds. It is responsible for assessing our own and other's affect states, for regulating our own affect, and for mediating affective transactions with others through the use of implicit communications.

The ANS and HPA Axis

The limbic system regulates affect by regulating the autonomic nervous system (ANS) and hypothalmic-pituitary-adrenal (HPA) axis, an endocrine system made up of a series of hormonal glands. Together these systems generate the arousal level and hedonic tone of affect.

The ANS consists of sympathetic and parasympathetic branches. The sympathetic aspect of the ANS is often compared to a car's accelerator. Among other things it increases heartbeat and respiratory rate, and in this way contributes to homeostasis by vitalizing and activating the system (upregulation). Without sufficient restraint, it generates dysregulated hyperaroused affect states. The parasympathetic aspect of the ANS is likened to a brake. It inhibits sympathetic arousal (downregulation) and thereby serves to modulate the effects of the sympathetic nervous system. If overly dominant, the parasympathetic nervous system generates dysregulated states of hypoarousal such as depression. Optimally, the sympathetic nervous system and parasympathetic nervous system are balanced and operate reciprocally, each acting as a counterbalance to the other and contributing as necessary in response to the demands of the internal and external environments.

Let's look at this reciprocal action first in a frightening situation. The parasympathetic brake on the sympathetic nervous system is released in response to a perceived threat. The now uninhibited sympathetic nervous system drives the fight-or-flight response. If neither fight nor flight is a survival option—when one is trapped and fear becomes terror—a component of the parasympathetic nervous system called the dorsal vagal system is activated. It then overrides the sympathetic nervous system and we freeze.

The survival importance of the freeze response can be seen in the feigned death (freezing) of mice when trapped by cats. Activation of the freeze response involves a metabolic collapse and immobilization of the mouse and, if all goes well, loss of interest by the cat. This inborn system serves to conserve and restore resources for a potential mad dash to safety. For humans faced with life-threatening situations, freezing also involves a psychological escape: a disconnection from somatic experience and horrifying reality into a state of dissociated detachment and numbness. At the neural level it serves to prevent cell death due to the neurotoxic conditions created by such severe states of stress.

But what of normal circumstances? It is essential to well-being that we spend most of our time in homeostatic states. Maintaining and returning to homeostatic states requires a balanced ANS, that is, a reciprocal equilibration of the sympathetic and parasympathetic nervous systems. The reciprocal cycling provides a feathering effect that modulates the intensity of affect, allows a fluid shifting between states, with recalibrations and corrections.

Through a reciprocal activation of its two branches, the ANS provides a flexible means of accelerating and decelerating heart rate and respiration to maintain homeostasis. Without such autonomic balance, we are prone to chronic states of sympathetic or parasympathetic arousal or abrupt shifting between extremes of hyper- and hypoarousal.

We need to add an important refinement to our understanding of the parasympathetic nervous system. Porges (2011) has proposed that parasympathetic regulation is mediated by the vagus nerve, which connects the parasympathetic nervous system directly to the heart. The vagus has two branches. The dorsal vagal system is activated in the presence of inescapable danger, induces a massive decrease in heart rate, and is the mechanism of the freeze response. It induces a sudden metabolic collapse manifesting in immobility and feigned death. A later-forming, "smart," ventral vagal system mediates graduated and nimble parasympathetic responses suitable for navigating social environments that require flexible responsiveness. Porges calls this the social engagement system.

To regulate affect, the limbic system also regulates the HPA axis, a series of hormonal glands (hypothalamus, pituitary, and adrenal) responsible for regulating the arousal level and hedonic tone of affect. It is often referred to as the stress system. Stress encompasses a broad range of physiological reactions from mild to severe and from chronic to acute. For our purposes, stress may be thought of as negative affect.

The HPA axis induces physiological change through the release of hormones. Primary among them are epinephrine and norepinephrine (aka adrenaline and noradrenaline), which accelerate the cardiovascular and respiratory systems, and cortisol, which calms them down. These hormones induce the reactions of the sympathetic and parasympathetic nervous systems. The HPA axis also releases neurotransmitters. For example, endogenous opioids such as endorphins have an analgesic effect that allows us to persist during survival experiences without experiencing pain. These may combine with dopamine to counteract stress or simply generate a sense of well-being.

Dual Circuits Connecting the Limbic System to the ANS

There is one last and crucial piece that must be added to complete the picture of the primary affect-regulating system. We have seen that the limbic system processes and integrates physioemotional and socioemotional information in order to regulate the ANS. It is connected to the ANS via two circuits: (1) the ventral tegmental limbic circuit connects the limbic system through the HPA axis to the sympathetic aspect of the ANS; and (2) the lateral tegmental limbic circuit connects the limbic system through the HPA axis to the parasympathetic nervous system (Figure 3.3).

The development of this dual circuit linking the limbic system to the ANS is the final and critical moment in the development of the primary affect-regulating system. Before this we are largely dependent on our caretaker for inducing sympathetic and parasympathetic arousal in order to maintain homeostasis. After the dual limbic circuits come on line, we are able to regulate our affect state with increasing autonomy.

Again, the dual limbic circuits regulate the sympathetic nervous system and parasympathetic nervous system reciprocally. That is, when the sympathetic nervous system is activated, the parasympathetic nervous system is deactivated, and vice versa. When balanced, this rapid, on-off, arousal-inhibition relationship allows for the modulation of affective intensity and the gradual shifting of affect states— affect tolerance, flexibility, and resilience.

In Part III we will see the pathological manifestations of an imbalance in the ANS, that is, when either the sympathetic or parasympathetic system dominates. In such cases, the ANS loses its flexibility and has a bias toward either hyper- or hypoarousal. This imbalance in the ANS results in a developed set point toward hyper- or hypoarousal and hyper- or hypoaroused responses to stress—core personality characteristics.

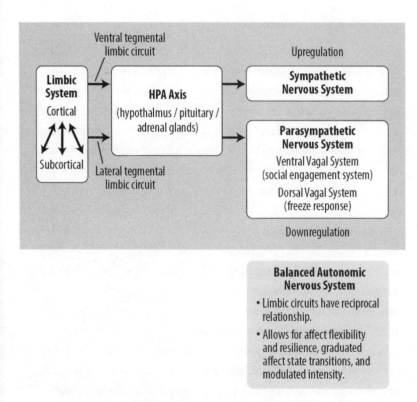

Figure 3–3. The Primary Affect-Regulating System

We saw this in the Strange Situation Procedure in Chapter 1. In the case of Kenneth (avoidant), the activation of his attachment system put him in a parasympathetic dominant state from which he was unable to extricate himself. When Barbara's (ambivalent-resistant) attachment system was activated, she found herself in a sympathetic dominant state. She was also unable to shift into a homeostatic state that would allow her to explore. On the other hand, Frances (secure) seemed to have had a primary affect-regulating system that was autonomically balanced, and she was able to return from dysregulated affect states to homeostasis and play.

Summary and Conclusion

In this chapter we have looked at the brain generally as a self-organizing, open, complex system that interacts with and is capable of commingling with other brains to achieve maximal complexity. When affect is regulated, the brain is in an integrated and flexible state—an optimal state for meeting the ongoing demands of the inner and outer environments. However, when dysregulated, the brain is disorganized and dissociated and unable to effect flexible responsiveness.

We then looked at the combined workings of the limbic system, the ANS, and the HPA axis in the regulation of affect. The limbic system appraises and integrates affective information coming from within and outside the self and, based on these evaluations, regulates the ANS (sympathetic and parasympathetic branches) and the HPA axis. Together, they regulate the arousal level and hedonic tone of affect that make up the core of self-states.

A well-organized limbic system is dominated by the orbitofrontal cortex. It provides the highest-order integration of affective information used to regulate the ANS and HPA axis. A well-organized ANS is balanced and provides affective resilience, tolerance, and stability. This maximizes the amount of time spent in homeostatic states, in which our affective experience is available to us as information and we are available for intersubjective relatedness.

A poorly organized primary affect-regulating system has system-wide ramifications: psychological, somatic, and relational. Without affect tolerance and resilience, we are subject to chronic states of dys-regulated hyperarousal (Barbara) or hypoarousal (Kenneth) or vacil-lations between the two (Douglas).

Without the somatic and psychological integration provided by a cortically dominated limbic system, subjectivity is disordered. With-out the integrated processing of implicit communications, intersubjec-tivity is disordered. The limbic system can be thought of as the center of social and emotional intelligence (Golemen, 2006, 2007).

Finally, let's look again at self-states. Recall from Chapter 2 that they comprise a system of cortically based attentional, representational, per-ceptual, memory, and reflective processes organized by affect. We saw that each of these processes may be dissociated by dysregulated affect and that the quality of cognitive functioning is affect state dependent.

Schore's understanding of the primary affect-regulating system illuminates the neurobiological mechanisms by which the intensity and hedonic tone of affect shapes and colors: our perceptions of the present; our representations of self and objects in the past and the future; the memories that are accessible; the capacity for our attention to move flexibly between interoception and exteroception; and the quality of our reflective capacities. Ultimately, our affect state orga-nizes our subjectivity and our capacity for intersubjective engagement.

CHAPTER 4

The Right Brain, Implicit Processes, and the Implicit Self

IF YOU REMOVE the brain from the skull and place it in your hands, you can separate the hemispheres by simply moving your hands apart. They are connected only by the corpus callosum, a band of nerve fibers that mediates the interhemispheric transfer of information (see Figure 4.1). Evolution has provided us with two hemispheres so different from each other that they are commonly referred to as the right and left brains. McGilchrist (2010) argues that they "bring different worlds into being," a world of entities as they are and another of entities to be used—worlds of subjects versus objects.

Schore (1994, 2003a, 2003b, 2012) proposes that the right brain is dominant in early attachment development, in the pathogenesis of developmental disorders, and in the psychotherapeutic treatment of disorders of affect regulation. This chapter summarizes his and Iain McGilchrist's (2010) understanding of right-brain, implicit processes. Along with describing the qualities of implicit processes in comparison to left-brain, explicit processes, my aim is to illuminate the preeminent role of the implicit right brain in listening to, understanding, and responding to our patients.

Schore's understanding of right- and left-brain processes may be thought of as an update of Freud's topographical model of primary and secondary processes and of unconscious, preconscious, and conscious levels of awareness. Like Freud, Schore proposes that unconscious (implicit) processes are foundational and that they underlie the problems that our patients bring to us,. Unlike Freud, Schore proposes that the problems originate in unconscious affect-regulating processes that are poorly organized and that they are changed through the affect-regulating, attachment relationship with the therapist.

Having two brains does not distinguish us from many other species. Birds, for example, have two identical hemispheres. The redundancy allows them to fly for days at a time with one hemisphere asleep while the other is active. This may seem attractive in an age when there are never enough hours in the day. However, the advantages of redundancy come at a high price. A brain with hemispheres that process information differently allows greater complexity and flexibility.

Our right and left brains process different kinds of information in different ways and perform different functions (Gazzaniga &

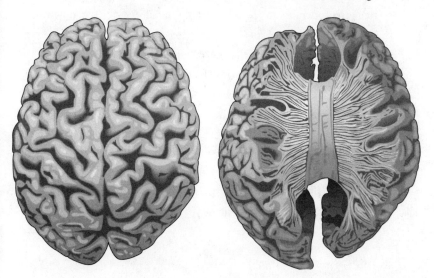

Figure 4-1. The corpus callosum and hemispheres of the brain.

LeDoux, 1978). The integration of two brains generating two very different ways of thinking, experiencing, and being in the world has enormous adaptive advantages. Let's look at the information processing of each hemisphere.

The right brain mediates implicit processes: implicit memory, implicit cognition, and implicit communications of affect. These processes are fast, unconscious, nonverbal, and automatic. *The left brain mediates explicit processes*, which are slower, conscious, verbal, and deliberate. Implicit processes are primary and precede the secondary, explicit processes. They are largely unconscious because of their speed—the threshold for consciousness is 250–500 milliseconds of focused attention.

Let me qualify this left- versus right-brain scenario by noting that, in actuality, virtually all mental activities utilize both hemispheres. It is more accurate to say that particular functions are right- or left-brain dominant and to keep in mind that they are relatively independent systems that operate reciprocally. It is the reciprocity of the systems that generates the complexity.

The right brain mediates the expression and reception of nonconscious, nonverbal communications of affect —facial expressions, prosody of voice, and gestures—whereas the left brain processes words.[28] Thus, the output of a patient's right brain can be processed only by the right brain of the therapist, and that of the patient's left brain by the left brain of the therapist.

The right brain is dominant for the primary, automatic, unconscious processing of emotions. The left brain performs their secondary, conscious processing in words. The right brain processes

---

28 Wernicke's area for receptive language and Broca's area for expressive language are both in the left hemisphere.

affective information first. So, for example, by the time we have consciously thought and felt something, we have already thought, felt, and made up our implicit minds about it. The left-brain, explicit mind is left with the job of rationalizing and putting a positive spin on it (Gazzaniga, 1989) or having second thoughts about the first reaction.

Attributes of Implicit and Explicit Processing

The right brain processes information holistically. Unconscious implicit processes assemble a gestalt—a integration of information presented without awareness of the operations that led to its construction. Images, for example, are processed in the right brain and provide us with a whole picture at once; all information is presented simultaneously. Complex ideas may receive the same treatment. Intuitions and insights, knowings that come to us all at once, are products of right-brain implicit processes that may take paragraphs to unpack verbally with the left brain.

The speed of right-brain processing is crucial for the processing of socioemotional information involved in the real-time assessment and navigation of the complexities of the relational environment. We not only need to process the split-second back-and-forth of emotional transactions but also need to have panoramic, all-at-once views of relationships that encompass the immediate context and considerations based on past and future.

Right-brain holistic processing allows multiple ideas to be held together simultaneously. It supports the complexities of synthesis; the apprehension of the layered meanings expressed in metaphor; the integration of past, future, and present experience; and a real-time appreciation of the complexities of subjective and intersubjective life.

The left brain processes information serially. It processes language, one word after another, in a linear sequence. It mediates logical and analytical thinking utilized in mathematics and the sciences, logistical planning in business, and reflection about everyday life. It processes information consciously, voluntarily, and relatively slowly. Clinically, left-brain explicit processing supports verbal reflective therapeutic actions such as observations and interpretations.

Thus, our lateralized brains provide the advantages of rapid thought for real-time relating and of slower processing, using words, for purposes of reflection, planning and explication. The speed of the right brain helps to explain why the left brain tends to find itself rationalizing conclusions already arrived at by the right—the source of unconscious biases.

McGilchrist (2010) describes the assimilative quality of left-brain processing. It evolved to grasp and control the environment. It uses words to categorize objects by fitting them into the scheme of things it already knows. It breaks the world into parts; it analyzes, categorizes, and reduces it to logic and certainty.

In stark contrast, the right brain apprehends each object as unique. It takes in the world as it is, accepting it with all its ambiguities and contradictions. Unburdened by the logical and sequential requirements of the left brain or by the limitations of language, the right brain is open and receptive, accommodating experience rather than assimilating it into known categories delimited by words. Right-brain, nonconscious, holistic processing is the basis of creativity, playfulness, humor, and spontaneity. Transitional experiencing (Winnicott, 1971) is mediated by the right brain.

McGilchrist (2010) notes that the left brain evolved for predicting and that it operates with known information and is adaptive for routine situations. The right brain "alone can bring us something other than what we already know" (p. 40). Indeed, the right brain evolved for novel situations, is alert for novel stimuli, can accept ambiguity, and has the capacity to continue to operate under the stress that comes with novelty. The left brain deactivates under severe stress.

The left and right brains mediate attentional systems congruent with their serial versus holistic modes of information processing. The left brain focuses narrowly, like the beam of a flashlight. It zeros in on specific targets, one at a time. The right brain attends globally, like the light of a lantern, taking in the surround as a whole and providing context and complexity. Novel information tends to come from the periphery of consciousness.

The fast right brain assembles the perception of the present and puts us in the moment. By processing information simultaneously, it has the speed necessary to provide us with our real-time inner and outer realities—to think about, for example, what we are saying while saying it. Right-brain fast thinking may be conscious, or it may be semiconscious and glimpsed out of the corner of our mind's eye at the periphery of consciousness; or it may be nonconscious.[29] When we do become aware of it, right-brain thinking may be experienced as an elusive, impressionistic mentalese that we simply call nonverbal. It is what Freud called the system preconscious, what Bollas (1987) called the unthought known, and what Donnell Stern (1997) refers to it as unformulated thought.

In contrast to this, the slower-acting left brain constructs con-

---

29 Such unconscious processing is often called *nonconscious* to distinguish it from Freud's understanding of the repressed, dynamic unconscious. In Freud's model, repression is required to keep unconscious content from our awareness. The implicit unconsciousness described here involves processes that occur too quickly for consciousness. (Recall that the threshold for consciousness is 250–500 milliseconds of focused attention.)

scious, verbal representations used for thinking about the past or future. Whereas the right brain presents the present, the left brain re-presents and thus removes us from the here and now. Its slow, linear processes are insufficient for monitoring the internal and eternal object relations of real-time relating while remaining in the moment.

In western culture there is a tendency to think that our left-brain, rational processes are in control. This is a central theme of McGilchrist's book *The Master and His Emissary* (2010). The left brain *thinks* it is in charge, but in reality it is unaware that it is the emissary of the right brain's emotionally based bidding. We can see this in the sequence by which the right and left brains process affective information.

Body-based affect ascends via the brainstem and is first processed by the subcortical components of the right limbic system. After this subcortical processing, the right orbitofrontal cortex integrates this physioaffective information with socioemotional information received from relational transactions. Subsequent to this right-brain primary processing, the emotional information travels across the corpus callosum to the left hemisphere for secondary, verbal, serial, conscious thinking and then back into the right for a final, most complex integration. Using Freud's scheme, Schore (2012) proposes that the right subcortical processing is unconscious (cannot be made conscious), that right cortical processing is preconscious (can be made conscious), and that left-brain, secondary processing is conscious (see Figure 4.2).

Left- and right-brain processing each have their benefits and limitations, and their integration or the flexible use of one or the other is an adaptive advantage. Although a chronic dominance of one hemisphere over the other may generate notable intellectual or artistic strengths, the limitations represent significant adaptive drawbacks.

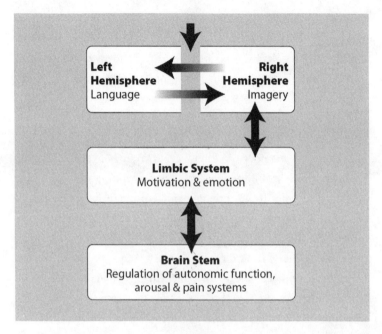

Figure 4-2.

The right brain is the seat of emotional and social intelligence. Left to its own devices, the left brain, with its sequential, logical processes, would set up a rule-bound, decontextualized, overly objectified, emotionally removed, utilitarian relationship to objects. However, in conjunction with right-brain implicit processes, the left brain can reflect on affect states in self and others and use this information to think more complexly. Deficits in right-brain processing, with left-brain dominance, lead to an emotionally barren, empty subjectivity and a lack of intersubjectivity. Without the foundation of right-brain processing of physiological and socioemotional information, we would be left with an absence of empathy for ourselves and others. Indeed, as we will see, psychotherapy is first and foremost a right-brain endeavor.

Let's now turn our attention to the different implicit processes mediated by the right brain. There are three crucial to the understanding of affect regulation. I begin with implicit memory, followed by implicit cognition, and end by returning to a discussion of implicit communication.

Implicit Versus Explicit Memory

The study of memory distinguishes two major types: explicit memory, which can be thought of as the encoding of *what*—what happened or what things are; and implicit memory, which can be thought of as the remembering of *how*—the encoding of procedures for doing things.

Explicit memory, also called declarative or semantic memory, is the remembering of facts and events. The learning of explicit memories requires focal attention and is conscious, for example, learning the structures of the limbic system. The encoding and storage of explicit memories are mediated by the hippocampus. It puts a time and date stamp on experiences and registers their emotional salience, to be used in assessing similar stimuli.

Explicit memories vary in duration. Working memory is short term, used when planning or problem solving. If I ask you to repeat your phone number backward, you would figure this out using working memory. It's a buffer, sometimes called the chalkboard of the mind. Explicit memories may be long term but do not last beyond several months. They may then be consolidated into permanent memory, by which time they are likely to have been considerably altered, and after which they will continue to be altered.

Finally, explicit memories include autobiographical memories of events with subjective experience at the center. These are called episodic or narrative memories and are crucial to exploring not only the past but also the future. They depend on the right brain to provide the emotional information that gives personal meaning to the episode.

Implicit memory, also called procedural or early memory, is fully functional at birth and, for some implicit memory systems, in utero. It is encoded through repetitive experiences. When implicit memories are activated there is no sense of remembering. Using a keyboard, riding a bike, and making automated relational moves employ implicit memory systems.

The activation of automatic neurobiological processes for regulating affect also employs implicit memory systems. It is a remembering of psychobiological and behavioral procedures engrained during infancy through repeated affect-regulating interactions with one's caretakers.

The behaviors of the children described in the Strange Situation Procedure described in Chapter 1 are manifestations of activated implicit memory systems. They were automated reactions to a fearful situation that tapped relational, attentional, and emotional patterns. The attachment patterns were scripted procedures engrained as the children adapted to their caretaking environments. Such remembered procedures include an anticipation of what is going to happen next and may be the basis of the expectancy effect.

Transference, too, can be understood as an activation of implicit memory systems in response to unconsciously perceived likenesses between a present relationship and a past relationship to which one has adapted. Attachment transferences involve the activation of procedures learned through repetitive experiences in an early attachment relationship, including relational behaviors, representational patterns (internal object relations), selective perceptions, attentional patterns, and patterns of affect regulation. Character traits consist of implicit memory systems developed as adaptations to different situations and activated in specific contexts. Our different ways of being in different contexts are assemblages of implicit memory systems.

Implicit memories serve as the operating instructions for the primary affect-regulating system. Automatic procedures for regulating affect are imprinted during the early mother-infant relationship—psychoneurobiological procedures for autoregulation, as well as relational procedures for dyadic regulation. When the attachment system is activated, implicit memory systems mediate our sense of self and others and ways of co-regulating one another. We are overwhelmingly and most basically implicit beings. Alterations to implicit memory systems are changes of the most basic kind—changes to the way we are, changes to our implicit selves.

Implicit Cognition

Implicit cognition refers to a nonverbal knowing that comes to us fully formed as a gestalt. It is immediate and made up of things that have often been learned without awareness (implicit learning). Intuition and insight are implicit cognitions that are fully formed by the time they become conscious. I have mentioned that the speed of implicit cognition is adaptive for monitoring real-time social interacting.

Citing a 2006 study by Volz and von Cramon, Schore (2011) notes that intuition is not "expressed in . . . language but 'embodied' in a 'gut feeling' or in an initial guess that subsequently biases our thought and inquiry" (p. 30). Intuitions may be expressed in images, metaphors, and physical sensations (Marks-Tarlow, 2012). Implicit communications, mediated by the right limbic system and transmitted below the threshold of consciousness, inform the therapist of the subjective experience of the patient and manifest as intuitions in the right brain of the therapist. Such intuitions guide therapists as they pursue hunches and impressions and are arguably the primary factor influencing therapeutic interventions.

Let's say that as a therapist I am onto something and begin to convey it to a patient. I know the gist of what I want to communicate and have confidence that the words will come even though I have yet to formulate them. The implicit cognition has developed only that far. Verbalizing it (left brain) often clarifies it to *me* as I am speaking. What came to me all at once as some kind of nonverbal mentalese and provided me with an immediate full sense of things may take several sentences to make explicit. The slowness allows me adjust the initial hunch as I put it into words.

Implicit Communication

The introduction noted that implicit communications mediate the nonconscious exchange of affect via facial expressions and gaze, the prosody of voice, and posture and gestures. They are the means by which we read others' affect states and reveal our own. Let's focus on the regulation of the infant.

Initially, the infant's affect regulation takes place through body-based proximal communications, including touch and holding. As the infant develops and becomes mobile, distal regulation via implicit communications becomes increasingly important. Visual perception of the mother's face and mutual gaze have the strongest effects.

The distal implicit communication of affect can be thought of as touch at a distance. It may be soothing or exciting, disturbing or pleasing, and it effects us through the body—from the bottom up. When the implicit communication is contingent, and especially when the expressed affect states are in synchrony, there is a felt psychobiological connection: a visceral sense of intimacy. Such limbic-mediated connecting-at-a-distance remains the fundamental mechanism by which we know and nurture one another throughout the life span.

Affect is at the heart of our subjectivity, and implicit communications of affect are the fundamental means by which we convey our subjectivity and encounter the subjectivity of others. The exchange of implicit communications of affect establishes the intersubjective field. Trevarthen (1993) refers to such immediate, intimate affect exchanges as "primary intersubjectivity." In Schore's model these are understood to be communications between "implicit selves."

The Implicit Self

The *implicit self* (Schore, 2010b, 2012) refers to the psychobiological state of the self at a given moment. Assembled automatically by the right brain, the sense of the implicit self usually hums in the background below levels of consciousness and is communicated nonconsciously via implicit communications.

Schore's ideas about the implicit self are, I believe, an update of Winnicott's "true self" (1965, pp. 37–55) based in spontaneous experience and of Stern's (1984) observations of the subjective sense of self. The detached experience of dissociation can be thought of as a detachment from implicit self-experience—from the experience of the bodymind.

Schore places implicit communication at the center of the therapeutic relationship. The implicit therapeutic relationship is co-constructed through involuntary, unconscious transactions between the implicit selves of the patient and therapist. These mutually influential, nonconscious communications are at the core of the therapeutic encounter and constitute the relational unconscious.

Implicit communications are the primary means by which trust and the therapeutic alliance are established. Facial expressions, eye contact, gestures and posture, and prosody convey *unequivocally* the therapist's interest, receptivity, recognition, and acceptance of the patient's implicit expressions of self-experience. Implicit communications have a greater impact than anything we might say in words about whether or not we care. Therapeutic sensitivity and nurturing intentions are implied, communicated unconsciously from implicit self to implicit self.

Implicit self-states, communicated involuntarily, may be very different from the conscious, explicit self-state communicated in words via the left brain. The left brain is responsible for constructing verbal narratives of our experience and tends to put a socially acceptable, self-enhancing spin on things (Gazzaniga, 1989). Implicit communications, on the other hand, are involuntary, direct communications from one nervous system to another, without editing. There is a certitude that accompanies implicit communication that is unmatched in explicit communications. When the explicit communication is different from a simultaneous implicit communication, we do well to trust the implicit—the implicit self cannot fake it.

Finally, therapeutic trust is based in perceived intentions, feeling recognized and accepted, and a sense of the therapist's emotional competency. All are derived from implicit communications. The patient learns implicitly of the therapist's capacity to receive and respond sensitively to his or her implicit communications of affect and about the therapist's capacity to tolerate strong or negative affects. All this is established psychobiologically and nonconsciously, right brain to right brain, in the split-second world of the patient-therapist implicit relationship.

TABLE 4.1 RIGHT BRAIN IMPLICIT VERSUS LEFT BRAIN EXPLICIT PROCESSES

	IMPLICIT	EXPLICIT
MEMORY	Procedural memory: nonconscious memory of how things are done; not experienced as memory.	Declarative or semantic memory of events and what things are; experienced as memory.
COGNITION	Fast, nonverbal knowing that integrates information and presents knowledge as a gestalt; used for knowing the present.	Verbal, slow, linear thinking about the past or future; used for rational analysis of the past or future.
COMMUNICATION	Fast, nonverbal, nonconscious, automatic/ involuntary; conveys affect states.	Slow, verbal, conscious, deliberate; used for conveying the past and future

Part II

Theory of Development

Secure Attachment
and the
Development of Affect Regulation

CHAPTER 5

Classical Attachment Theory

CLASSICAL ATTACHMENT THEORY[30] provides a foundation for understanding how the capacity to regulate affect develops.[31] It is built on the original theorizing of John Bowlby and studies by his student Mary Ainsworth and of her student Mary Main. Chapter 1 described the different attachment patterns as they present behaviorally in the Strange Situation Procedure. In this chapter I discuss Bowlby's contributions, with an emphasis on the *internal working model*, a central theoretical concept providing attachment theory with much of its clinical value. I then take up the work of Mary Main, who advanced attachment theory from the classification of behavioral patterns in the mother-infant attachment relationship to the classification of narrative patterns of adults; a measure of the individual's verbal representational capacity. She called her measure the Adult Attachment Interview.

---

30 There is no better source for a comprehensive, historical and theoretical appreciation of classical attachment theory than Robert Karen's beautifully written *Becoming Attached* (1994).

31 I use the term *classical attachment theory* in relationship to Schore's (1994) integration of attachment theory with developmental affective neurobiology, which he calls "modern attachment theory."

Bowlby and the Internal Working Model

Bowlby brought the concept of the attachment system to psychoanalysis from ethology,[32] where it was understood as a behavioral system activated by fear. It was viewed as part of the survival system, which includes the fight-flight-freeze reactions. It looks like this.

When an immature primate goes off exploring and finds itself too far from its mother's side, it becomes afraid. With the onset of fear, the exploration system is deactivated and the attachment system is activated.[33] The young primate first looks for the location of its mother and assesses whether she is paying attention and if *she* is alarmed. If it returns to her side, she is performing a *safe haven* function. If it is reassured of safety by referencing its mother's face from a distance, she is performing a *secure base* function. Both facilitate the deactivation of the attachment system and reactivation of the exploration system.

Bowlby theorized that the aim of the attachment system was to restore a background sense of "felt security", which allows the child to explore. We saw this in the Strange Situation Procedure when, after becoming distressed at separation from her mother or the arrival of a stranger, the secure infant was calmed and returned to play (exploration). Put in terms of affect regulation, the function of the attachment figure is to return the frightened child to a regulated state.

---

32 Ethology is the study of animals in their natural habitat. He was influenced by the work of Konrad Lorenz and Niko Tinbergen, the fathers of the field. Bowlby took the general idea of a model of self-in-the-world from ethology and conceived of it in object relational terms (Hinde, 2006). He sought to integrate psychoanalysis and biology (Freud and Darwin). Schore's work is a direct extension of this effort.

33 The exploration and attachment systems have a reciprocal relationship.

The Internal Working Model—Ways of Being in Relationships

The secure and insecure patterns Ainsworth observed are conceptualized by attachment theory as adaptive strategies: adaptations to the caretaking environment that serve to maintain the relationship with the mother and a sense of safety. They are at the core of attachment relationships.

Bowlby theorized that such mother-infant interactions become "imprinted"[34] as "interiorized actions"[35]—a repertoire of automated ways of acting and being with the attachment figure. He referred to this system as the "internal working model of attachment." Bowlby conceived of these patterns in psychoanalytic terms as the object relations of attachment: a system of self and object representations that mediates our attachment relationships.

The internal working model provides a basis for understanding how infant attachment patterns develop into adult personality patterns. Clinically, it is a framework for understanding attachment-based transferences. Let's examine this more closely. The internal working model (Bowlby, 1973; Bretherton, 2005; Cobb & Davila, 2009; Pietromonaco & Barrett, 2000) is conceived of as a dynamic template—a schema that mediates patterns of interpersonal behavior, attention,

---

34 Bowlby believed that imprinting, a single-trial means of learning, is the learning mechanism of attachment. He was influenced in this by Konrad Lorenz's studies with geese that became attached to him through imprinting— he merely passed through their line of sight during a critical period. This idea, that *an image can encode attachment procedures*, is important for Schore's theory of development and therapeutic action. Schore (1994) proposes that the mother's face is imprinted, that it is the representation activating attachment patterns, and that the therapist's face is a key determinant of therapeutic action.

35 We can now appreciate that such imprinted interior actions are implicit-procedural memories.

perception, representation, and affect arousal in the relationship with the attachment figure. Using such packages of cognitive-affective-behavioral patterns, the internal working model serves to evaluate, predict, and manage the attachment relationship in the service of safety and regulated affect.

Evaluation and Prediction

The evaluation and prediction components of the internal working model play leading roles. The real-time status of the self in an attachment relationship is assessed by processing the socioemotional information emanating from the attachment figure: Are we connected? Are you available, interested, positive? Depending on the evaluation, expectations based on prior experiences are activated.

For example, a secure child with a history of sensitive, responsive caretaking reaches to pick up a delicate figurine for some joyful banging. Seeing the alarmed and disapproving look on his mother's face and hearing her abrupt "NO-NO," he is first stunned and then bursts into tears. Immediately he looks back to her face while extending his arms to be picked up. He expects his empathic mother's face to change for the better. She is known to him as emotionally flexible and able to switch affect states efficiently. He expects to be received with open, reassuring, soothing arms, to have his distress relieved and the ruptured relationship repaired. Such positive expectations distinguish him from insecure infants. Their negative expectations are based in repeated entreaties for reassurance and reconnection that have been met with dismissal or anger.

Anticipating the future is essential to a strategy for safety. Because we normally do not have time to think through every interaction, we rely on learned expectations to organize our reactions. *Our expectations of how the attachment figure will respond guide the attachment system.* Attention, perception, representation, and interpersonal behavior, the other components of the attachment package, are primed by these expectations. An attachment figure who is expected to be dismissive will activate patterns of attention, behavior, and so forth, that the child has developed to cope with a lack of sensitive responsiveness and with being left alone in a distressed state. Attention will be diverted from the caretaker's face, which is the most immediate source of stress. Perception and representation of the event will be based on past negative experiences. Behaviors are likely to be aimed at self-soothing, given that dyadic distress relief is not anticipated.

The expectancy effects embedded in the internal working model infuse the attachment relationship with trust or distrust. The secure child's attachment interactions are dominated by the attachment figure's reliable accessibility, interest, and sensitive responsiveness. Expectations based in such experiences establish trust in the intentions and emotional competency of attachment figures.

Mediating Relationships

Bowlby proposed that the internal working model, developed in infancy, mediates attachment relationships throughout the life span. For example, the return-to-mother safe-haven behaviors develop into procedures of interactive affect regulation. The later-developing, look-to-mother-for-reassurance secure-base functions mature into representational processes employed for autoregulation. Ideally, we develop both auto- and dyadic ways of managing stress and returning to regulated states.

The clinical implications are noteworthy. Whether or not patients tend to use us as a safe haven can be considered a core aspect of the transference. Whether or not they use us as a secure base might be considered a measure of the effectiveness of the therapeutic relationship (Eagle & Wolitzky, 2009). If they do use us as a safe haven, do they do so with positive expectations, or anxiously? If they have internalized us, is it as a shaming or nurturing regulatory object?

Assimilative Function

The internal working model has an assimilative dynamic that filters and absorbs experience into the schema. It interprets the transactions of the attachment relationship according to pre-formed expectations and guides attention, perception, and representations accordingly.

The assimilative function of the internal working model is adaptive. In real time we often do not have the time to think deliberately about how to interact with others. The internal working model serves to automatically regulate attention, filtering what enters into awareness, and performs a predetermined shaping and coloring of perceptions and representations of the self in relationship to the others. There are also maladaptive aspects to this that may manifest as transference and impede therapeutic progress.

The influences of the assimilative aspect are of the self-fulfilling-prophecy variety. Positive expectations derived from secure attachment experiences are communicated implicitly and elicit positive responses from others. Negative expectations, born of insecure attachment experiences, work in the opposite direction. This recursive quality stabilizes the internal working model by reinforcing the expectations. It also works against changing it therapeutically and can be thought of as the mechanism underlying what Freud called "transference resistance."

Finally, the assimilative aspect of the internal working model determines a sense of self according to a model formed in early attachment experiences. For example, the sense of worthiness associated with secure attachment derives from the readily available interest and the contingent, nonjudgmental responsiveness of the secure caretaker. Feeling worthy is part of the package when a secure attachment pattern is activated. A sense of self as unworthy, based in a very different history, comes as part of the package when insecure attachment patterns are activated.

Working Model

Bowlby's use of the term internal *working* model includes the idea of a work in progress. That is, it matures along with a growing appreciation of the realistic limitations of the attachment figure and the developing capacities of the self and as the means for achieving felt security develop. Thus, the internal working model not only assimilates reality but also accommodates it. Such developmental updates give rise to increasingly complex and flexible schemas for being in relationships.

The complexity and flexibility of our attachment system go beyond the maturation of a single model. Bowlby appreciated that we develop multiple internal working models in relationships with different attachment figures or variations in their capacities at different phases of development. The same caretaker that provides secure conditions during an early developmental period may not be as well suited to subsequent, more complicated phases.

There is agreement among attachment researchers that there are primary and secondary internal working models derived from primary and secondary attachment figures. Their interplay is thought to account for the blends and mixtures of attachment patterns that we observe clinically. Adding to the complexity, the activation of attachment patterns is context specific: different patterns are activated in response to different attachment figures and variations in the same attachment figures. One can easily appreciate the parallels between the model of multiple internal working models and the model of multiple selves and the context-dependent activation of self-states.

Mary Main and Adult Attachment

Bowlby's theorizing about the internal working model set the stage for Ainsworth's research on its behavioral component. Following her research, Mary Main devised the Adult Attachment Interview (AAI) (George, Kaplan, & Main, 1985; Main & Goldwyn, 1998; Main, Kaplan, & Cassidy, 1985). This was the next major advance in the development of attachment theory. Whereas the Strange Situation Procedure is a measure of infant behavior, Main conceived of the AAI as a measure of what happens in the minds of individual adults when their attachment system is activated—the "adult state of mind with respect to attachment." Her work has played a crucial role in extending attachment theory to the clinical level and served as a basis of mentalization theory (Fonagy et al., 2002).

The AAI is a semistructured interview in which an adult is asked questions about his or her attachment experiences. It is shockingly blunt and begins by asking interviewees highly personal questions about the relationship with each parent: for example, which parent they felt closer to, what would happen during times of distress, whether their parents were ever threatening, and so forth. Importantly, it is not the content of responses but, rather, the psychological processes that differentiate between attachment patterns.

The AAI measures the coherency of the narrative provided by adults when they are asked about their early attachment relationships.[36] Main was particularly interested in memories of loss and trauma: whether they could be spoken of and, if so, whether they affected the quality of the narrative. Her assumption was that the coherence of the verbal narrative reflects the relative integration or dissociation of the mind,

---

36 Main's doctorate was in linguistics, which is concerned with coherence.

which in turn reflects the integration or dissociation of the brain (Main, 1991, 1996; Main et al., 1985).

By eliciting memories of the early attachment relationship, the AAI activates the attachment system. Responding to questions requires that the interviewee communicate memories of the attachment relationship while coping with the powerful affects that accompany them. More specifically, it requires that they access episodic memories, organize them into a coherent narrative, and communicate them collaboratively with the examiner (Hesse, 1996).

The individual's collaborative capacity during the interview has proven to be more important than initially imagined. For one thing, it is an indication of the flexibility of attention when the attachment system is activated. That is, it is a measure of whether the interviewee can alternate between interoception, in order to retrieve and organize the memories, and exteroception, in order to collaborate with the examiner. While organizing and verbally communicating a narrative, interviewees must also keep track of whether the interviewer understands their communications and what the interviewer already knows and may need to know (Hesse, 1996). All this occurs while needing to regulate the affects that infuse attachment memories. From the point of view of affect regulation, the AAI can be thought of a stress test of the capacity to maintain an integrated-flexible organization of mind.

A key component of secure attachment involves metacognition. For Main, the ongoing metacognitive monitoring of transactions with the examiner—the capacity to "step back and consider his or her own cognitive processes as objects of thought or reflection" (1991, p. 135) while accessing memories of early childhood experiences, is a crucial component of the capacity for coherence and collaboration. This proved to be a key observation that led to the study of mentalization, the topic of Chapter 6.

Although the scoring of the AAI takes content into account—for example, Main's concern with memories of loss and trauma—the primary concern is the coherent or incoherent structure of the subject's narrative. A coherent narrative is understood to be one that is truthful and succinct without distortion or contradiction. It is measured according to a fascinating set of maxims developed by philosopher of language Paul Grice (1975):

Maxim of Quantity

Make your contribution as informative as is required (for the current purposes of the exchange).

Do not make your contribution more informative than is required.

Maxim of Quality

Do not say what you believe to be false.

Do not say that for which you lack adequate evidence.

Maxim of Relation

Be relevant.

Maxim of Manner

Avoid obscurity of expression.

Avoid ambiguity.

Be brief (avoid unnecessary proxility).

Be orderly.

From Essays 2 and 3, first published in *Syntax and Semantics,* vol. 3, P. Cole and J. Morgan, eds., and vol. 9, P. Cole, ed. (New York: Academic Press, 1975, 1978). Copyright © 1975, 1978 by Herbert Paul Grice.

It is interesting to think about Grice's maxims in relationship to the hyper- and hypoaroused arousal patterns associated with preoccupied and avoidant attachment. The preoccupied pattern of hyperarousal under stress generates hyperactive mentation that precludes a succinct, orderly, and unambiguous narrative. Swept away by affect, the mind flooded with too many thoughts to organize, those with preoccupied attachment patterns tend to distort events through exaggeration, go off on tangents, and offer contradictory evaluations. At the other end of the continuum, the hypoarousal and deactivated mentation associated with an avoidant attachment pattern will produce narratives that lack sufficient information and evidence. The restricted mentation and detachment from affect of the avoidant produce sparse narratives, distortion through minimization, simplistic and often idealized evaluations, and a paucity of memories.

Securely attached adults are better able to maintain regulated affect in the midst of attachment memories. They produce believable narratives that are what Main and Goldwyn (1998) called "truthful and collaborative." Their narratives include a range of negative and positive evaluations of their early attachment experiences that lend them believability. They are able to integrate negative memories of attachment experiences with positive memories and can regulate the associated affects sufficiently to produce a coherent narrative. They are able to keep track of what they have said and intend to say and are able to assess the examiner's reactions and adjust accordingly.

The AAI was used in research that further underscored the relevance of attachment theory for clinical work. Longitudinal studies found that scores in the Strange Situation Procedure were highly correlated with AAI outcomes in adulthood, pointing to the stability of attachment patterns across the life span (van IJzendoorn, 1995; Hesse, 1999). Attachment studies using the AAI also detected different attachment patterns for a particular child in relationship to each of his or her parents (Main, 1995; Steele, Steel, & Fonagy, 1996), supporting the clinical observation that we tend to develop multiple attachment patterns that are activated in different contexts.

Robust correlations were also found between the attachment category of parents in the AAI and classifications of their relationship with their children in the Strange Situation Procedure (Fonagy, Steele, & Steele, 1991; van IJzendoorn, 1995). This is a stunning finding. Mother-infant behavior is related to the mother's capacity for narrative coherence when stressed. That two such disparate measures are strongly related is an indication that attachment research taps into something fundamental and far-reaching. Regulation theory proposes that that "something" is the capacity to regulate affect.

Studies demonstrating correlations between the attachment patterns of parents, measured by the AAI, and the attachment patterns of their children, measured in the Strange Situation Procedure, are of particular importance. Caretakers whose primary attachment pattern was measured by the AAI as preoccupied were associated with children with ambivalent-resistant patterns. Caretakers whose primary patterns were dismissive were associated with children who were avoidant. Parents with disorganized attachment patterns in the AAI tended to raise children classified as disoriented. Secure adults tend to have secure children.

Studies that separate out genetic factors and inborn temperament provided further support for Bowlby's theory and Ainsworth's observations that parenting plays a significant role in the development of attachment patterns. It is clear from twin studies that attachment patterns are heavily influenced by experiences in the attachment relationship and do not simply reflect the genetic transmission of temperament (Bokhorst et al., 2003; O'Connor, Croft, & Steele, 2000; O'Connor & Croft, 2001).

Finally, "earned security" studies give heart to psychotherapists: they find that attachment patterns can change as a result of psychotherapy or experience with secure spouses (Main & Goldwyn, 1998; Lichenstein Phelps, Belsky, & Crnic, 1998).

The correlations between the AAI and the Strange Situation Procedure set off a search to answer the problem of the "transmission gap" (van IJzendoorn, 1995), the holy grail of attachment research.[37] The hope is that understanding the mechanism by which attachment patterns are transmitted from parent to child will provide insights for intervention with struggling mother-infant dyads in order to avert the intergenerational transmission of insecure patterns and for understanding how to alter attachment patterns in psychotherapy.

This brings us to the two theories of affect regulation that have developed from attachment theory. Chapter 6 is an overview of the work of Peter Fonagy and his collaborators. Their mentalization studies illuminate what I am calling the secondary affect-regulating system. Chapter 7 focuses on Allan Schore's work on modern attachment theory, which elucidates what I am calling the primary affect-regulating system.

---

37 When you think about it, the correlation of the attachment patterns of parents measured by the AAI and the Strange Situation Procedure measures of their children's attachment patterns is an extraordinary finding: a verbal measure of an adult's narrative coherence predicts the behaviors of their child in a novel situation. What underlies the relationship between such apparently different phenomena? What is responsible for the transmission of this underlying variable?

CHAPTER 6

Mentalization

The Secondary Affect-Regulating System

MENTALIZATION (Fonagy et al., 2002; Allen & Fonagy, 2006),[38] understood as the secondary affect-regulating system,[39] is a left-brain-dominant, cortically based, voluntary, conscious, slow affect regulation system that is later developing than the primary system. It may seem odd to present the secondary system in the midst of discussing the primary system. However, because mentalization theory uses Mary Main's work, introduced in Chapter 5, as a jumping off point and, like it, is concerned with the verbal-explicit domain of mental life, mentalization theory is a direct extension of classical attachment theory[40] brought to the clinical level.

Although this book focuses on the primary affect-regulating sys-

---

38 Mentalization theory draws from philosophy (theory of mind), developmental social cognition, cognitive neurobiology, attachment theory, and psychoanalysis. It is, along with regulation theory, an example of how major advances in psychotherapy are being made by the integration of disciplines.

39 Regulating affect is only one of the responsibilities of the mentalizing system.

40 Mentalization theory integrates classical attachment theory with philosophy (theory of mind), the object relations school of psychoanalysis, the study of the development of social cognition, and cognitive neuroscience.

tem, psychodynamic psychotherapy requires working with both the primary and secondary systems. I devote this chapter to the latter so that we can discuss both in the chapters that follow, and I encourage the reader to consult other texts that present mentalization theory and its clinical application more fully. We begin by looking at the mentalizing system as Main first observed it.

Main (1991) noted that in the process of taking the Adult Attachment Interview, securely attached adults were able to "step back and consider their own cognitive processes as objects of thought or reflection" (p. 135). She called this "metacognitive monitoring," which mentalization theory extends into studies of "reflective functioning" or "mentalizing."[41]

Main also noticed that secure adults monitored not only their own minds, considering and reevaluating their stories as they assembled them, but also the minds of the examiners. This involved keeping track of what the examiners understood, already knew, needed to know, and so forth. It proved to be a key observation. Secure adults monitored and assessed, with reasonable accuracy, both their own and the examiner's mind as part of the process of producing coherent narratives.

Main theorized that a breakdown of coherence occurred when a narrative touched on unresolved loss. We can now say that if the affect associated with the loss were regulated, the memory could be thought and felt about clearly and woven into a coherent whole.[42] It is the unresolved, traumatic losses that hinder metacognition and narrative coherence.

---

41 *Reflective functioning* is a technical term used specifically for the empirical operationalization of *mentalization*. In practice, the two terms are often used interchangeably.

42 Recall that, when affect is dysregulated, reflective capacities are deactivated or compromised. Note the catch-22 here: if affect is regulated, reflective functioning can perform its functions, which include regulating affect; when affect is dysregulated, reflective functioning is deactivated or compromised.

Main's insights about metacognition, unresolved trauma, memory, and narrative served as the springboard for the field of mentalization studies (Fonagy et al., 2002; Allen & Fonagy, 2006; Allen, Fonagy, & Bateman, 2008; Busch, 2008; Jurist & Meehan, 2009). Like Main, Fonagy and his colleagues use the coherence of the narrative as a measure of underlying disturbance in mental functioning. However, whereas Main measured the coherence itself, Fonagy and his collaborators focused on the processes involved in the construction of coherent narratives (Holmes, 2006). In so doing, mentalization theory extends classic attachment theory into a model with direct clinical application. Significant theoretical and clinical advances have been made in a variety of areas.

Theoretical and empirical studies demonstrate that the mentalization of affect contributes to affect regulation, provides a sense of agency, and acts as a bulwark against potentially traumatizing experience (Fonagy et al., 2002; Allen et al., 2008). Empirical studies also demonstrate that mentalization-based treatment is effective in the treatment of borderline personality disorder (Bateman & Fonagy, 2004).

Slade et al. (2005; see also Fonagy & Target, 2005) have taken an important step toward solving the problem of the transmission gap. They found a strong association between the mentalizing capacity of mothers and the development of secure attachment, suggesting that mentalizing is a mechanism in the intergenerational transmission of attachment patterns. The implications are profound for both development and psychotherapy. Encouraging studies are taking place utilizing mentalization based interventions with at-risk mother-infant dyads to prevent the intergenerational transmission of insecure attachment (Slade, 2012);. Fonagy and his collaborators propose that mentalization is an underappreciated therapeutic action common to all psychotherapies.

So, what exactly is mentalization and what are the processes targeted by a mentalization-based psychotherapy? In the most general sense mentalization concerns the representation of mental states[43]— the reading of one's own and others' mental states. More specifically, mentalization theory is concerned with the capacity to verbally represent intentional states.

Intentional refers to the aspect of mental states that indicate possible action. Motives, goals, beliefs, desires, and emotions indicate intention and precede and predict actions. Reading our own intentions and the intentions of others provides critical evolutionary advantage (Fonagy & Target, 2006). At the level of individual selection, detecting the intentions of others supports competition with rivals. At the level of group selection, communicating intentions supports cooperation—a key advantage for the human species.

As noted with regard to collaboration with the examiner in the AAI, this capacity for mind reading is closely associated with attachment status. Securely attached people are better able to mentalize than those with insecure attachment. Caretakers who mentalize well facilitate the development of securely attached children (Fonagy et al., 1991; Steele et al., 1996; Slade et al., 2005; Fonagy & Target, 2005).

Mentalization theorists use the felicitous phrase "having mind in mind" to depict the role of mentalization in the development of secure attachment. They propose that the child first comes in contact with its own mental state by seeing it reflected back to them. To do this with reasonable accuracy the mother must be able to imagine and mirror

---

43 The initial measure of mentalization used the term *reflective function* often used synonymously with mentalization. In these ground breaking studies narratives taken using the AAI were assessed for the caretakers' use of mental state language (Fonagy et al. 1991). It is understood to be an assessment of the capacity of caretakers to think about their own and others' mental states and, importantly, it predicted the attachment status of their children better than studies using the AAI.

the infant's mental state. The mind takes form from the outside-in, its state reflected in the caretaker's face.

Once language comes into play, the outside-in process takes the form of mind talk, in which the mother represents the child's mind through words depicting mental states.[44] Slade and colleagues (2005) refer to this as "minding the baby." The mother's capacity to verbally represent and reflect back her child's mind with reasonable accuracy is crucial.

A mother's capacity for mentalizing her child is at the heart of the mentalization theory of optimal development and pathogenesis. For example, the accuracy of the caregiver's mentalization of the child—reflecting the child's mind back to him in words—has ramifications for developing a real-seeming versus false self (Allen et al., 2008; Fonagy et al., 2002).

The Development of Mentalizing Processes

We tend to take for granted the idea that intentions precede actions and that they take the form of desires, motives, emotions, and so on. However, reading intentions with reasonable accuracy is a developmental achievement.

To mentalize one must first develop a sense that the mind is representational in nature, that it depicts things in the inner and outer worlds and that a mental representation is distinct from the thing represented. One must also learn that intentions can be represented and that they indicate possible actions. And one must learn that others have minds like one's own and that, although they are like-minded with regard to processes, they may be very un-like-minded with regard to representational content.

---

44 For example, with increasing precision, "upset, frustrated, angry" and "upset, confused, scared."

Eventually, one must come to understand that we construct representations with varying degrees of accuracy. Representations are merely our take on things in our inner and outer worlds. We *interpret* signs of others' intentions. Not until sometime in the sixth year of life is all this in place. With this in mind, let's examine what the mentalizing processes are and their developmental progression.

Mentalization theory has delineated four modes of mentalizing that develop sequentially. The first three to develop—the teleological, psychic equivalence, and pretend modes—are considered prementalizing processes. Full mentalizing involves an integration of psychic equivalence and pretend modes.

Teleological Mode

In the *teleological mode* intentions can be understood only in terms of actions. (This might be thought of as a sensorimotor stage of mentalizing.) There is no sense yet of a mind that is representational in nature or that actions are preceded by thoughts. For example, if you were thinking ideologically and saw someone throw a piece of paper that landed next to a wastepaper basket, you would believe they intended to do so. There is no distinction between intent and action.

In the teleological mode the result of an action indicates the intention. If someone steps on your toe, they intended to hurt you. On the expressive side, the only way to communicate intentions is through action. Anger can be represented only through violence. It is not until the second year that a child has the representational capacity to understand that intentions precede actions and that the end result does not always signify intention.[45]

---

45 Note that this is after attachment patterns have been established. The mentalization system is not part of the attachment system, although they are reciprocally related. When the attachment system is activated (and thus we are dysregulated), the mentalization system is deactivated. When the attachment

Psychic Equivalence Mode

In *psychic equivalence mode*, the next step toward full mentalizing, the child has a sense of the representational nature of his mind but does not distinguish between the representation and what it represents. What is in the mind is in the world, and it is in the world just the way that his mind represents it. If, for example, he thinks that you did something on purpose, you *did* do it on purpose—if you are not admitting to doing it on purpose, you are lying. Additionally, because the child has not yet developed the capacity to transcend egocentrism, he believes that everyone else also thinks you are lying. It is not that it is uncommon to function in a mode of psychic equivalence, to take the accuracy of our representations for granted and assume that others share them but, rather, whether we relinquish psychic equivalence and generate alternative perspectives when necessary.

Pretend Mode

The third step toward full mentalizing is *pretend mode*. In this mode a mental representation is experienced as separate from the thing represented, but too much so. Thus, representations do not have a sufficient sense of reality attached to them. You can get a sense of this from a patient of mine who remembered being fascinated by a game in which he repeated a word over and over until it became "just a sound meaning nothing," severed completely from its referent. Left to its own devices, the pretend mode would create a barren and valueless representational world.

---

system is deactivated, and we are again regulated, mentalizing processes are available (Fonagy et al., 2002; Jurist, 2009). The primary affect-regulating system, on the other hand, is the core of the attachment internal working model.

Full Mentalization

Full mentalization is achieved when the psychic equivalent and pretend modes are integrated. Mental representations are neither too attached nor too detached from their referents in the real world. One can vacillate between the two modes and integrate them. Representations seem real and meaningful and can be questioned. They can be appreciated as one's subjective understanding of reality rather than reality itself. At this point mentalizing is capable of achieving its full adaptive and humanizing potential. It serves an array of functions.

An accurate reading of one's intentions as antecedents of actions allows for the possibility of a sense of agency. Indeed, a mentalization-informed therapy has the development of an "agentic self" as a goal. I have found that asking patients "What do you want to have happen?" to be a particularly potent intervention. It encourages the mentalization of intentions and seems to startle and awaken them to themselves and the possibility of their own agency.

Developing the capacity to mentalize in psychotherapy provides the means for correcting pathological thinking.[46] Mentalizing traumatic experiences serves as a buffer against the sequelae of trauma. Mentalizing has an existential value, allowing for an examined life worth living. Mentalization allows us to represent our emotions for interpretation, reinterpretation, modification, regulation, and adaptive use.

The Mentalization of Affect

There is consensus that the core clinical value of mentalization theory lies in the mentalization of affect (Allen & Fonagy, 2006; Fonagy et

---

46 Mentalization-based therapy can be thought of as a mixture of psychoanalytic and cognitive behavior therapies (Allen & Fonagy, 2006).

al., 2002; Jurist, 2005). To appreciate this, let's review the distinction between primary affect and categorical affects.

Primary affect is the body's response (our first response) to salient stimuli in the inner and outer worlds. It is the physiological experience of what is happening in our autonomic nervous system and vital organs, especially the heart. It has two basic dimensions: continuums of hyper- and hypoarousal and positive and negative hedonic tone.

The categorical affects (aka explicit or discrete affects) comprise primary affect that has been subjected to a higher-level cognitive appraisal. I know, for example, that I am ashamed because I am severely hypoaroused (head hanging, muscles flaccid, heart slowed), the hedonic tone of my affect is intensely negative, and, at a higher cognitive level, there is something about me that a valued person will find repellant and I will be rejected if this thing about me is exposed.

With the addition of more elaborate cognitive appraisal there is now a word, *shame*, that represents the experience and makes it available for verbal reflective thinking. Shame has thus migrated from being only a physiological experience to a word in the mind. *I have made something nonmental mental.* I have mentalized affect by naming it, and in doing so I have formulated (Stern, 1997) the categorical affect. Recall that Darwin observed that there are seven categorical affects (shame, sadness, joy, anger, surprise, fear, and disgust). They each have distinct facial expressions and exist across all cultures, suggesting that these have evolutionary advantages and have become inborn.

Primary affect is processed and regulated in the right brain, nonverbally. Categorical affect is the product of the left and right brains working together whereby unformulated somatic experience becomes increasingly intelligible. Keeping this distinction between primary and categorical affect in mind, let's see what the mentalization of affect involves.

Affect establishes our relationship to the object, including what it means to us.[47] Primary affect does this at the most fundamental level: opportunity or danger, positive or negative, approach or avoid. With mentalization, the subjective meaning of the object is known with increasing precision. It takes primary affect to the verbal level and begins a cognitive refinement of meaning.

Recall the incident with the snake described in Chapter 3. My snake-jump-run reaction engaged the primary affect-regulating system acting in the service of survival—an automatic "mindless" reaction. Here's some mentalizing that followed in which I adjusted the intensity of the affect and action based on it: "That was a snake! Wait. That was a black snake. No need to panic. I'll go look at it. On the other hand, I am not so sure. I'll risk erring on the side of caution and keep on walking."

Here's an example of more complex mentalizing by a patient. "I was so tense throughout the evening. I realize now that I was still angry with him from yesterday. He never apologized. I'd feel differently if he had. He never does. The more I think about it the angrier I get. But he didn't mean to embarrass me. Maybe he doesn't even know." In the snake incident my mentalizing was applied only to *my* mental state. The second example involves mentalizing of self *and* object. In both cases the initial appraisal was given more thought. The refinement of meaning through the mentalization of affect is central to getting the object relationship right. This is a key function of the secondary, verbal processing of affect.

The mentalizing system regulates affect first by identifying it. Naming the body-based experience provides a cognitive grasp that contains the intensity and brings the unformulated experience into focus.

---

47 Kernberg (1975) and Schore (1994) place affect at the heart of the object relationship, linking the self to the object (self–affect–object).

Naming the affect is often accompanied by a sense of relief: "Oh *that's* what I was feeling."[48]

Once the affect is identified, a process of elaboration is possible, and the initial take undergoes reevaluation(s). Elaboration is the work of fine-tuning the meaning of affect. It requires the effortful focusing of attention on (usually) negative or stressful affect and the deliberate use of imagination to do the necessary cognitive appraisal.

Elaboration regulates affect by changing meaning. After elaboration, my relationship to the snake went from panic to cautious. It meant something different to me, and the arousal level of my fear was diminished but not eliminated. I stopped running but kept walking.

Here's an example of mentalizing affect that includes the use of the past to get the affect right. Note the amplification and dampening of arousal as the original take is honed and the meaning changes:

> I was furious at him and then I realized it's because I was hurt. At first he returned calls immediately. Actually, now that I think more about it, it was humiliating to be kept waiting so long. My brother still treats me like that. Really pisses me off. Actually, there's really no reason to feel so humiliated. But I was embarrassed. He led me on. I thought he was more interested than he was. I even told my friends. I wonder if I misread him or if I did something that changed his mind.

Mentalization theorists emphasize that full mentalization involves the thinking through of a feeling in the midst of live affect. From the point of view of interpersonal neurobiology, mentalizing is not simply a left-brain operation. Rather, the left brain is fed *regulated primary*

---

48 Note that, in the case of traumatic affect, naming can be terrifying, as though naming the affect makes it real and because it triggers the memory.

affect that has been processed in the right brain. The left brain then makes further sense of it using reflective-verbal processes.[49] Effective mentalization requires optimal hemispheric integration supporting "thinking and feeling about thinking and feeling" (Allen & Fonagy, 2006, p. 62). It is only when left-brain-dominated cognition is suffused with *felt* affect first processed in the right brain that we can generate complex, cognitive-affective blends of thoughts about emotions (e.g., a judgment about a feeling), emotions about thoughts (e.g., shame about a thought), and emotions about emotions (e.g., shame about being angry).

Finally, mentalization theory emphasizes a close relationship between mentalizing and the sense of agency. A sense of mastery and responsibility emerges from the mentalization of affect. This sense of mastery comes primarily from the regulation of primary affect and its refinement by the secondary affect-regulating system. The sense of responsibility builds with the increasing capacity to elaborate and refine meaning through the processing of categorical affect by the secondary affect-regulating system.

The Primary and Secondary Affect-Regulating Systems

We can now further define and distinguish between the primary and secondary affect-regulating systems and discuss their relationship. We have seen that the mentalization of affect provides a cognitive

---

49 Mentalization theorists think of the nonverbal, automatic-involuntary processing of the socioemotional information that takes place in the limbic system as the implicit mentalization of affect. However, using the term *mentalizing* for this may imply more refinement and deliberation than the primary affect-regulating system is due. In this book I reserve the term *mentalization* to refer to left-brain, voluntary, reflective, high-level processing. Additionally, as I am using the term, *mentalization* refers to the identification and elaboration of *categorical* affect: the work of the secondary affect-regulating system. The primary affect-regulating system is involved with the regulation of primary affect.

grasp and fine-tuning of meaning that serves to cognitively adjust the level of arousal and modify its hedonic tone. It is a left-brain-based, conscious system of reflective-verbal processes that subjects primary affect, presented by the right brain, to a higher-order cognitive assessment. Ultimately, the mentalizing of affect and the object relations it defines are woven into a coherent narrative.

The two affect-regulating systems come together at the point where primary affect, processed in the right brain, is further processed in the left; where somatic experience becomes words in the mind; where the nonmental becomes mental; where preconscious, right-brain implicit processing is superceded by the conscious, explicit processing of the left.

It is important to note that the mentalizing of affect is dependent on the primary system's regulation of affect, not only because the reflective processes are compromised or deactivated in dysregulated states but also because, if affect is dysregulated-dissociated, it is not available for conscious processing.

The left-brain, verbal, linear, deliberate processes of the mentalizing system are too slow for real-time interactions. However, they enable us to reflect on our own and others' affect states that occurred in the past or that we imagine will occur in the future. Crucially, they allow us multiple assessments of what happened or will happen, provide a nuanced understanding of affects, and correct or confirm the gut reactions generated by the primary system. They provide additional complexity, flexibility, and stability.

The explicit, top-down mentalizing of the secondary affect-regulating system may be our highest achievement (Fonagy & Target, 2006)—the refining of meaning and getting object relations right. The implicit processing of the primary system regulates affect from the bottom up. It is a relatively primitive system that we share with other mammals. The functioning and development of the secondary system depend on the primary system. Lewis and Todd (2007) write of the relationship between the two systems when we are functioning optimally:

> To speak of cognitive regulation versus emotion regulation may be misleading. However, some forms of regulation are carried out by executive processes, subject to voluntary control, while others are carried out by "automatic" processes that are far more primitive. Both sets of processes are in constant interaction, and that interaction gives rise to a stream of activity that is both cognitive and emotional. (p. 407)

Chapter 7 focuses on the development of the primitive, primary affect-regulating system.

Modern Attachment Theory

The Development of the Primary Affect-Regulating System

THIS CHAPTER PROVIDES an overview of modern attachment theory (Schore, 1994, 2003a, chaps. 2, 3, 4, and 6, 2006; Schore & Schore, 2008). It returns our focus to the primary affect-regulating system. I begin with a brief review of neurobiological developments and then discuss the mother-infant interactions that influence them.

Modern attachment theory is the centerpiece of Schore's regulation theory, in which he advances classical attachment theory beyond the behavioral and psychological spheres, studied by Ainsworth and Main, to a psychoneurobiological theory of the development of self-regulation.[50] He delineates the neurological structures and the psychobiological dynamics of the primary affect-regulating system and links their development to the affect-regulating experiences of the attachment relationship.

Schore proposes a biphasic critical period in the development of the primary affect-regulating system—a neurological growth spurt

---

50 This is a direct continuation of Bowlby's overarching project integrating psychology (psychoanalysis) and biology.

that begins prenatally and continues through 16–18 months of age. During this time the structures of the limbic system come online sequentially and are organized hierarchically, with the later developing, cortical structures inhibiting the subcortical structures. During the same period circuits develop that connect the limbic system first to the sympathetic and then the parasympathetic aspects of the autonomic nervous system (ANS; see Figure 3.3). With these developments the infant possesses a functioning limbic system for appraising body based affect and socioemotional information linked to a system that regulates arousal: the hypothalamic-pituitary-adrenal (HPA) axis and ANS. How it is organized will depend on the infant's affect-regulating experiences. This is where affective neurobiology meets attachment theory.

The development of the primary affect regulating system has two distinct phases that intersect with a qualitative change in the attachment relationship. In the first phase the infant becomes increasing mobile and is increasingly in need of inhibition. In this phase (through 12–14 months), the limbic circuits that regulate sympathetic arousal undergo innervation. During this time the mother-infant dyad engages in repeated emotional transactions encoded in implicit memories that script the automatic procedures of upregulation. In the second phase (12–14 to 16–18 months) when the infant becomes mobile, limbic circuits that regulate parasympathetic arousal innervate,[51] and mother-infant affect-regulating transactions become encoded as the automatic procedures of downregulation.

At the same time, the right orbitofrontal cortex is forming connections to subcortical structures of the limbic system. This allows it to inhibit body-based urges mediated by subcortical structures and per-

---

51 The ventral tegmental limbic circuits mediate sympathetic arousal, and the lateral tegmental limbic circuit mediate parasympathetic arousal.

form the executive functions of the primary affect-regulating system. Now the limbic system, with the right orbitofrontal cortex at its apex, is able to appraise opportunities and dangers and provide instructions to the ANS for up- or downregulation supporting engagement or disengagement from the environment. To understand how such optimal development happens, let's look at the attachment experiences of the securely attached mother-infant dyad during the first phase of the critical period.

The Development of the Capacity to Regulate Sympathetic Arousal

Twelve-month-old Frances (secure) squiggles down from her mother's lap and speeds off on all fours in quest of whatever. When she reaches the other side of the room, her energy seems to wane. She slows and becomes tentative. She turns and appraises her mother's face, and their eyes meet. Reassured *and revitalized*, our intrepid explorer resumes her adventure with new energy.

When Frances slowed and referenced her mother's face, her mother's expression indicated availability, interest, and reassurance *and* generated sympathetic arousal that supported further exploration. Mahler, Pine, and Bergman (1975) observed this "emotional refueling" during the early, practicing phase of separation-individuation when children begin making forays away from their mother's side.

What has happened psychobiologically during this secure base transaction? Why did Frances perk up and reengage with the world? For an explanation, Schore looks to implicit communications that generate sympathetic arousal. He calls this the "psychobiology of affective reunions" and proposes that the revitalization of the infant is caused by the impact of eye contact on the sympathetic nervous system.

There is no more intense implicit communication than eye contact.

It directly links two nervous systems.[52] Mother-infant dyads begin prolonged face-to-face play and mutual gaze transactions when the infant is about two months of age. Looking deeply into one another's eyes generates mutually amplifying joyful states of intensely heightened arousal. Such mother-infant mergers into a single psychobiological unit of shared joy mark defining moments of the "symbiotic" stage (Mahler, Pine and Bergman (1975; Mahler, 1979). Schore proposes that moments of shared joy stamp in the positive attachment bond and establish a disposition to engage in dyadic regulation.

Experiences of shared joy provide opportunities for learning to regulate sympathetic arousal. During these interactions the infant must occasionally avert its gaze to avoid becoming overwhelmed. The contingently responsive mother allows for gaze aversion and synchronizes with the infant's rhythms of engagement and disengagement (Beebe, 2000; Stern, 1986). The mother attunes to the infant's levels of arousal, is sensitive to the infant's affect tolerances, and makes room for the infant to downregulate by adjusting her gaze aversions accordingly.

Positive states of attuned hyperarousal are growth enhancing and essential to adaptive development. They give rise to metabolic conditions that support neural growth. Face-to-face, shared, arousal-amplifying, joyful experiences accumulate as implicit memories that encode relational moves and neurobiological processes that regulate sympathetic arousal.[53]

---

52 The retina is the one place that the nervous system extends to the surface of the body and is exposed. Schore draws attention to the fact that even the constriction and expansion of pupils is an unconscious, hidden regulator of one another's affect.

53 Adding a cognitive perspective, Tronick (2007, chap. 29) proposes that a shared state, a merging of the two subjectivities in which each partner is infused with the experiencing of the other, forms a superordinate system generating an expanded state of consciousness. In this state of deep intersubjectivity, each individual system maps onto the other, and the mutual cognitive-affective

Note the importance Schore gives to the face in the development and subsequent operation of the primary affect-regulating system. The face is the richest source of affective information—"the display board of the self" (Tomkins, 1962). Moreover, in the early phase of the critical period, vision is the infant's dominant sensory modality.

Schore proposes that implicit memories of *sequences* of affective experience are encoded in presymbolic representations of the mother's face. Once stored, they are available to match against perceived faces and, when activated, set off automatic regulatory processes.

Let's return to what happened with Frances during her excursion into the world beyond her mother. Frances's refueling illustrates infants' dependency on emotional engagement with attachment figures to maintain vitalizing affects that support a sense of "going on being" (Winnicott, 1958). Such secure base transactions also generate the arousal level required for active engagement with the environment; the motivation to "go on doing". The extent to which this is true is dramatically demonstrated by its opposite, operationalized in the still face experiment. What happens when the need for emotional connection is frustrated for too long?

The still face experiment (Tronick, 2007, chap. 20, pp274-292) starts with a secure mother-infant dyad engaging in regulated, face-to-face play.[54] At a prearranged signal, the mother goes still, her face impassive. Typically, infants are immediately alerted by their mother's nonresponsiveness. They become increasingly distressed and disorganized

---

enrichment increases complexity and coherence of both the neurological and mental systems.

Lewis Sander (1992) refers to such states as "moments of meeting." They occur both in psychotherapy and everyday life and between mothers and infants. Whatever the content that is exchanged, there is a shared experience of deep intersubjectivity and a shared sense that "I know that you know that I know what you know, and that this is a unique experience constructed by just *us*."

54 To see a video, search YouTube for "still face experiment."

as they make futile attempts to reengage them. Left long enough in this state of dysregulation, an infant will eventually collapse, physically and emotionally, and disengage from the environment. They undergo a profound metabolic shutdown, probably an activation of the dorsal vagal aspect of the parasympathetic nervous system—a response to overwhelming fear, helplessness, and hopelessness.

The still-face experiment can be thought of as a compressed version of Bowlby's observations of institutionalized children without parental contact who, after a period of angry distress and then despair, became detached. In the experiment, the mother comes back to life and reconnects to the infant, who is then regulated and able to reorganize and return to a regulated state. Neglected infants are not so fortunate. Indeed, there is consensus that neglect is more harmful that abuse to the primary affect-regulating system.

As development proceeds, the autonomy-supporting mother depicted in the exploratory refueling episode goes on to engage in increasingly complex and subtle secure base interactions with her infant. Through her implicit communications she will be instrumental in establishing the sense of self in relationship to the outside world.

Sroufe (1979) quotes a 1846 passage by Kierkegaard that describes an ideal version of the attuned caretaker's support of exploration and emerging autonomy:

> The loving mother teaches her child to walk alone. She is far enough from him so that she cannot actually support him, but she holds out her arms to him. She imitates his movements, and if he totters, she swiftly bends as if to seize him, so that the child might believe that he is not walking alone . . . and yet, she does more. Her face beckons like a reward, an encouragement. Thus, the child walks alone with his eyes fixed on his mother's face, not on the difficulties in his way. He supports himself by

the arms that do not hold him and constantly strives towards the refuge in his mother's embrace, little supposing that in the very same moment that he is emphasizing his need for her, he is proving that he can do without her, because he is walking alone. (p. 462)

Through her gestures and face, this "loving," contingently responsive, exploration-supporting mother provides just the right amount and kind of help needed. Note her capacity to shift states and calibrate her arousal levels with her infant's as she shares in the joy of mastery and the ups and downs of getting there. She does not intrude yet helps maintain a positive state of optimal arousal. She allows the infant to test developing competence while acting as a backup when needed. In doing so she instills pride, positive expectations, and the disposition to keep on doing.[55]

Demos (1986) writes about two different maternal responses to negative affects in their infants. One rushes in whenever the infant cries, depriving it of optimal levels of stress (Tronick, 2007, chap. 27) and opportunities for developing stress tolerance and self-mastery. The other, with a higher tolerance for negative affect and an intuitive sense of her infant's capacities, stands helpfully by and intervenes when the level of negative arousal threatens to disorganize her infant.

The need for emotional connection (Tronick, 2007, chap. 35) and the regulation of sympathetic arousal have extensive implications for pathogenesis and for psychotherapy. Imagine a chronically stressed infant coping with a avoidant caretaker who cuts short or fails to engage in joyful face-to-face interactions. There is a failure to enter into shared positive states in which the attachment bond

---

55 It is also, I think, an ideal description of our regulating role in psychotherapy as our patients delve into stressful subjective experiences.

is first fastened and then deepened. There is also a failure to establish a disposition toward interactive regulation. This same caretaker is likely to be insensitive to breaks in connection and need for reconnection.

It is equally stressful for the infant confronted with a preoccupied caretaker who is capable of positive emotional engagement but whose own needs frequently intrude. Prone to abandonment anxiety herself, she may be unable to accommodate her infant's need to gaze avert, disconnect, and downregulate (Beebe, 2000). She may take it personally. Or, in contrast to Kierkegaard's exploration-supporting mother, she may be unable to contain herself and interfere with too much help. Her prideful excitement may crowd out the infant's.

In psychotherapy, mutual gaze and facial expressions are indications of our interest and intentions. Even as we listen silently, these visuoaffective stimuli provide emotional support—a dopaminergic, metabolic boost—that bolsters patients as they struggle to explore shameful aspects of their inner and outer worlds. Trust is established as our face transmits our nurturing intentions, emotional competency, and nonjudgmental recognition. Just as the infant learned implicitly that stressful states of depletion can be tolerated and counteracted, our patients are developing positive expectations and encoding upregulating procedures that support continued engagement with stressful thoughts and memories.

Something else both subtle and profound happened during Frances's refueling process. When her energy flagged and she looked to reconnect with her mother, her face and body expressed her lowered state of arousal and deteriorating hedonic tone. Her mother first momentarily matched Frances's downregulated, stressed affect state. Then, via energy-expanding mutual gaze and graduated changes in her face, she upregulated her daughter. Frances was then able to resume her engagement with the environment, recharged and empowered.

The initial match with the infant's downregulated state provided an emotional embrace—a resonant, felt experience of reassuring recognition (Benjamin, 1990). The mother acted intuitively and spontaneously. No words were spoken—rather, it was a "vitalizing attunement" (Schore, 2012) initiated by the caretaker's state matching and followed by graduated sequences of split-second, upregulating, visuoaffective implicit communications.

Transactions of vitalizing attunement are right-brain to right-brain, implicit-self to implicit-self communications. It is obvious to all involved when this kind of connection is made. One feels felt through the shared emotional resonance and experiences an immediate sense of safety. It is deeply reassuring and intrinsically regulating. Vitalizing attunement modulates the intensity of the affect at the same time that it produces a resonance that deepens and prolongs it.

Schore proposes that attunement involves a "psychobiological synchrony" involving microadjustments to one another's arousal states. Think, for example, of mother-infant face-to-face play or, for that matter, the empathic interactions of everyday life. We are constantly, mutually calibrating our arousal levels to be in emotional synchrony with each other. Attunement is essentially a synchronization of nervous systems as we match the ebbs and flows of one another's arousal. By linking her nervous system to the infant's, the mother is able to up or down regulate the infant's level of arousal.

Of course, the good enough mother is not always able to attune, and not all interactions are positive. In the next phase of development, in which the infant learns to modulate parasympathetic arousal, recurring mutually stressful episodes of misattunement complicate the mother-infant relationship. During the second phase of the critical period the system for the regulation of parasympathetic arousal comes online, the infant becomes mobile, the mother and infant are often at odds, and the regulation of shame takes center stage.

The Development of the Capacity to Regulate Parasympathetic Arousal

This section examines emotional transactions of securely attached mother-infant dyads during the second half of the critical period (12–14 to 16–18 months). Circuits responsible for parasympathetic regulation myelinate, and the developmental task is to establish implicit processes for downregulation.

The optimal outcome enables infants to inhibit themselves through *modulated* activation of the parasympathetic nervous system. This provides the capacity to remain regulated while delaying action. When fully developed, it permits access to a full range of memories, allows us to think and feel clearly, and maximizes response flexibility while downregulating. Note that I emphasize *modulated* activation of the parasympathetic nervous system. Recall that Kenneth, the avoidant child described in Chapter 1, was a consummate inhibitor and endured a prolonged, dysregulated parasympathetic state.

Neurobiological structures responsible for parasympathetic regulation come online during the period when the infant is becoming mobile.[56] The onset of mobility creates considerable complications for the attachment relationship.[57]

Until this point, attachment interactions have been predomi-

---

56 The lateral tegmental limbic circuit becomes myelinated and connects the right frontal cortex with the parasympathetic nervous system. Schore (1994) proposes that the implicit memories of experiences of caretaker-induced downregulation are recorded in these circuits and thus establish the procedures of parasympathetic activation.

57 As we will see in Part III, some emotionally engaged caretakers who were able to facilitate the establishment of upregulation are not up to this new task of facilitating downregulation. Depressed caretakers, who struggle with sharing joy states, are again without sufficient emotional resources at this stage of their infant's development.

nantly positive, and the infant has come to expect nothing less than a steady diet of pride-amplifying mirroring. However, with the need to restrict the exuberant infant's forays into the world, the attachment figure's role now includes inducing shame states—states of negative hypoarousal. Mother-infant interactions go from 90 percent positive caretaking, play, and affection to a prohibition every nine minutes! (Schore, 1994, p. 199).

The caretaker now must enforce restrictions on exploration by inhibiting the infant—by activating and modulating parasympathetic arousal. The capacity of the caretaker to induce shame moderately is key for this period of development. Let's return again to Frances (secure) and the "bangable" episode, this time to understand what goes into moderate shaming.

Frances sets off from her mother's side, speeding toward a coffee table. Pulling herself up to a standing position, and feeling quite good about this newfound ability, she picks up what to her is a "bangable." To her mother it is a porcelain figurine. Frances looks to her mother for a shared state of joyful banging but instead encounters misattunement: a facial display of disapproval accompanied by a vocalization of alarm. Rather than the expected mirroring and amplification of joy, her mother's face displays fear, disgust, and perhaps anger.[58] The attachment bond has been severed unexpectedly, inducing intense fear.

Positive expectations shattered, Frances is stunned. She undergoes an abrupt switch, occurring in the span of a heartbeat, from a state of positive hyperarousal to an intense state of negative hypoarousal, a metabolic implosion in which, among other things, her muscles lose

---

58 Disgust, one of the categorical affects common to all cultures, is the often displayed but usually unconscious face of disapproval. It consists of a closing of the nostrils, exhaling through the mouth, squinting, and constriction of the pupils. Try it and you'll find yourself feeling disgust/disapproval. From a survival point of view, closing the nostrils and eyes and exhaling protects us from noxious material.

tonus. Involuntarily, she releases her bangable and drops to her seat with a thud. After a moment she recovers enough to begin a helpless, downregulated crying. She reaches up to her mother, expecting to be picked up, soothed, and brought back to a regulated state.

Her expectations are fulfilled. Her mother is able to switch her attention to the impact of her reaction on Frances, and, most important, she is able to efficiently shift states. Her own hyperarousal drops to align with Frances's state of hypoaroused distress, enabling her to reestablish a psychobiological connection and begin the process of restoring her daughter to a regulated affect state. Reassured of her mother's attachment and revitalized, Frances returns to the business of infancy.

Schore's model is illuminating in unpacking this communication. Let's start with shame. It holds a special place in his regulation theory. The bangable episode represents a paradigmatic example of shame induction and regulation. How so? What is shame? How does the capacity to regulate shame develop?

The capacity to process shame adaptively is crucial for personal and social development. It serves as a regulator of self-esteem and signals the need for self-correction. However, despite its centrality in our emotional economy, shame has a history of being ignored as a pathogenic force. Helen Block Lewis (1987a) called it the "sleeper" emotion that, despite its pervasive role in psychopathology, tends to go unrecognized by patients and therapists alike. Lewis depicts shame as a state of acute distress involving imagery of being looked at by a devaluing, valued other. This visual imagery is accompanied by an urge to hide, expressed by burying one's face in one's hands or a wish to "crawl into a hole." When shamed, we are rendered speechless and suffused with painful aloneness and exposure. It is an all-encompassing experience of hopelessness and helplessness in which the self, in its entirety, is felt to be devalued and shunned.

Lewis (1987b) notes the rapid onset and acute nature of shame: it catches "the self at the quick and can be experienced as paralyzing the self" (p. 17). She goes on to understand shame as the internalization of the experience of "loss of love."[59] It may be the most painful of the categorical affects.

Shame theorists take pains to distinguish between guilt and shame. Although both serve social functions, shame is earlier developing and more fundamental than guilt and has greater intensity.[60] Yet despite (actually because of) its intensity and painful nature, it is often "bypassed," a term used by Lewis that suggests that shame becomes "dissociated." She notes that dissociated shame may take the form of a complete lack of feeling or a defensive anger she calls "shame-rage."[61]

Schore (1994) proposes that shame originates in experiences of intensely painful affect states induced by unexpected misattunement. When engulfed by shame, we suffer a profound physiological and psychological collapse. There is a loss of tonus that causes the head to hang involuntarily, eyes cast downward, breaking visual connection with others. The chest cavity contracts, constricting and slowing the heart. Attention is focused inwardly on a negatively valanced, shut down, and shuttered self. Any previous object-oriented intentions are replaced by an all-encompassing sense of aloneness, self-

---

59 Facial displays of shame are first observed at about 14 months of age and thought to be the earliest developing of the categorical affects. Given that shame is a state of hypoarousal induced by a facial display of disgust and thwarted mirroring, it is easy to understand its adult iteration as lost love.

60 Translated into a current understanding of emotion, guilt may be understood as shame that has been further mentalized to include ideas of having done something wrong and the consequences for others. I discuss the distinction between shame and guilt further in Chapter 11.

61 We can now understand this as hyperaroused and hypoaroused manifestations of dissociated shame.

debasement, and wish to hide. The hung head and slumped posture of shame exude a collapse of subjectivity and preclude the possibility of intersubjectivity. This is the abject state from which Frances's mother rescues her.

Schore's (1994) microanalysis of the prototypical experience of shame induction illuminates its power. He depicts an abrupt onset of a rapid and painful sequence of state switches. The infant goes from a state of positive hyperarousal, with expectations of joyful state sharing, to extreme fright or terror, to a stunned (frozen) state of profound negative hypoarousal. Shame thus may be understood to represent the sudden, painful collapse induced by unexpected, disapproving misattunement .

In a secure attachment relationship, the sequence is followed by reattunement that returns the infant to a sense of connection, safety, and well-being, with a refreshed capacity for interest in the world. Such moderate shaming is imprinted as a sequence of misattunement–shame–collapse–repair. Moderate shaming is critical to the development of tolerance for negative affect and resilient shifting from dysregulated to regulated affect states.

To shame moderately, caretakers must regulate their own strong negative affects. In the "bangable" example, Frances's mother recovered from a complex affective blend, including startled fear and anger (hyperarousal) and disgust (hypoarousal). After regulating herself, she had to drop down several registers to attune to her infant's hypoaroused shame state. The attunement modulated the intensity of Frances's shame and revitalized her. Moderate shaming is a test of the caretaker's emotional competence.

By shaming moderately, the securely attached caretaker's emotional resilience and tolerance for strong negative affects are passed along to her infant. The infant matches the caretaker's emotional states and encodes the sequence. Rapid enough interactive repair and moderate intensity mark a critical difference in the development of secure and insecure attachment and, ultimately, in the capacity to process shame adaptively.

Note that to attune to the infant and bring her out of a shame state, the caretaker herself must be able to tolerate shame. As we will see in Chapter 8, the incapacity to regulate shame is a hallmark of insecure attachment. Note also that moderate shaming involves a successful rupture-repair sequence (Tronick, 2007, chap. 27). Shaming sequences are imprinted as implicit memories into the limbic system of the infant and encode neurobiological procedures for tolerating and bouncing back from states of negative hypoarousal.

Schore proposes that encoded sequences of misattunement–dysregulation–attunement–reregulation are at the core of the secure internal working model. The imprinting of such rupture-repair sequences includes the outcome of repair. The happy ending is encoded into the internal working model and creates the positive expectations characteristic of secure attachment.

Here, then, is Schore's answer to the problem of the transmission gap: the transmission of secure attachment has been effected through implicit communications of affect. The infant has implicitly learned the arousal patterns of the attachment figure. There has been an intergenerational transmission of secure attachment in the form of the capacity to manage negative affect and shift efficiently from dysregulated to regulated states. The primary affect-regulating system of the attachment figure is internalized by the infant.

The Neurobiology of Secure Attachment

Schore proposes that secure attachment experiences facilitate the optimal organization of the limbic structures. Also, implicit memories of secure regulatory experiences become the operating instructions for a balanced autonomic nervous system (ANS) enabling affect tolerance and resilient affect regulation. They act as algorithms derived from experiences of affect regulation during the critical period.

Up to this point our focus has been on the interactive, affect-regulating experiences that become engrained procedures for up- and downregulation. Let's now look at the development of the hardware. (You may wish to refer to Figure 3.3, a chart of the connections of limbic nervous system and ANS.)

During the critical period, the limbic system is organizing into a cortical-subcortical hierarchy, with the right orbitofrontal cortex at the apex performing a final analysis of interoceptive and exteroceptive emotional information. Schore (1994) proposes that implicit memories of rupture-repair sequences of dysregulation and reregulation are stored in the ventral and lateral tegmental limbic circuits. They are internalized as operating instructions for sympathetic and parasympathetic regulation.

During the first phase of the orbitofrontal critical period (10–12 months), when the capacity to upregulate is established, the ventral tegmental limbic circuits connect the right orbitofrontal cortex to the HPA axis and the sympathetic nervous system. The HPA axis is the endocrine system—hypothalamus, pituitary, and adrenal glands—responsible for delivering adrenaline and noradrenaline to the upregulating, energy-expanding sympathetic nervous system.

During the second phase of the critical period (12–18 months), when the capacity for downregulation is established, the lateral tegmental limbic circuits innervate and connect the right orbitofrontal cortex to the HPA axis and parasympathetic nervous system. In this case, the HPA axis is called upon to deliver cortisol, endorphins, and endogenous opiates to the downregulating, inhibiting, energy-conserving parasympathetic nervous system. The infant is now on the road to building resilient self-regulation, affect tolerance, and flexible responsiveness even when stressed.

An additional and crucial neurobiological development occurs during the critical period. Recall that a balanced ANS involves *reciprocal*, equilibrating activations of the sympathetic and parasympathetic nervous systems (when one is on, the other is off). Developing a balanced, coupled, reciprocal cycling of sympathetic and parasympathetic arousal will regulate the intensity and duration of affect states, facilitates efficient and fluid state shifting, and allows for the delay necessary for real-time corrections of primary affect.

Optimal Neurological Development of the Primary Affect-Regulating System

At the end of the critical period of securely attached infants, a balanced ANS has been established. The limbic circuits that link the right frontal cortex to both the sympathetic and parasympathetic aspects of the ANS are coupled into a reciprocal system enabling affect modulation, tolerance of sympathetic and parasympathetic arousal, and fluid state shifting. The right orbitofrontal cortex has achieved hierarchical dominance over the subcortical components of the limbic system and is flexibly responsive to fast-changing socioemotional events. Resilient operating instructions, encoded as procedural memories in presymbolic representations of the mother's face, have been stored and govern the HPA axis and ANS. The internalization of procedures and expectations involved in shared joy states and moderate shaming supports the flexible use of dyadic or autoregulation.

Summary and Conclusion:

Let's take a moment to review what Schore's modern attachment theory proposes and then examine the relationship between the development of the primary and secondary affect regulating systems. The essential role of the attachment figure is the regulation of the infant's affect states. The secure caretaker is sufficiently emotionally competent to facilitate the development of a balanced ANS. Repeated experiences of successful affect-regulating transactions are internalized as implicit memories that become the automated relational moves, representational and perceptual schemas, and neurobiological procedures of the primary affect-regulating system—life-long psychobiological patterns of dyadic and autoregulation.

The secure caretaker's capacity for autoregulation and affect tolerance are key. When shaming the infant, the empathically attuned attachment figure is able to modulate the intensity of the shame and efficiently reestablish a psychobiological connection with the infant. The securely attached infant comes to expect the reestablishment of the attachment relationship, contributing to shame tolerance.

The primary affect regulation system of secure attachment figures is robust enough to cope with the stresses of regulating an infant: to tolerate the infant's dysregulation, to modulate their own disgust and anger, and to attune to the highly stressful, hypoaroused shame states induced in the infant. Secure attachment figures have tolerance for both hyper- and hypoaroused affect and, when dysregulated, are able to self-right and repair ruptures in the attachment relationship.

A balanced ANS enables the regulation of hyper- and hypoaroused affect states. It facilitates the capacity to experience joy and enter into states of shared joy without becoming overwhelmed. The regulation of positive hyperarousal also allows us to experience pride states without crossing over into grandiosity and to pursue exciting objects and goals without becoming manic. The capacity to regulate negative hyperarousal allows the processing of anger and its modulated expression—crucial to the development of autonomy.

We must be able to regulate negative states of hypoarousal in order to manage the induction of shame for the socialization of children and to process our own shame and use it for self- and social development. Ultimately, the regulation of sympathetic and para-sympathetic arousal underlies the regulation of the pride-shame axis (Nathanson, 1987, 1992) and the management of narcissistic equilibrium.

These developments are mediated by the right brains of infants and caretakers. Caretakers must be able to receive implicitly communicated affect, match it, and stay regulated. They must have access to implicit cognition for split-second assessments of the infant's affect states and of the emotional transactions. The right brain of the infant is also at work receiving, appraising, and expressing implicit communications and storing implicit memories

With the completion of the development of the right-brain-based, primary affect-regulating system, the development of the left-brain-based, secondary affect-regulating, mentalization system begins (Schore, 1994; Fonagy et al., 2002; Jurist, 2005). The emergence of mentalizing capacities is an extraordinary evolutionary advance onto-genetically and phylogenetically. It provides a secondary assessment after the primary processing of emotional information in the right brain and thereby increases the capacity for emotional correction and response flexibility.

The development of the mentalizing system depends on the effectiveness of the already developed primary affect-regulating system. The capacity for delay provided by the primary system allows the mentalizing system to develop a wide array of categorical affects and more complex understandings of self and others. Just as a well-developed primary system supports the development of mentalization, a poorly developed one impedes it.

The mentalizing system can be understood as the exploratory system of the inner worlds of self and others. Like the exploratory system of the external environment, it is activated only when the attachment system is deactivated: when we are in regulated states. An efficient primary system provides maximum time in regulated states and thus maximum time for the development of the mentalizing system. Securely attached children not only feel safe in exploring their own and others' inner states but also are more often in regulated self-states, in which they are *able* to do so. Regulated states facilitate clear thinking and feeling and support higher-order development.

Part III

THEORY OF PATHOGENESIS

Relational Traumas and Their Sequelae

CHAPTER 8

Relational Traumas

Developmental Origins of Disordered Affect Regulation

AFFECT TELLS US what matters. It alerts us to salient stimuli, disposes us toward engagement or withdrawal, and indicates whether our goals and needs are being met. Hedonic tone signals adaptive value—positive/approach or negative/avoid. Intensity signals how much it matters. Accurate appraisal of internal and external stimuli is crucial for adaptive functioning. It relies on our capacity for self-regulation. The relational traumas of insecure attachment are the source of deficient affect regulation. How that happens is the topic of this chapter.

In Chapter 7 we saw that in a secure attachment relationship the caretaker's empathically guided, contingent emotional responsiveness facilitates the development of a hierarchically organized limbic system and a balanced ANS. The resulting optimally developed primary affect-regulating system supports affect tolerance and resilient state shifting. These are the emotional capacities necessary for managing the strains of continued development.

We now look at the traumas of insecure attachment. In this circumstance attachment figures are less emotionally competent—less able to keep the infant in homeostatic, vitalized, growth-facilitating states. Rather, the infant chronically suffers prolonged exposure to neurotoxic, growth-inhibiting states of bodymind at a time when the primary affect-regulating system is first being established.

Relational trauma may be defined as exposure to chronic misattunement and prolonged states of dysregulation in the context of the early attachment relationship. It results in an altered development and deficient functioning of the primary affect-regulating system. When seeking affect regulation, the infant encounters responses that exacerbate rather than modulate her dysregulation. The attachment figure is without the emotional capacity to sufficiently regulate the infant. The stressor is the relationship resulting in relational triggers, generalized social anxiety and impaired attachment relationships=

The extraordinary contributions of Herman (1997) and van der Kolk (2005, 2014) in the understanding of "complex trauma" or "developmental trauma" has focused on sexual, physical and verbal abuse, and neglect within the attachment relationship. "Relational trauma" as Schore uses the term refers to unobvious, invisible trauma that occurs in the early attachment relationship. It has only recently begun to be studied empirically (See, for example, Bureau et al, 2010 and Liotti, 2004). Like later developmental traumas, these very early attachment traumas lead to impaired development and disordered personalities. Indeed, early relational trauma during the critical period of development is a likely precursor of later developmental trauma.

In this chapter I summarize Schore's theory of pathogenesis (1994; 2003a, 2003b, 2012). I first introduce relational trauma and how it manifests as disordered affect regulation. I then discuss the different types of relational trauma at the neurological, psychological, and behavioral levels. I end with a summary of the book to this point.

Schore proposes that chronic, misattuned affect-regulating transactions result in psychoneurobehavioral defects in the primary affect-regulating system.[62] Prolonged states of dysregulation generate neurotoxic conditions that adversely alter the developing limbic-autonomic structures. Chronic episodes of misattuned regulation also leave an imprint of maladaptive neurobiological, behavioral, and psychological procedures for responding to stress.

Schore further proposes that different types of neurological trauma are induced in each of the insecure attachment relationships. Each results in distinct deficits that manifest as the regulatory deficiencies we observed in the arousal patterns of the insecurely attached infants in the Strange Situation Procedure described in Chapter 1.

Different Types of Relational Trauma Resulting in Different Types of Disordered Affect Regulation

The avoidant infant emerges from the early attachment relationship predisposed toward parasympathetic responses to stress. This is an energy-conserving, "minimizing" strategy that supports passive coping, social withdrawal, deactivated mentalization, and hypoaroused categorical affects, including despair, shame, and disgust. The bias toward hypoarousal and overdependence on autoregulation interfere with resilience. This results in protracted periods of hypoaroused dysregulation, a hypoaroused set point (learned temperament) and social isolation.

Recall Barbara's hyper-aroused, hyper-activated, response to stress. The preoccupied disposition toward hyperarousal underpins an internal working model characterized by a maximizing strategy. This includes hyperengagement with the relational environment, hypervigilance, and hyperactive and compromised mentalizing. The

---

62 We will see in Chapters 9–11 that disordered affect regulation sets up vulnerabilities to Axis I and II psychiatric disorders, dissociation at low levels of stress, and pervasive shame.

bias toward hyperarousal interferes with resilience and results in prolonged periods of hyperaroused dysregulation and a hyperaroused set point. Overdependence on dyadic regulation and ambivalent attachment generate enmeshed and fraught relationships.

The disorganized infant emerges from the attachment relationship vulnerable to abrupt state changes and extreme hyper- or hypoarousal in response to stress. This chaotic and unregulated emotional system sustains incompatible internal working models and underlies behavioral and psychological instability.

Rather than a balanced ANS supporting response flexibility, robust affect tolerance, and resiliency, the stress response patterns of insecure attachment are rigidly hyper- or hypoaroused or an unstable mix of the two. We saw this in the Strange Situation Procedure.

When faced with the stressful arrival of a stranger or departure of his mother, Kenneth (hypoaroused) became apathetic and disengaged from the environment. He was limited to passive coping and enduring the situation. Barbara (hyperaroused) became simultaneously frightened and angry and remained tightly engaged with her mother at the expense of exploring. She was limited to active coping, in this case controlling her mother. Douglas (disorganized) displayed unexpected and confusing state shifts. He vacillated between states of hyper- and hypoarousal. He experienced extreme disengagement observed in his frozen, dazed look.

In Chapter 5 we also saw these arousal patterns manifest in the Adult Attachment Interviews of avoidant and preoccupied individuals. The impoverished mentalizing and minimal narrative of avoidant adults reflect their hypoaroused and deactivating responses to stressful memories of their attachment relationships. In contrast, the hyperactivation of mentalizing processes and elaborate but unruly narrative of preoccupied adults reflects hyperaroused, hyperactivated responses to stress.

All the insecure arousal patterns limit adaptive responses to the environment, exploration, and growth. What accounts for these different maladaptive responses to stress? Infants adapt to the socioemotional conditions of their particular caretaking niche. The emotional environment established by each type of insecurely attached caretaker is stressful in its own way. Each constitutes a subtype of relational trauma that requires a different adaptation. Each strategy is driven by a different autonomic response.

Schore understands the autonomic response to be at the core of the internal working model. It supports the physiological, experiential, cognitive, and behavioral components of the strategy. The avoidant, overregulated pattern underpins coping passively with the rejecting, barren, hypoaroused socioemotional ambiance set by the dismissive caregiver. The preoccupied, underregulated adaptation supports a strategy of active coping with inconsistent and intrusive caretaking, and a hyperaroused socioemotional ambiance. The chaotic and extreme arousal levels seen in the responses of disorganized infants reflect the lack of a solution to the problem of unpredictable, fear-generating or profoundly neglectful responses of the disorganized caretaker. Note that in each case the primary affect-regulating system of the caretaker is imprinted onto and internalized by the infant.

That is the big picture. However, to fully appreciate the psychobiology of relational trauma, it must be seen through a microanalysis of the emotional transactions of insecure attachment. The split-second world of insecure attachment illuminates the nature of the trauma. Seeing relational trauma in the raw provides an appreciation of its cumulative effect and of the internal working model as a strategy for adapting to the attachment relationship. This is crucial to understanding attachment transferences such as emotional distance versus enmeshed engagement.

The Psychobiology of Relational Trauma

The internal working models of insecure attachment are adaptations to a stressful socioemotional environment. They are strategies that anticipate and preempt or endure the emotional deficiencies of the caretaker. As a point of comparison, let's return briefly to the regulatory capacities that account for the secure caretaker's contingent emotional responsiveness.

During the first phase of the critical period, the securely attached caretaker has the capacity for co-regulated shared joy with her infant. During the second phase she is attentive and adept at nonintrusive regulation as the infant begins to venture into the world. In the "bangable" episode she demonstrates robust affect tolerance and resiliency as she shames the infant moderately and efficiently repairs the rupture in the attachment bond. The key to the repair of the rupture and return to homeostasis was the mother's capacity first to modulate her disgust and anger and then to switch states efficiently and attune to her infant's dysregulated shame.

The secure attachment relationship infuses the infant with sense of self-worth and trust based in experiences of attentive and competent dyadic regulation. Positive expectations develop that go on to bridge the gap between rupture and repair. Sturdy affect tolerance and emotional resiliency are established. A very different picture emerges of the emotional transactions of insecure attachments—scenes of aggravated and prolonged dysregulation.

Relational Trauma as a Neurodevelopmental Disorder

Insecurely attached infants experience chronic prolonged states of stress that generate neurotoxic conditions during the critical period in the development of their primary affect-regulating systems. Schore (1994) marshals extensive evidence that early relational trauma interferes with optimal development of the limbic system and the circuits connecting it to the ANS and alters the functioning of the hypothalamic-pituitary-adrenal (HPA) axis.[63] A variety of processes are involved.

Cortisol, a hormone secreted in dysregulated states and crucial to returning to homeostasis, becomes neurotoxic if left in the system for a prolonged period. Excess cortisol impairs the myelination of limbic structures. Further, it results in a thinning of connections between the right orbitofrontal cortex and the amygdala and thus a reduction in the capacity to inhibit amygdala reactions.

Overexposure to endogenous opioids such as endorphins, important for calming and returning to homeostasis, may lead to alterations in opioid secretion and reception. This condition impairs the functioning of the HPA axis. The metabolic conditions of chronic stress also hinder the balanced development of the lateral and ventral tegmental limbic circuits, which connect the limbic system to the ANS.

Excess neurons are produced during the critical period. Parcellation, a natural process that "prunes" excess neurons, favors the most robust store of affect-regulating transactions. In the case of insecure attachment, implicit memories of sequences of dysregulation followed by misattunement and shame and exacerbated by prolonged dysregulation survive at the expense of less established imprints of dysregulation–attunement–reregulation interactions.

Finally, Schore proposes epigenetic influences involving the experience-dependent expression of genes. Under conditions of chronic stress, there is insufficient environmental inducement of metabolic

---

63 Recall that the limbic system appraises and responds to body-based affect and socioemotional information. It regulates the ANS and the endocrine glands of the HPA axis responsible for the discharge of neurohormones, including adrenaline, endogenous opiates, and cortisol. For the limbic system to function optimally, the right orbitofrontal cortex must be well connected to and able to inhibit the subcortical limbic structures.

conditions that support the genetic expression of proteins necessary for limbic development. Additionally, because limbic structures myelinate sequentially, defects reflect the timing of the trauma.[64]

The Mechanism

Recall that the capacity to regulate the sympathetic nervous system sets up during the first phase of the critical period.[65] During the second phase the capacity to regulate the parasympathetic nervous system is established.[66] Working reciprocally, they provide a balanced ANS, each acting as an antagonist to the other. Optimally, the parasympathetic nervous system is dominant, able to inhibit and release sympathetic arousal.

The reciprocal counterbalance allows affects to be modulated and tolerated and thus be available for assessment. It also allows for sympathetic or parasympathetic responses as necessary for recovery from

---

64 Schore (2010a) writes that "a critical period of amygdala development occurs from the last trimester of pregnancy through the second postnatal month, followed by a critical period of limbic anterior cingulate development from 3 to 10 months, and lastly an orbitofrontal developmental period at 10 to 18 months. Depending upon the nature, severity and timing of the relational trauma in these critical periods, traumatic attachments are imprinted into the developing limbic (amygdala), then anterior cingulate, then orbitofrontal and autonomic (insula) nervous systems of the early maturing right brain. Thus the overwhelming stress of the very early life attachment trauma (abuse and neglect) alters the developmental trajectory of the right brain which is dominant for coping with negative affects . . . and for 'regulating stress—and emotion related process.' . . . This developmental model asserts that sexual abuse in later stages of development impacts later maturing left hemispheric, hippocampal and dorsolateral prefrontal verbal systems, as well as the callosal system that integrates the two hemispheres. These later forms of life trauma will overlie earlier attachment right brain nonverbal imprints" (p. 145).

65 During this period the ventral tegmental limbic circuit is myelinating, linking the limbic system to the sympathetic nervous system.

66 During this period the lateral tegmental limbic circuit is myelinating, linking the limbic system to the parasympathetic nervous system.

dysregulated states. Affect modulation, toleration, and resilience are critical to further development. For example, parasympathetic inhibition provides us with a capacity to regulate anger, crucial to the development of autonomy.[67] Conversely, a well-established capacity for sympathetic arousal provides a counterforce to parasympathetic arousal and establishes the capacity for moderate shame.

Let's now look at the psychobiology of each of the insecure attachment patterns. Recall that during the early phase of the critical period the infant is not yet fully mobile and the interactions between the caretaker and infant have been overwhelmingly positive. Mobility and shaming begin in earnest during the second phase.

The Psychobiology of Avoidant Trauma

When stressed, dismissive caretakers enter a negative, hypoaroused, withdrawn state. The paucity of emotional connection in the caretakers' own early attachment experiences has left a deep imprint of insensitivity, shame, and disgust about attachment needs and an overreliance on autoregulation. They tend to dismiss appeals for dyadic regulation, which, in any case, they are deficient in providing. In general, they establish a barren socioemotional environment for the infant marked by deficient empathy and insufficient expression of positive affects.

The avoidant infant develops an adaptive response that anticipates and guards this against rejection and shame and endures emotional austerity. His downregulated internal working model employs a strategy of avoidance, deactivation, and passive coping.

Difficulties begin for the avoidant-dismissive dyad during the first phase of the critical period when the capacity for regulating sympa-

---

67 See Schore (1994, chap. 26) for an important integration of affective neurobiology and developmental psychoanalysis regarding the regulation of infantile rage.

thetic arousal is developing. The chronically hypoaroused and withdrawn caregiver finds it stressful to join the infant in the shared joy states that put their stamp on the early infancy of secure attachment. These are the very stuff of positive attachment and remain so throughout the life span. They also generate ideal neurochemical conditions for the growth of limbic circuits that regulate hyperarousal (the ventral tegmental limbic circuits).

Without sufficient positive connection, and with a surfeit of negative affect infusing caretaker dismissals, the attachment bond that forms is based in expediency rather than attraction. Without the caretaker's participation, the opportunity for the infant to develop a capacity to generate and modulate states of positive hyperarousal is derailed. Schore (1994) also suggests that the chronic misattunement in the first phase induces shame prematurely, further contributing to the avoidant infant's parasympathetic bias.

With the onset of the second phase and the infant's increased mobility, the dismissive caretaker is called upon to set limits with moderate shaming. Here again the caretaker's emotional shortcomings are problematic. Recall that moderate shaming requires efficient repair of misattunement ruptures and that successful rupture-repair sequences engender resilient regulatory processes. Recall also that reregulation of the shamed infant begins with the caretaker's attunement to the infant's hypoaroused shame state. This is followed by a gradual, sensitively calibrated upregulation of the infant into a homeostatic state. Both are beyond the emotional capacities of the dismissive caretaker.

When stressed by the infant, the dismissive caregiver is hypoactivated, emotionally numbed, and disengaged. In this diminished state the caregiver is without the capacity or inclination to alleviate the infant's distress. Rather, the infant is left alone in highly stressful, intensely negative, hypoaroused states of shame and despair, the result of austere shaming.

The metabolic conditions generated by chronic states of negative hypoarousal are a growth-inhibiting neurological environment for the development of neural circuits responsible for hyperarousal. Rather, they facilitate the growth of circuits mediating hypoarousal. Additionally, there is an inadequate store of implicit memories scripting procedures that generate moderate sympathetic arousal. Instead, there is a buildup of implicit memories encoding procedures for parasympathetic arousal.

Together, the paucity of joy and effects of cold shaming result in deficient regulation of sympathetic arousal and a bias toward the parasympathetic—hallmarks of avoidant attachment. The parasympathetic bias supports a downregulated set point and parasympathetic responses to stress. The incapacity to regulate sympathetic arousal results in a fear of being overwhelmed by sympathetic affects (anger, fear, joy, pride) that becomes a core anxiety for those with this attachment pattern.

Avoidant patients tend to dampen or avoid shared joy states. They shy away from empathetic attunement for fear being emotionally overwhelmed by the amplification created by affect resonance. This is exacerbated by their shame at having attachment needs. They tend to defend heavily against anger and lose control when expressing it. Severely avoidant patients with whom I have worked have often become overwhelmed and cry when I induce pride.

In summary, the avoidant infant adapts to an emotionally impoverished environment not only lacking in joy but in which any hyperaroused affect may be discouraged. Attachment needs are dismissed or shamed. Shame is administered austerely and endured alone, with autoregulation providing the only refuge. At the neurological level, the metabolic conditions of avoidant trauma favor a parasympathetic bias and incapacity to regulate hyperaroused affect states. The stage is set for subclinical, shame-permeated depression and overregulation of anger, fear, joy, and pride.

Parasympathetic arousal dominates as a default state and as a response to stress. Without a balancing counterforce between sympathetic and parasympathetic arousal, there is difficulty modulating the intensity of affect. Affect tolerance is deficient, dysregulation-dissociation occurs at low levels of stress, and returning from dysregulated to regulated states is inefficient.

Disengagement from the attachment figure, avoidance of attachment concerns, emotional avoidance and detachment, and autoregulation develop as adaptations to socioemotional impoverishment. As personality develops, fear of being overwhelmed by the intensity of affect, chronic dissociation of affect, and negative expectations support a characterological joylessness, stoicism, and rationalized despair.

These traits, coupled with a low emotional intelligence and avoidance of dyadic regulation and shared states, pose substantial obstacles to therapeutic progress. Moreover, the lack of emotional expressiveness and characterological hypoarousal is stressful and may create negative countertransference. On the other hand, unlike preoccupied patients, avoidant patients are directly affected by shame. They have a ready appreciation of their shame and are interested in its discovery and the effects it has on their lives. Their capacity for objective, albeit emotionally detached self-assessment also provides therapeutic opportunities.

Therapists often despair of helping avoidant patients and may be put off by them, derisively referring to them as schizoid. Understanding them as traumatized assists empathy that includes allowing them the emotional distance they need as they develop the capacity to regulate hyper- and hypoarousal.

The Psychobiology of Preoccupied Trauma

The ambivalent-resistant infant adapts to a hyperaroused, vibrant, and volatile socioemotional environment. The preoccupied caretaker is sympathetically biased and deficient in parasympathetic regulation. The incapacity to modulate parasympathetic arousal is defended against with hyperarousal. Shame is bypassed with anger. The lack of parasympathetic inhibition is responsible for difficulties with delaying action and renders the caretaker inconsistent as a regulatory object.

When stressed, preoccupied caretakers become hyperaroused and dedicated to assimilating the infant to meet their needs. Deficient at autoregulation, they typically rely on the infant for their own self-regulation. They may, for example, intrude on the infant's quiet to pressure a smile as a way of reassuring themselves of the infant's love—a use of the infant for mirroring when the infant may prefer to attend to something else or be left alone. The caretaker's own fear of abandonment and need for regulation crowd out the needs of the infant.

Preoccupied caregivers are often emotionally sensitive, capable of attunement and interactive regulation, and predisposed to caretaking. However, their deficient capacity for autoregulation renders them inconsistently available. Their inconsistency engenders pronounced abandonment anxiety in the infant, who develops an internal working model that serves as a defense against it.

During the first phase of the critical period, when the capacity to regulate sympathetic arousal develops, the preoccupied caregiver is able to join enthusiastically in mutually amplified joy states. An orientation toward dyadic regulation and a capacity for a positive attachment bond are established in the infant. Problems arise when the caretaker's vulnerabilities come into play. For example, when the infant needs to gaze avert in order to regulate his own level of arousal, the preoccupied caretaker may experience the turn away as abandonment and intrusively disrupt the infant's gaze aversion. Rather than being allowed to develop procedures for autoregulation, the infant is pressured to respond to the needs of the caretaker.

With the onset of the second phase, the preoccupied caretaker's emotional limitations are uniformly problematic. This is the time for the infant to establish the capacity to regulate parasympathetic arousal, a core deficiency of the preoccupied caretaker. Optimally, experiences of dyadically regulated, moderate parasympathetic arousal are encoded as implicit memories. They serve as a means of regulating shame and as a break on sympathetic arousal. Nowhere are the vulnerabilities of preoccupied caretakers more evident than in their difficulties inducing shame moderately and repairing the rupture efficiently.

The preoccupied caretaker shames intensely, driving the infant into a state of extreme shame without repair and hyper-aroused shame-rage as a means of defense. For example, as the toddler inevitably gets into trouble, the preoccupied caregiver may become angered by the child's failure to live up to the idealized child she needs for her own self-regulation. Driven by her anger, she induces shame with a ferocity that drives the infant into intensely painful states of hypoarousal. Additionally, because of the caretaker's inefficient autoregulation, she remains dysregulated for a protracted period and is unavailable to reregulate the infant. Rather, the caretaker's hyper-arousal impels her into a tight, negative engagement with the infant, who remains in an exacerbated state of agitated shame.

Experiences of such "hot" traumatic shaming are encoded as procedures of unmodulated activation of the parasympathetic nervous system. Shaming episodes involve an extremely painful and frightening metabolic collapse of the self. Counteractive, hyperaroused defenses against shame develop and become a signature trait of preoccupied personalities.[68]

Anticipation of virulent shaming and the need to keep the care-

---

68 Some preoccupied parents suffer a shame phobia and fail to shame their infants sufficiently.

taker regulated and ensure his or her availability become a centerpiece of the child's internal working model. The strategy is to preempt the caretaker's shame and rage at feeling abandoned. Compulsive caretaking often develops and serves to maintain the attachment relationship.

At the neurobiological level, Schore (1994) argues, the severe and prolonged stress of unregulated shame sets up metabolic conditions that favor the development of the ventral tegmental limbic circuits that mediate sympathetic arousal. These same conditions inhibit the development of the lateral tegmental limbic circuits that mediate parasympathetic arousal.

The inability to regulate parasympathetic arousal leaves the infant without sufficient counterbalance to sympathetic arousal and, thus, deficient in the capacity to regulate both hyper- and hypoarousal. Without the ability to modulate the intensity of affects, dysregulation-dissociation occurs at low levels of stress, and affect is chronically dissociated. Without the counterbalancing activations, resilience is inefficient, resulting in prolonged dysregulated states.

In summary, preoccupied trauma results in underregulated sympathetic arousal, hyperaroused responses to stress, fear of hypoarousal, and thus the incapacity to process shame. Autoregulation is deficient, and manic defenses against depression are prominent. The preoccupied caretaker's fears of abandonment, assimilative disposition, and overreliance on dyadic regulation result in chronic intrusions and use of the infant for the caretaker's self-regulation. Examples of how this manifests are found in the caretaker's interference with gaze aversion, overinvolvement in the infant's budding independence, intense shaming, and inefficient repair of attachment ruptures. Adaptation to the preoccupied caretaker's regulatory deficiencies results in a hyperactivated internal working model involving enmeshed and ambivalent object relations, hypervigilance and hyperreactiveness to misattunement, and other signs of abandonment.

Hypervigilance for misattunement and abandonment, coupled with shame-rage, hyperactivated and often faulty mentalization, and enmeshment with and ambivalent caretaking of the therapist, pose substantial impediments to therapeutic progress and a difficult therapeutic terrain to navigate. The therapist may find herself seduced by the mirroring or walking on eggshells. On the other hand, the need for dyadic regulation, emotional expressiveness, and heightened distress about ambivalent attachments provide strong motivations and therapeutic opportunities.

The Psychobiology of Disorganized Trauma

Disorganized caregivers are subject to unpredictable extremes of hyper- and hypoarousal and states of profound, hypoaroused dorsal vagal dissociation. They lack the capacity to regulate and process shame and, instead, may suffer extreme episodes of depression or anger. They cannot shame moderately. There is extensive evidence that most have themselves suffered childhood abuse and/or neglect and are vulnerable to abusing or neglecting their own children (e.g., Carlson et al., 1989; Cicchetti & Toth, 1995; Van der Kolk, Fisler, & Rita, 1994).

Disorganized parents are deficient in both auto- and dyadic regulation. When stressed, they may become frightening or frightened, both of which induce extremely intense fear and terror[69] in the infant. Whereas the structured insecure caretaker's emotional deficiencies pose a problem to which there is some sort of a solution, the disorganized attachment environment poses an insoluble problem.

Schore (2013) illuminates the split-second traumatic emotional

---

69 Note the isomorphism between isolated-event trauma and the chronic situation of the disorganized child—fear with no escape. There is also overlap between the sequelae of isolated-event trauma, associated with posttraumatic stress disorder, and disorganized attachment. For example, both are subject to chronic severe dissociation and to sudden and unpredictable extremes of arousal in response to internal or external triggers.

transactions in a disorganized attachment relationship by referring to Beebe et al.'s (2012) ground-breaking research. They wrote:

> Clinically we observed that this maternal "closing up" of her face often occurred at moments of infant distress, as if the mother is "going blank." If she remained empathic to infant distress, she might fear finding herself in the original traumatized state of her own history. For example, as one future disorganized infant sharply vocalized distress and turned his head abruptly away with a precry face, the mother's head jerked back, as if "hit" by the infant's distress; she then looked down with a "closed-up" face . . . these mothers . . . may shut down their own emotional processing and be unable to use the infant's behaviors as communications in a momentary dissociative process. (p. 364)

Note the dissociated state of defensive withdrawal by the mother, which is matched and imprinted by the infant.

The damage to the primary affect-regulating system caused by disorganized trauma is qualitatively more severe than that caused by avoidant or preoccupied insecure trauma. Recall that secure attachment involves a reciprocal, counterbalancing relationship between the activations of sympathetic and parasympathetic nervous systems. In cases of structured insecure attachment, these two components of the ANS become biased but remain coupled. Although unbalanced, *there is still a moderating effect*. This is key for understanding why structured attachment results in less severe levels of dysregulation-dissociation compared with disorganized attachment.

Schore (1994) argues that, in the case of disorganized attachment, the neurochemical assault is so severe that the two aspects of the ANS become uncoupled. Lacking the reciprocal counterbalance, the disorganized personality is subject to extremes of hyper- and hypoarousal. The sympathetic and parasympathetic aspects may be activated simultaneously, but they do not serve as a moderating counterforce for one another. Additionally, the blank, dorsal vagal states of the mother are matched and imprinted by the infant. Thus, in the disorganized personality, sympathetic and parasympathetic arousal are unregulated, and there is a vulnerability to profound states of hypoaroused dissociation.

Summary of the Book Thus Far

We have covered a lot of ground. Part I discussed Schore's ideas about the primacy of right-brain implicit processes and the mechanics of the primary affect-regulating system. The body reacts first to salient stimuli. Affect represents the body's reaction. Ideally, the affect can be regulated, assessed, and made available to consciousness. It can then be further assessed and integrated into one's sense of self and relationship with others.

Schore proposes that for the primary affect-regulating system to function optimally, the right orbitofrontal cortex must operate at the apex of the hierarchically organized limbic system. It inhibits subcortical limbic structures that mediate body-based motivations and initial reactions to external stimuli. A balanced ANS develops around a store of implicit memories that encode affect modulation and resilient responses to dysregulation.

I extended these ideas into a model of the bodymind depicting regulated-integrated versus dysregulated-dissociated self-states. Dissociated self-states manifest with automaticisms, detached states of consciousness, and compartmentalized content. The availability of memories and the quality of attention deployment, perceptual and representational disposition, and reflective functioning depend on the unconscious, automatic, affect-regulating, implicit processes of the right brain.

In Part II we saw the effects of secure attachment experiences on the development of the primary affect-regulating system and on the capacity for self-regulation. I also described mentalization as a secondary affect-regulating system in relationship to the primary system. It is "secondary" not only in that emotional information is first processed by the primary system, but also in the sense that the conscious mental processes are supported by, and their quality is dependent on, the unconscious and preconscious processes of the primary system.

In Part III I have begun to present Schore's theory of pathogenesis. We have seen that relational trauma results in deficient affect regulation involving biased or chaotic responses to stress, a low affect tolerance, chronic dissociated affect and misappraisal of salience, and difficulty returning from dysregulated to regulated affect states. As a result, insecurely attached patients suffer frequent and prolonged hyper- or hypoaroused dysregulated-dissociated affect states. These core deficiencies in regulating affect underlie the sequelae of relational trauma: chronic dissociation, personality disorders, and pervasive dissociated shame, the focus of the next three chapters.

CHAPTER 9

Chronic Dissociation

A Sequela of Relational Trauma

WE HAVE SEEN that relational trauma results in deficits in the primary affect-regulating system and in dysregulated-dissociated affect at low levels of stress. Relational trauma refers to the cumulative effect of chronic misattunement, immoderate shaming, and repeated episodes of prolonged dysregulation that occur in insecure attachment relationships during the critical period in development of the primary affect-regulating system.

Dissociated affect may be defined as information about the state of the body that cannot be assessed and used for adaptive responses to one's internal or external environments. It cannot be integrated into our sense of self and others. Without this crucial information subjectivity and intersubjectivity break down. At the neurological level, Schore (1994, 2012) argues, the primary affect-regulating system itself dissociates. The structures of the system are no longer integrated and reciprocally exchanging information. As a result affective information is not processed in the right hemisphere, does not receive primary implicit processing, and thus cannot be transferred to the left brain for secondary, conscious formulation and appraisal.

In the next chapters I discuss three sequelae of relational trauma:

chronic dissociation, personality disorders, and pervasive dissociated shame. This chapter addresses chronic dissociation.

Recall that I've understood dissociative phenomena to share three characteristics: automaticity, compartmentalization of content, and altered states of consciousness. I've also distinguished dissociative phenomena as either hyper- or hypoaroused and moderate or severe. (See Chapter 2.) In this chapter I propose that the different types of insecure attachment are associated with severe vs moderate and hyper-aroused vs hypo-aroused types of dissociation. I focus on moderate dissociation as an underappreciated sequela of relational trauma.

Deficits in affect regulation result in dysregulation-dissociation at low levels of stress (Ogawa et al., 1997). As a result we frequently find ourselves more automated, reduced to encapsulated parts of our personality, and in altered states of consciousness. Higher-order cognitive processes are hindered. We cannot read our own or others' inner states resulting in reduced subjectivity and intersubjectivity. Agentic and autonomous functioning is compromised. Schore (1994, 2012) proposes chronic dissociation as a key factor in developmental arrest[70] and a primary obstacle to therapeutic progress (for the latter, see also Bromberg, 2006).

In what follows, I propose developmental origins of different types of dissociation. Dissociative phenomena are discussed as moderate versus severe and hyperaroused versus hypoaroused. I distinguish between moderate and severe in terms of the intensity of arousal and the associated degree of compartmentalization, automaticity, and altered consciousness. I suggest that moderate forms of dissociation originate in the *structured* insecure attachment patterns. Preoccupied

---

70 There is evidence of arrested development at the neurobiological level as well (Schmahl et al., 2010).

trauma results in proneness to moderate hyperaroused dissociation. Avoidant trauma results in proneness to moderate hypoaroused dissociation. Disorganized trauma results in greater damage to the primary affect regulating system and greater degrees of dysregulation. It is the developmental origin of severe forms of both hyper- and hypoaroused dissociation. (See Figure 9.1)

The scheme shown in Figure 9 is based in my clinical observations. It is at odds with the common use of the term *dissociation* to refer only to hypoaroused dissociation. However, it is consistent with many (see,

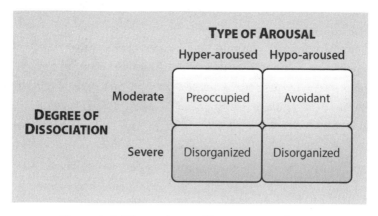

Figure 9–1. Dissocation and Insecure Attachment

e.g., Bremner, 1999; Ogden, Minton, & Pain, 2006; Schmahl et al., 2010) who find empirical and clinical support for hyper- and hypoaroused subtypes of dissociative phenomena. Lanius and colleagues (Lanius, Bluhm, Lanius, & Pain, 2006; Lanius et al., 2002) have found neural correlates for hyper- and hypoaroused subtypes.[71]

---

71 Lanius et al. (2005) have also found support for the hypothesis that posttraumatic dissociative phenomena are of the same type as the peritraumatic dissociative response, which may be either hyper- or hypoaroused. Note also

There is consensus that dissociative phenomena have a spectrum of severity. For purposes of discussion I've proposed moderate vs severe subtypes. Severe dissociation has received the lion's share of attention in traumatology and is represented in diagnostic manuals as dissociative disorders. Moderate dissociation, although more common and critically important in clinical work, has been relatively neglected. It can be thought of as "subclinical" or "subsyndromal" dissociation. It is debilitating but not necessarily disabling and often passes unobserved, which may account for the lack of attention it has received.

I begin with a discussion of severe dissociation, crucially important for understanding patients with disorganized attachment patterns.

Severe Dissociation

Severe dissociative symptoms fall into hyper- and hypoaroused subtypes (Bremner, 1999; Schmahl et al., 2010; Van der Kolk et al., 1996). Liotti (2004) describes manifestations of both in clinical interviews.

...dissociation is suggested either by such a degree of unwitting absorption in mental states that ordinary attention to the outside environment is seriously hampered, or by a sudden lack of continuity in discourse, thought or behavior of which the person is unaware (supposedly due to intrusion of dissociated mental contents in the flow of consciousness). Thus, for instance, a dissociative patient may suddenly interrupt her speech during a therapeutic session, stare into the void for minutes, and become unresponsive to the thera-

---

that Lanius et al. (2010a) distinguish between two types of PTSD: one suffering from "dissociation" referring to what I'm calling hypoaroused dissociation, and the other suffering from reliving symptoms which I count among hyperaroused dissociative symptoms.

pist's queries as to what is happening to her. Or a patient suffering from post-traumatic stress disorder (PTSD) may suddenly utter fragmented and incoherent comments on intrusive mental images (usually related to traumatic memories) that surface in his consciousness and hamper the continuity of the preceding dialogue with the therapist. (p.474)

Utterances that intrude like the one described are hyperaroused automatisms that derive from tightly compartmentalized content. Staring into the void and becoming unresponsive suggest profound hypoarousal—a dorsal vagal freeze state and an absence of content. Both phenomena involve an extreme alteration of consciousness and full automatization.

Severe Hypoaroused Dissociation

Freeze states involve immobilization without loss of consciousness. Sometimes called "feigned death," they are adaptive in the face of life-threatening danger. The metabolic retardation and immobilization conserve energy needed for physical escape. Pain numbing endogenous opioids are released. Such states tend to be accompanied by depersonalization and derealization, providing a psychological escape when physical escape is impossible (Putnam, 1997). Adaptive for peritraumatic dissociation, the activation of freeze states become pathogenic if they become a characterological response to trauma related cues or levels of stress that should be tolerable.

Porges (2011) proposes that the dorsal vagal component of the parasympathetic nervous system is the mechanism generating freeze states. Dorsal vagal activation generates an abrupt metabolic shutdown involving slowed heart rate and respiration—an extreme parasympathetic response. Schore (1994, 2009) asserts that the dorsal vagal response is associated with disorganized attachment and generates the type of dissociation observed in the blank faces, glazed looks, and stilled activity of some disorganized infants (Main & Solomon, 1986) and their caretakers (Hesse & Main, 1999), in the collapse of infants during the still face experiment (Tronick, 2007), and in states described by some borderline personality disorder patients as "falling into a black hole."

Severe Hyperaroused Dissociation

Extreme sympathetic arousal and dissociation are adaptive peri-traumatic responses to threat. They support the fight and flight systems. Speed is of the essence—deliberate, higher-order cortical processes such as verbal reflection are deactivated and replaced by automated reactions. Cannabinoids are released that provide a numbing defense against pain (Corrigan, 2014). Altered states of consciousness occur that may involve attention becoming hyper-focused and narrowed, total absorption and often a sense of time slowed down.

Severely hyperaroused, posttraumatic dissociative phenomena manifest as reliving experiences—vivid intrusive memories, real-seeming flashbacks, and nightmares. Intrusive memories come on us inducing total absorption. In reliving nightmares, there is total immersion in the virtual reality and intense hyper-arousal over-ridden by immobilization. In flashbacks the hyperarousal is unre-strained. They too sweep one into a total immersion in content that is normally strictly quarantined; behavior is completely automated. Note the blends of sympathetic and parasympathetic arousal, with one or the other dominating.

Moderate Dissociation

Although moderate dissociation has not been studied empirically, it has been addressed in the clinical literature without labeling it as such. Bromberg's pioneering work on dissociated self-states (1998, 2006, 2011), for example, is concerned with moderate levels of hyperaroused dissociation. Regulation theory has focused thus far on severe hypoaroused dissociation (Schore, 1994, 2003a, 2009, 2012). In this section I further these ideas based on patients' reports of moderately dissociated self-states.

Moderate dissociative phenomena are often subjectively known but not objectively apparent. Although they impede therapeutic progress, they are infrequently addressed in psychotherapy. Many of the patient descriptions of moderate dissociation that contributed to what follows were not offered spontaneously, but rather because I pursued a reference to their subjective experience. Most of my patients were ashamed of their moderate dissociative symptoms, which contributed to their failure to report them. However I have found that they are inevitably relieved to discuss them, their shame ameliorated by understanding their origins and grasping the subjective experience.

Moderate dissociation is distinguished by the mid-level intensity of the hyper- or hypoarousal and concomitant moderate degree of dysfunctionality. There is some modulation of the intensity of affect but not enough to stay regulated. One is hypoactivated but not immobilized, or hyperactivated but not completely out of control. The degree of automation and altered consciousness also seems to vary with the intensity of arousal. Let's look at some moderate dissociative phenomena.

In moderate states of absorption, unlike the absorption in reliving experiences, we are able to snap out of it. If involuntarily pulled away from the present by absorption in our own preoccupations, we are able to catch ourselves and return. Generally, recovery from such absences from the present occurs before they are noticed by others. Context remains influential. We remain responsive to environmental cues, and interpersonal automaticisms provide sufficient appearance of engagement for us to recover unnoticed.

One avoidant patient reported that in social situations he was unable to keep his attention focused on what others were saying. His mind kept wandering off, and when he returned he sometimes had no idea what was being discussed. Sometimes he was attentive enough to figure it out. This was exacerbated in groups, but at least there he was able to "disappear." It also occurred in conversations with individuals and proved embarrassing. We understood this as an avoidant, hypoaroused response to social anxiety. He had entered into a hypoaroused-dissociated state and lost control over his attention which was rigidly focused inward on non stressful topics—typically his hobby.

Here's an example of moderate hyperaroused dissociation. A preoccupied patient mentioned that she often could not keep from acting provocatively and bringing attention to herself in social situations. Even when she attempted not to she would find herself in hyperaroused-dissociated states. She would lose control of her behavior and her attention, which was focused on whether others were paying attention to her. Sometimes she was acutely aware of this as it was happening, sometimes only afterward.

Both of these patients had become dysregulated-dissociated because of the stress of the social situation. Both had become automated. Both had normal-seeming social lives but were unsuccessful in intimate attachment relationships.

Moderate emotional detachment and altered consciousness do not reach the level of an out-of-body experience or a severely altered sense of reality. However, in this condition somatic sensations are not clearly felt or available for processing. One is neither fully out or nor fully in one's body. In varying degrees there is a remove from oneself and the reality of what is happening. There is a breakdown in subjectivity without complete collapse. Whereas severe detachment fully disrupts the sense of going-on-being (Winnicott, 1958), moderate detachment generates experiences of "sort-of-going-on-being." The subjective experience of dissociation has been captured in the term "not-me" (Chafetz & Bromberg, 2004). "Not-really" might be added to refer to the experience of what is happening. The subjective experience of moderate dissociation inhabits a middle ground of "me-but-not-me" and "real-but-not-really."

Finally, moderate dysregulation generates partially dissociated self-states (Howell & Blizard, 2009) that are not as tightly compartmentalized as the alters of dissociative identity disorder. There is an overlap of memories and identity associated with other self-states. For example, although they are likely to be dismissed, representations of self and others as experienced in other states remain accessible. We may remember that the person with whom we are angry is not all bad but not be influenced by the idea. The idea comes through, but the affect associated with it is dissociated and faint at best.

Instances of moderate dissociative phenomena abound: for example, speaking involuntarily (and self-consciously) to one's child as if channeling a hated aspect of one's own parent; standing at the refrigerator eating mindlessly or automatically yet self-consciously; absorption in one's own thoughts while seeming to listen to a patient; intruding involuntarily into a patient's narrative with your own agenda; or automated, involuntary false-self and as-if relating.

Take the example of eating mindlessly at the refrigerator. Such automated eating occurs in a state of moderate dysregulation-dissociation. There is a detachment from self experience involving dissociation from affect, and sensations, including taste or the feeling of being full, are diminished. We may be uncomfortably aware of our behavior but continue it anyway. Discordant thoughts that present themselves about the resolve to diet have no traction. Agency has been disrupted by automaticity. Note that one is detached from somatic experience but not fully depersonalized. Content is compartmentalized but not fully. One is in a partially dissociated self-state.

Moderately hyper- and hypoaroused-dissociated self-states vary in their degree of intensity and subjective discomfort. We are usually able to "pass" in these states—"pass" to others and even to ourselves. However, when we are aware of being in this state, there is often a sense that something is "off" (Bromberg, 2006), that one is not thinking and feeling clearly.

The subjective experiences of moderately hyper- and hypoaroused-dissociated states differ dramatically from one another. Let's look first at hyperaroused dissociation.

Subjective Experience of Moderate Hyperaroused Dissociation

Moderate hyperaroused dissociation is associated with the preoccupied, underregulated attachment pattern. Appreciating the subjective experience is crucial to both patient and therapist; a place from which to begin change. One patient reported feeling overwhelmed with "thoughts coming all at once." Another described thoughts coming "too fast, one thought after another, but they don't go together. My mind gets all messed up. First I believe one thing, then another. It's nuts." Another patient said, "It's like I feel everything and nothing at the same time. I don't know what I am feeling. I just start talking and cannot stop." Another reported feeling numb while crying and yelling at her boyfriend.

Perhaps because the term *dissociated* is often used simplistically to mean "unfeeling" or "checked out," and because preoccupied personalities are emotionally expressive, driven by and often overtly overwhelmed by affect, it is not obvious that they experience detachment from affect. However, several of my patients have reported numbing. Moreover, the primary affect regulating system itself is dissociated and somatic experience cannot be fully processed and integrated into the appraisal of the present or one's overall sense of self and others. Although they can't help but know they are experiencing emotion, they are highly vulnerable to misinterpreting what what those emotions are. It is as though the affects take over one at a time presenting a confusing mix. Conflicting affects can't be blended and resolved but rather contribute to splitting. There is a sensory overload.

The subjective experience generated by moderate hyperaroused dissociation is characterized by affective flooding accompanied by scrambled or fragmented thinking. Thoughts seem to slip through without traction and drive what preoccupied patients say. There is a sense of being swept away. The inability to grasp, accurately appraise, and make sense of their emotional experiences, sometimes in addition to numbing, renders preoccupied personalities detached from their affects in the midst of being buffeted by them.

Thoughts and actions that occur while in a hyperaroused-dissociated self-state cannot be integrated into a coherent sense of self. When preoccupied patients can reflect on their thoughts and actions, they are likely to think "I didn't really mean that," or "That's not the real me." They have been in a hyperaroused, partially dissociated self-state. They can remember but disavow the state.

Subjective Experience of Moderate Hypoaroused Dissociation

States of moderate hypoaroused dissociation are associated with the avoidant, overregulated attachment pattern. Patients report feeling nothing, "grayed out," or in a "foggy," "dreamy" slowed state of consciousness. A musician patient described the experience as one in which "everything is delayed a beat, like everything is an echo."

Participating in social interactions can be highly stressful for these patients. One, referring to his slightly too long pauses and very deliberate style of speaking, described experiences where sentences were fully constructed before being said "as though everything I say is written out first in my mind." He sometimes experienced difficulty following what others were saying, had to repeat it to himself, and was unable to keep up.

The symptoms of moderate hypoaroused dissociation may be known by their absence: a generalized deactivation and withdrawal, a lack of attention paid or thought given, an absence of full engagement, a sense of distance from oneself and others, a sparse inner life, and an experience of feeling nothing. There is sensory deprivation.

Hyperaroused Versus Hypoaroused Moderate Dissociation

Hyperaroused and hypoaroused-dissociated states stand in stark contrast to one another. A preoccupied patient (Barbara) wanted her depressed, avoidant husband (Kenneth) to start therapy and brought him to a session. After a brief period of being solicitous and making an effort to get him to speak, she seemed to forget her original intent and launched into an attack. She was furious that the day before the appointment he had forgotten to call to say he would be late from work. She was sure that he had done it as a way of getting revenge. Like the ambivalent-resistant infant in the Strange Situation Procedure, she alternated between attacking and pleading with him, crying during both. Note her egocentrism and prementalization. She assumes the accuracy of her representations (psychic equivalent mode) and bases her interpretation of Kenneth's intentions on the outcome: its effect on her (teleological mode).

Kenneth seemed stupefied as she yelled at him. He was mystified by her interpretation and coolly told her, "I really don't know what you're talking about. I barely remember the incident you think I am taking revenge about. I didn't think at all about you. I wasn't angry or anything. I just got lost in my work until you called. I am really not as complicated as you think." Whatever may have led to his avoidant absorption in work, Kenneth's depiction of his mental life needs to be appreciated. The diverting of his attention from his stressful relationship and the lack of mentalization and of any felt affect are all representative of a state of hypoaroused dissociation.

Whereas Barbara manifested a confusing array of hyperaroused-dissociated self-states, Kenneth was mired in a stressed, devitalized, deactivated state of parasympathetic dominance. Whereas Barbara was thinking fast and furiously about attachment concerns, Kenneth gave it little thought at all and reacted to Barbara with the aim of being done with the topic as quickly as possible. Whereas Barbara's misattribution demonstrated prementalizing processes, Kenneth failed to mentalize at all. Whereas Barbara was hypersensitized, Kenneth was in a stupor.

Barbara's and Kenneth's verbal expressions during above incident reflect differences of hyperaroused, overwhelmed, scrambled dissociation and hypoaroused, deactivated, barren dissociation. Barbara's narrative came as an escalating torrent laced with powerful emotions. As she became increasingly swept away, her narrative lost coherency. Although parts of the narrative were emotionally compelling, ill-fitting fragments—often memories of past incidents—intruded. She was flooded and expressed a confusing mix of angry, pleading, crying diatribes that overwhelmed Kenneth. Kenneth was unable to take all this in and said little.

Barbara's core anxiety is of abandonment; Kenneth's, of being overwhelmed by affect. Barbara's intensity drove Kenneth into a state of hypoaroused dissociation. Kenneth's withdrawal was experienced by Barbara as abandonment, which further inflamed her, which further frightened and deactivated him, which further frightened and inflamed her, and on and on in a recursive and escalating loop.

Summary and Conclusion

Barbara's hyperactivated, overwhelmed, fragmented dissociative state was marked by intensity, an inability to take hold of and make sense of affect, and overwhelmed confusion. Kenneth's hypoactivated, distanced dissociation manifested as sluggishness, and dazed confusion. Both were dissociated from their affects and both were automated—running scripts of their insecure internal working models. Kenneth was coping passively, Barbara actively. Each was without the capacity to mentalize fully or operate with agency. For both, subjectivity and intersubjectivity had collapsed.

Recall that Schore proposes that the relational trauma of avoidant and preoccupied attachment leave the sympathetic and parasympathetic systems coupled. This provides a degree of mutual counterforce—the parasympathetic system acting as an antagonist to the sympathetic and vice versa. However, one system dominates, and there is insufficient reciprocity, resulting in under- or overregulation of affect. Moderate dissociation is the psychological and phenomenological manifestation of an ANS biased toward hyper- or hypoarousal.

This may explain why those experiencing moderate dissociation can usually "pass." The coupled but biased ANS provides Barbara with sufficient inhibition and Kenneth with sufficient outward-directed motivation to function, albeit suboptimally, in the social realm. One can often make do in moderately dissociated self-states, although the degree of success depends on one's location on the avoidant and preoccupied spectrums.

CHAPTER 10

Personality Disorders

A Second Sequela of Relational Trauma

ALONG WITH THE neurological impairments and regulatory deficits it causes, relational trauma give rise to character traits that serve to preempt and/or cope with expected misattunement, dysregulation, and shame. Relational trauma results in a sense of self as unworthy and a distrust of the intentions and emotional competency of attachment figures. The insecure internal working models, the object relations of insecure attachment observed in the Strange Situation Procedure, portend an adult who frequently struggles to maintain a positive sense of self and is on guard against rejection or abandonment.

Beginning with Bowlby (1977), attachment theorists and researchers have been concerned with the implications of attachment patterns for personality and psychopathology. A wealth of research has explored associations among insecure attachment patterns, personality disorders, and vulnerability to Axis 1 psychiatric disorders that are commonly comorbid with personality disorders.[72]

---

72 Among the many studies on insecure attachment patterns and psychiatric disorders, see, for example, Agrawal, Gunderson, Holmes, and Lyons-Ruth (2004); Atkinson and Zucker (1997); Bradley and Westen (2005); Cassidy and Shaver (1999); Collins and Read (1990); Fonagy (1999); Grossmann, Grossmann,

In his theory of pathogenesis, Schore (1994, 2003a, 2012, 2013) proposes that disordered affect regulation, born of insecure attachment, is the core deficiency underlying vulnerability to personality disorders and other developmental Axis 1 disorders. In this chapter I summarize and build upon Schore's ideas about how differing regulatory disorders underlie the type of personality disorder one develops. I end the chapter with psychobiological profiles of personality disorders.

A brief word first about vulnerability to Axis 1 psychiatric disorders. Schore (1994) proposes that all developmental psychiatric disorders represent a "limitation of adaptive stress regulating capacities" (p. 390). From the point of view of regulation theory, a vulnerability to psychiatric disorders is another sequela of relational trauma. An avoidant bias toward hypoarousal supports disorders of overregulation manifesting as overt depression, covert/underlying anxiety, and chronic hypoaroused dissociation. The preoccupied bias toward hyperarousal supports disorders of underregulation that present as agitated depression, hypomania, overt anxiety, and chronic hyperaroused dissociation.

As we are about to see, disordered regulation is also at the core of personality disorders. There are hyperaroused and hypoaroused types of narcissistic personality disorder. The borderline personality disorder includes vulnerability to extreme states of both hyperarousal and hypoarousal.

Insecure Attachment and Personality Disorders

In this section I describe how insecure internal working models manifest as adult personality disorders. The autonomic response to stress is at the core of the internal working model. Different responses to

---

and Waters (2005b); Lyons-Ruth, Melnick, Bronfman, Sherry, and Llanas (2003); Main (1995); Mikulincer and Shaver (2007); Obegi and Berant (2009); Sroufe (1996); Westen, Nakash, Thomas, and Bradley (2006); and Widiger (2003).

stress support different strategies: flexible in the case of secure attachment, active *or* passive coping strategies in the case of preoccupied and avoidant attachment, and no adaptive strategy in the case of disorganized attachment.

Character traits of disordered personalities are manifestations of insecure internal working models developed in the early attachment relationship to avoid or preempt misattunement and shame. The insecure internal working model is activated by relational cues associated with the relational trauma suffered. As a result, social anxiety is an ongoing problem for insecure personalities.

Deviations from Ideal Type

In what follows I offer personality profiles proposed as "ideal types" rarely encountered. Deviations from such models and mixtures of traits are to be expected because of variations in inborn strengths and weaknesses, adaptations to multiple attachment figures, and idiosyncratic developmental experiences.

Appreciating the uniqueness of a personality requires taking into account inborn temperament, as well as the learned temperament we have been discussing. Culture and gender also play a role in shaping personality. Clinicians commonly note, for example, the differences between male and female avoidant personalities. Regulation theory focuses on the part of the puzzle that derives from the early attachment relationship and its effects on the primary affect-regulating system.

Finally, with regard to deviation from an ideal type, one of the most intriguing influences on personality is hemispheric dominance. Stereotypically, avoidant personalities are associated with left-brain dominance, and preoccupied personalities, with dominance of right-brain dominance. The hemispheric dominance seems central to the personality. For example, with preoccupied personalities, the fast, holistic processing of the right brain, responsible for processing socio-emotional information, is a foundation for their highly developed social ability. Its speed also facilitates impulsivity, which is common in preoccupied personalities. In contrast, left-brain-dominant avoidant personalities, typically maladept in understanding and navigating the socioemotional environment, are hindered by an underdeveloped right brain and overreliance on the slow linear processing of the left. The lack of social intuition leaves them reliant on reflective functioning, which is too slow for real-time interacting and is compromised under stress.

Things look quite different when the stereotype is broken—when left-brain dominance is combined with preoccupied attachment or right-brain dominance is combined with avoidant attachment. I am currently treating an avoidant man with right-brain dominance. He has a well-developed emotional intelligence. He is aware of, indeed, focused on his own and his wife's emotional dynamics. His assessments are reasonably accurate. However, he is accepting to a fault. Everything is "interesting." He registers almost no somatic experience of the emotions he knows about. He can talk about anything, including a very significant trauma as a 7- to 8-year-old that he reports had no outward or inward effect on him at the time. He thinks he was emotionally detached already. He often feels disturbingly distant from others. Most patients with avoidant personalities that I have treated require emotional education and must develop interest in and the capacity to attend to and think about attachment themes. For this patient, all this was in place when treatment began. His treatment has consisted almost entirely of me amplifying his dissociated affect and him becoming vitalized.

With these qualifications about ideal types in mind, let's now look at psychobiological profiles of attachment patterns. I begin with characteristics originating in secure attachment as a point of comparison.

The Psychobiology of Secure Attachment

A well-developed primary affect-regulating system operates at the core of the secure internal working model. The right orbitofrontal cortex is densely connected to subcortical limbic structures, allowing it to inhibit their initial reactions. It provides accurate enough appraisals of salient stimuli in the inner and outer environments and works in combination with a balanced ANS. There is a rich cache of implicit memories encoding resilient responses to dysregulation.

This optimally adaptive primary affect-regulating system provides emotional flexibility and a robust tolerance for both negative and positive affect. It supports the development of a wide array of categorical affects, a wide range of integrated self-states, and a reality-based, resilient regulation of the shame-pride axis. It is able to modulate negative and positive sympathetic affects including anger, pride, and joy. It can also regulate parasympathetic arousal, allowing for delay without repudiation of body-based urges, and modulate shame, which can be used for self-correction and emotional growth.

Empathically guided contingent emotional responsiveness by the securely attached caretaker promotes the development of an implicit sense of self as worthy and a capacity for self-acceptance and realistic self-confidence. The accessibility and competence of attachment figures during stressful interactions engender trust and positive expectations, as seen, for example, in the clear and direct expression of needs. The internal working model is flexible and can be adjusted as needed. It supports passive or active coping and the use of dyadic or autoregulation, depending on the situation.

School performance and peer relationships of securely attached children are more successful than those of children with insecure internal working models. As adults they are more likely to enter into mutually enhancing romantic and marital relationships in which conflicts can be resolved. They are capable of intimacy and autonomy. Finally, robust affect modulation and tolerance support the maturation of the secondary affect-regulating system and the capacity to reflect on one's own and others' inner states with reasonable accuracy in the midst of stressful affect.

Organized Insecure Attachment and Narcissistic Personality Disorders

Internal working models established to cope with the stressful regulatory environments of avoidant and preoccupied attachment may generate personality traits sufficiently maladaptive to warrant a diagnosis of narcissistic personality disorder. Psychoanalytic observations and attachment research have distinguished two types of narcissistic personality disorder (Gabbard, 1989; Broucek, 1991; Bach, 1985; Miller, 1986; Dickenson & Pincus, 1998; Kohut, 1977; Russ, Shedler, Bradley, & Westen, 2008; Wink, 1991). This section examines how the sympathetic bias of preoccupied attachment supports a disinhibited, extroverted narcissism, whereas the parasympathetic bias of avoidant attachment supports an inhibited, introverted type.

Although different in outward appearance and socioemotional dynamics, the two types of narcissistic personality disorder share key characteristics of deficient empathy, grandiosity, egocentrism, and social anxiety. Russ and colleagues (2008) find that "interpersonal vulnerability and underlying emotional distress, along with anger, difficulty in regulating affect, and interpersonal competitiveness," are features the two narcissistic personalities have in common. Both are chronically defending against low self-esteem and may be drawn to mirroring and idealizing object relations that function to regulate it (Kohut, 1971). Both are prone to dissociative states at low levels of stress.

Although they share these core characteristics, the differences in their object relations and character defenses—differences in their internal working models—are substantial and reflect sympathetic or parasympathetic biases. The hyperaroused narcissistic personality disorder derives from preoccupied attachment. This type has been variously termed grandiose, obvious, overt, fragmented, excited, and inflated narcissism, all reflecting the hyperarousal that is central to it. I prefer the term *preoccupied* or *hyperaroused narcissism*, enriched by their references to classical and modern attachment theory. The second, often overlooked type of narcissistic personality disorder derives from avoidant attachment. Variously called deflated, covert, and depressed narcissism, it is a parasympathetic-dominant, inhibited form that I shall refer to as *avoidant* or *hypoaroused narcissism*.

Hyperaroused Narcissism and the Psychobiology of Preoccupied Attachment

The preoccupied personality is centrally characterized by hyper-arousal. There is a reliance on externalizing defenses and a tendency toward enmeshed object relations. These are stereotypical narcissists, who chronically draw attention to themselves and fill and dominate the intersubjective field with their large personality and skillful assimilation of others to meet their mirroring needs.

Schore (1994) summarizes the characteristics of the preoccupied narcissistic personality disorder as "self-absorbed, arrogant and aggressive, unabashedly self-aggrandizing and attention demanding, insensitive to the reaction of others and overtly impervious to their hurt feeling, and seemingly shameless" (p. 423). He also notes that in these cases "the continuous activation of the grandiose self . . . minimizes the experiences of depression" and that they are "quick to experience narcissistic rage in response to a narcissistic injury" (p. 424).

This type of narcissism is a sequela of preoccupied relational trauma which results in an incapacity for moderate parasympathetic arousal, adaptive limitations imposed by having only hyperaroused responses to stress, a poor capacity for autoregulation, and overdependence on dyadic regulation. The hot shaming of preoccupied trauma has left a deep imprint of hypersensitivity and a virulent fear of shame. The inconsistent attunement and chronic intrusions incurred in the attachment relationship engendered a strategy of hypervigilance for signs of abandonment and strategies to preempt it.

The inability to regulate parasympathetic arousal makes it impossible to modulate and process shame. Rather than being able to use it adaptively for personal growth and real-time interpersonal adjustments, shame is reacted against with rage. Dissociated shame seems to fester at the core of the personality always needing countermeasures.

The inability to regulate parasympathetic arousal is central to the intergenerational transmission of preoccupied attachment. The caretaker's defenses against hypoarousal impede attunement to the shamed infant and interfere with bringing it out of shame states. Occasionally there is a fear of inducing shame, perhaps a residue of the shaming trauma the preoccupied caretaker has incurred. This deprives the infant of the adaptive stress required for the development of frustration tolerance, delay, and the inhibition of egocentrism and grandiosity.

Recall the environment with which the preoccupied internal working model is designed to cope. The preoccupied caretaker's dependence on the infant for dyadic regulation and the caretaker's own shame and anger in response to perceived abandonment by the infant creates a stressful ambient environment. The preoccupied caretaker's need of the infant as a narcissistic regulating object (Miller, 1986, 1997) offers the opportunity for a coping strategy that becomes a way of being in attachment relationships. At the expense of its own autonomy and out of fear of abandonment and shame, the infant learns to maintain the caretaker's sense of self with the needed mirroring and upregulation.

This active-submissive strategy comes with a deep-seated ambivalence and compensating grandiosity. A preoccupied patient described her jumbled object relations as follows: "I need to be with my friends all the time. I am ridiculously sensitive to them. But I don't really like them. They're just not what I want them to be. It's tiring and infuriating taking care of them so much." Another revealed her contempt for people she manipulated and, in the next moment, suddenly crying, her desperate need for them to admire her. As a child her need for dyadic regulation, ambivilance, and disposition toward shame-rage encountered the same traits in her mother. This set the stage for a chronically agitated relationship.

Hyperaroused self-states become emotional signatures of preoccupied narcissism: prone to feeling strongly indiscriminately, making too much of things, and investing objects with too much significance. They have hyperaroused responses to stress and have a hyperaroused set point. Without the capacity for moderate hypoarousal, preoccupied narcissists are unable to tolerate disappointment about the way things are. The avoidant personality suffers from opposite characteristics: making too little of things, failing to register the significance of objects, and hosting a ready despair about the way things are. They have hypoaroused responses to stress and a hypoaroused set point.

Hypoaroused Narcissism and the Psychobiology of Avoidant Attachment

A dearth of emotional connection, chronic rejection, and austere shaming are hallmarks of avoidant relational trauma. They leave an enduring shadow of parasympathetic dominance, deficient sympathetic regulation, an inability to register one's own or others' affect states, proneness to hypoaroused dissociation, and a barren inner world. Chronic dismissal and misattunement foster a strategy of avoidance of dyadic regulation and social isolation. Character defenses guard not only against rejection and shame but also, due to insufficient capacity to regulate hyperarousal, against losing control over sympathetic affects such as anger, joy, and pride. Parasympathetic dominance sets a disposition to shame, disgust, and despair.

Core character traits of the avoidant narcissistic personality are supported by hypoarousal. As with preoccupied narcissism, dissociated shame lies at the core of the personality. However, in the former, shame is masked with expressed anger, whereas in avoidant narcissism, shame manifests undisguised, taking the form, for example, of a collapsed posture, habitual gaze aversion, and an overly accommodating relational stance. Preoccupied narcissism actively reverses shame; avoidant narcissism personifies it. Despite its overt expression, shame tends to remain unknown to its carrier, who keeps it from consciousness with averted attention, blunted emotion, and covert grandiosity. Privately, avoidant personalities may harbor a comforting, albeit dissociated, sense of superiority that communicates aloofness when it seeps through.

The object relations of avoidant attachment are adaptations to the dismissive caretaker's disposition toward withdrawal, autoregulation, and intolerance of dependence. A strategy of hyperindependence, stoicism, and resigned/passive coping promotes an attachment relationship of mutual, proximal isolationism and avoidance of conflict. Such mutual distancing and avoidance of negative affect are peacefulness to a fault. It is a common arrangement in avoidant-avoidant marriages and a danger to be guarded against in avoidant-avoidant therapeutic dyads.

Schore (1994) notes that this type of narcissistic personality disorder manifests "low self esteem, rejection sensitivity, diminished energy and vitality," and "inhibited, shy, self-effacing" behaviors to "avoid being the center of attention" (p. 424). We saw the antecedents of these traits in the Strange Situation Procedure. Recall the infant

Kenneth's hypoarousal, avoidant attention and low-key behavior and his stoical, stressed, passive coping and minimized expectations.

Depending on the degree of impairment, the avoidant personality suffers a range of alexithymia and lack of responsiveness to others' affect states. Schore (1994) marshals extensive evidence that deficiencies in detecting and appraising body-based affect and socioemotional communications are due to an impoverished development of the right orbitofrontal cortex—the executive center of social and emotional intelligence. The numbing effects of endogenous opioids that accompany parasympathetic arousal and hypoaroused dissociation are additional factors contributing to the insensitivity to one's own and others' affect states.

Recall that avoidant trauma results in a deficient capacity to regulate sympathetic arousal. This results in a core anxiety of being overwhelmed by affect. Gaze aversion is deployed to avoid this. Not looking at the face has been understood to originate as an avoidance of the disgust displayed on the face of the dismissive caretaker. It also a defense against the intensity of arousal generated by eye contact. For example, fearful of hyperarousal, including positive hyperarousal, avoidant personalities tend to ward pride off, dampening it by dismissing compliments and averting their gaze. The gaze aversion serves to minimize emotional resonance and amplification of positive arousal.

It is noteworthy that avoidant personalities have the capacity to stifle sympathetic arousal, but often only up to a point. Remember that, although typified by a parasympathetic bias, there is also an inability to regulate sympathetic arousal. Anger is expressed predominantly indirectly or passively, or not at all, but avoidant personalities may have short fuses, with breakthroughs of intense anger. I have mentioned that the low tolerance for sympathetic arousal has manifested as crying when I have induced pride in avoidant patients. One avoidant patient shied away from concerts and sports events because he was unable to tolerate the intensities induced by affect resonance. He reported attending a political rally where he burst into tears as he entered the enthusiastic crowd. Another patient, in whom I had induced pride, looked at me crying and laughing and said, "I feel loved"—he had never before experienced it.

Borderline Personality Disorder and the Psychobiology of Disorganized Attachment

Although there seems to be consensus among clinicians that fundamental aspects of borderline personality disorder (BPD) derive from disorganized attachment, empirical research does not present such a clear picture (Bradley & Westen, 2005). Studies show that all three types of insecure attachment may result in a borderline personality. Most show that disorganized and preoccupied attachment patterns are strongly associated. A few show that avoidant attachment is associated, although it typically has the lowest correlation. Levy (2005) proposes the severity of the insecure attachment pattern as an explanation for the lack of consensus. According to this view, preoccupied and disorganized patterns are most closely associated, but the severity of the attachment disorder also determines the association with borderline personality disorder.

Fonagy (1996, 2002), Holmes (2003, 2004), and Liotti (2000) associate borderline personality disorder with disorganized attachment. Their studies focus on cognitive symptoms, including splitting, the fluidity (lack of constancy) of self- and object representation, and deficient reflective functioning. Schore (1994) also links borderline personality disorder with disorganized attachment. He approaches the problem in terms of the instability of affect, intensity of dysregulation, vulnerability to severe depression, and proneness to profound hypoaroused dissociation. He also notes that, "an extremely inefficient capacity to regulate shame underlies this affective and characterological disturbance" (p. 416).

In their review of the contemporary understanding of the dynamics of BPD, and reflecting the transition from a cognitive to affective emphasis in the field, Bradley and Westen (2005) write:

> Emotional dysregulation refers to a tendency for negative emotions to spiral out of control, to be expressed in intense and unmodified forms, and/or to overwhelm reasoning. *Empirically, emotional dysregulation is probably the most characteristic feature of the disorder as defined in recent editions of the* DSM. . . . Vulnerability to emotion dysregulation in BPD is characterized by high sensitivity to emotional stimuli, high emotional intensity, and slow return to emotional baseline once emotional arousal has occurred. (p. 393; my italics)

Reflecting the incapacity to use either auto- or dyadic regulation and the vulnerability to psychiatric disorders, they write:

> The emotional dysregulation seen in patients with BPD can be understood as a gross failure to engage in normal emotion regulation processes; i.e., conscious and unconscious procedures used to maximize positive and minimize negative emotional states. A number of maladaptive efforts at emotion regulation characterize patients with BPD. Some are behavioral, such as suicidal and self- harming behavior when these reflect efforts to obtain relief from experiences of intolerable or overwhelming affect. . . . BPD is also associated with a number of other maladaptive behaviors likely to serve in part as affect regulation strategies, such as substance use and bulimic episodes. (p. 394)

Schore (1994) highlights the instability and extremes of the socio-emotional environment to which the disorganized infant must adapt. An intensely stressful, emotionally chaotic ambiance is established by a caretaker catastrophically incapable of self-regulation. The ambient strain is punctuated by moments of extreme dysregulation and sudden, profound parasympathetic dissociation.

Concerning the dissociation, Schore proposes that the blank states observed on faces of disorganized infants in the Strange Situation Procedure are dorsal vagal freeze states and originate in matches with dissociative states of the disorganized caretaker such as those observed in the administration of the Adult Attachment Interview (Hesse & Main, 1999). Recall also that the disorganized infant is faced with an attachment figure that is the source of both safety and danger. Danger without escape activates dorsal vagal freeze states.

Thus, core features of disorganized relational trauma include exposure to unpredictable and extreme intensities of dysregulation and dissociation and a terror-inducing attachment dilemma from which there is no escape. We saw in Chapter 8 that the effects on the primary affect-regulating system include deficient development of the right orbitofrontal cortex, an imprint of traumatic implicit memories, and the decoupling of the sympathetic and parasympathetic nervous systems (Schore, 1994).

The emotional sequelae of disorganized relational trauma reflect these catastrophic deficits to the primary affect-regulating system and correspond to the socioemotional pattern of the borderline personality disorder. Characteristics include mercurial, severely disturbed internal and external object relations; frequent, unpredictable, and abrupt shifts to extreme and enduring dysregulated affect states; an incapacity to regulate or process shame; and proneness to severe dissociative states.

Summary and Conclusion

Preoccupied and avoidant narcissistic personality disorders are under- and overregulated personalities. The behavioral and psychological patterns and type of dissociation reflect their autonomic biases towards either hyper- or hypoarousal. Disorganized attachment and borderline personality disorder reflect a decoupling of the normal sympathetic and parasympathetic reciprocal activations. The mutually moderating effects of the sympathetic and parasympathetic nervous systems is lost, and the resulting psychological and behavioral characteristics reflect a disorder of nonregulation.

The internal working models of both types of narcissistic personality disorders may be understood as hyper- or hypoaroused defensive strategies aimed at preempting and/or coping with the repetition of traumatic shame. The internal working model of the borderline personality disorder represents a lack of a regulatory strategy and a corresponding failure of defenses against traumatic shame. It reflects nonregulation and manifests as chaotic and severe affect dysregulation,. Note that, despite their differences, all the insecure attachment patterns involve an incapacity to regulate and process shame. Dissociated shame is a central feature of all the personality disorders (Schore, 1994, 2003a, 2012).

CHAPTER 11

Pervasive Dissociated Shame

A Third Sequela of Relational Trauma

THE INCAPACITY TO process shame is a central feature of insecure attachment. Like other sequelae of relational trauma, dissociated shame is the result of regulatory deficiencies. Schore (1994, 2012) proposes that dissociated shame resulting from relational trauma is the primary pathogenic force underlying developmental psychiatric disorders, an important motive driving repression, and a key factor in developmental arrest.

In this chapter I discuss shame from the point of view of regulation theory (Schore, 1994, 2003a, 2003b, 2012). I begin by discussing the nature of shame and, along with pride, its centrality in our mental economy. I discuss the importance of the ability to process shame and the source of shame's pathogenic power and pervasive influence. I end with manifestations of dissociated shame in the clinical setting and the importance of dissociated shame (and dissociated pride) in the treatment of disordered affect regulation. I draw from Broucek (1991), Herman (1997, 2007), Kaufman (1992), Lewis (1971, 1987a,b), Nathanson (1987a,b, 1992), and Tomkins (1962,1987), in addition to Schore.

Let me remind you of what shame is by comparing it with guilt. Shame theorists take pains to distinguish between them. The two affects are often confused in part because they are often fused (Lewis, 1987b). Herman (2007) summarizes key distinctions between shame and guilt:

> Though shame and guilt are often spoken of interchangeably, and though both can be considered social or moral emotions, the two states are quite distinct. Whereas shame is focused on the global self in relation to others, guilt is focused on a specific action that the person has committed. Shame is an acutely self-conscious . . . painful and disorganizing emotion; guilt may be experienced without intense affect. Shame engenders a desire to hide, escape, or to lash out at the person in whose eyes one feels ashamed. By contrast, guilt engenders a desire to undo the offense, to make amends. Finally, shame is discharged in restored eye contact and shared, good-humored laughter, while guilt is discharged in an act of reparation (Lewis, 1987c).

Note that it is the repair of the emotional connection and the positive upregulation of laughter that end shame.

Shame's onslaught has an abrupt onset. It is intensely visceral and painful, all-encompassing, and disorganizing. It is represented imagistically through the eyes of a valued other. Being "looked down on" gets to the heart of the matter. Guilt, on the other hand, is known largely through reflective processes in which one imagines the plight of another. It is a step removed, more mind than body and less acutely painful.

Shame is the more basic emotion. It originates preverbally and remains a wordless state. Neither Darwin (1872/1965) nor Ekman and Friesend (1975) include guilt among the basic categorical affects. Schore (1994) notes that shame has a facial expression, whereas guilt does not.

Shame is more self-involved than guilt. "The experience of shame is directly about the *self*, which is the focus of evaluation" (Lewis, 1971, p. 18). When shamed, we match the other's disgust toward us and experience self-disgust. Guilt involves thinking about and experiencing *others'* emotions about what has happened to *them* and feeling badly about how we have affected *them*. Whereas shame paralyzes, guilt moves us toward reparation. Shame, with its self-involvement, wish to hide, and power to disorganize, can interfere with the capacity to experience and come to terms with guilt. There is frequently shame about shame, so shame can also interfere with the processing of shame!

The importance of the capacity to regulate and process shame cannot be overestimated. Nathanson (1987b) sees adaptive shame as a "mark of our humanity." Lewis (1971) notes that it supports our values and guards our privacy. Tolerance for shame is crucial to empathy and plays a role in altruism (Schore, 1994). Modulated shame applies a necessary break on grandiosity and egocentrism and engenders the acceptance and correction of deficient aspects of the self—key for continued development. Regulation theory proposes that moderate shaming is a crucial experience that imprints resiliency and sets the capacity for the regulation of parasympathetic arousal. The rupture-repair process of moderate shaming is dependent on the caretakers' capacities to regulate their own shame (Schore, 1994).

Attention must also be paid to pride's place in our emotional economy. Developing the capacity for moderate pride is no less important than the capacity for moderate shame in the maintenance of our well-being and adaptive socioemotional functioning. Freud (1957) understood pride to be essential to self-regard and a positive sense of self. Kohut (1971) illuminated the importance of healthy narcissism. The capacity to generate pride's positive hyperarousal is crucial for recovery from shame's negative hypoarousal and the restoration of narcissistic equilibrium. The capacity to generate moderate intensities of shame and pride is key for the regulation of the shame-pride axis along which self-esteem fluctuates (Nathanson, 1987a).

The preoccupied bias toward hyperarousal and incapacity to regulate hypoarousal give rise to underregulated pride and overt grandiosity and the overt expression of rage to bypass shame. The avoidant bias toward hypoarousal and deficient capacity to regulate hyperarousal support covert shame-rage and private grandiosity that serve to buoy against shame's undertow. In both types of narcissistic personality disorder, pride is no less dissociated than the shame against which it is meant to serve as a modulating counterforce. Those with insecure attachment may alternate between dissociated pride and shame states that are segregated from one another and cannot be integrated into the overall sense of self. Dissociated pride sits alongside dissociated shame at the core of the narcissistic personality disorder.

The Sources of Shame's Pathogenic Power and Pervasive Influence

Beginning with the angry, traumatizing shaming of Adam and Eve, through the shame-fueled revenge that motivated the Trojan War and the ruinous disgrace of Hester in Hawthorne's *Scarlet Letter*, to current understandings of oppressed and traumatized populations, Western civilization has depicted the power of shame and the enduring mark it leaves as it is passed down through the generations. Schore's (1994) understanding of misattunement and shame and his microanalysis of the shaming process reveal the source of shame's pervasive influence and pathogenic power.

Shame is a confounding feature of all post traumatic disorders. It is responsible for difficulties seeking help, changes in one's sense of self and the social isolation that so often result from trauma. This is true even for trauma induced by strangers or impersonal events such as accidents. It is especially true for chronic trauma induced by attachment figures. Attachment trauma comes from the one on whom one's sense of self worth depends and, experienced through the ego centrism of child, it is felt to be about the self, not the perpetrator. Such "complex" or "developmental" trauma (Herman, 1997; van der Kolk, 2005, 2014; Courtois, C. and Ford, J. 2012, 2014) leaves an imprint of shame that infuses the whole of the self, infiltrating every nook and cranny of the personality.

The terms complex and developmental trauma are used to refer to observable trauma; chronic physical, sexual or emotional abuse occurring in the attachment relationship, severe neglect and exposure to domestic violence. The definition can and, I believe, should be expanded to include the relational trauma that Schore has illuminated. Relational trauma refers to invisible complex trauma (Bureau et al, 2010). Like the observable complex traumas, it too leaves an indelible mark on the primary affect regulating system and on one's sense of self, and it too is an obstacle to further development. Moreover, the shame born of early relational trauma is dissociated during the traumatic interaction. It remains dissociated when reactivated making it an elusive therapeutic target.

The insecure internal working model is, at its core, an adaptation to chronic misattunement-shame—a strategy for defending against and coping with anticipated shame. Each time the insecure attachment system is activated, automated, defensive object relations are set in motion. The avoidant relational strategy is to become hypoactivated, withdrawn and compliant. The preoccupied strategy is to become hyperactivated, tightly engaged and coercive. At the same time they both enter an altered state of consciousness. The avoidant experiences a dulled, slowed, vapid state of consciousness. The preoccupied experiences a hyperalert, speeded up, entangled state of consciousness. Both are highly automated. Both suffer from ubiquitous shame that cannot be processed.

The *pathogenic power of shame* is revealed in the microanalysis of immoderate shaming. Shame represents an overwhelmingly frightening, unexpected severance of the attachment relationship and disorganization of the self. In a flash, one is exposed, shunned, and alone: in pain, paralyzed, and helpless.

Recall the paradigmatic shaming event described in Chapter 7, in which Frances is about to have a terrific time demonstrating her prowess with a fragile "bangable." She looks to her mother, expecting a face that mirrors her fabulousness and amplifies her joy about herself. Instead she encounters a face of disgust—a massive, unexpected misattunement. Stunned—terrified and immobilized—the infant is instantly taken down by a painful metabolic collapse. The self implodes. Shame's pathogenic power is in full view. The elements of acute trauma are present: overwhelming fear followed by what appears to be a freeze/dorsal vagal response—extreme frightened hyperarousal followed instantly by extreme hypoarousal.

A key factor in whether a traumatic event will lead to posttraumatic stress disorder is whether or not the victim is attended to in a timely fashion and whether supportive human contact is reestablished. Likewise, the failure to reestablish the attachment bond after shaming is a key component of immoderate shaming and relational trauma. If the shaming sequence includes a modulated induction of shame and soon enough restoration of the attachment bond with a return to a regulated state, the stage is set for emotional resiliency and the capacity for moderate shame. However, if the infant is shamed immoderately, the stage is set for shame-infused, posttraumatic pathology. Immoderate shaming can be understood as an ur-trauma of the self that leaves a shadow of disordered affect regulation and dissociated shame.

Manifestations of Dissociated Shame in Clinical Situations

We have seen that avoidant, downregulated narcissism manifests as a personification of shame and that preoccupied, upregulated narcissism supports personality traits of reversed shame. Dissociated shame permeates insecure personalities yet, despite its ubiquity, is veiled to those who suffer it and often to those who treat them.

Shame may be expressed as generalized personality traits. Broucek (1991) lists parasympathetic-dominant, inhibited personality traits that represent dissociated shame: "shyness, reticence, . . . self-consciousness, feeling of inferiority and inadequacy" (p. 5). Note that these traits are expressed implicitly but often not formulated explicitly. Also, keep in mind that dissociated shame will be represented by hyperaroused traits in preoccupied personalities.

Shame may be referred to verbally and still go unnoticed. Wurmser (1987) refers to a "shame family of emotions." They comprise a set of categorical affects delineating a spectrum of shame intensity—from mild embarrassment and chagrin through mortification. At the far end of the continuum lies humiliation, a soul-crushing emotion induced by angry shaming. (Contempt may be defined as anger plus disgust.) Although these words all refer to shame, they may simultaneously mask it. I am constantly impressed by the impact on patients when I call shame "shame." Perhaps due to the rawness of the word, shame seems to be the affect that dares not speak its name.

Implicit expressions of dissociated shame that go unnoticed include a patient's gaze aversion at a particular moment, a slowing of speech and/or a drop in volume, all typical of avoidant hypoaroused reactions. Hyperaroused indications include speeding up over some content, or a momentary stuttering or abrupt change of topic. Because such implicit communications may travel below the radar, we often know first of dissociated shame only through the emotional countertransference.

Shame in the Transference-Countertransference

The affect field of the patient-therapist relationship is mediated by implicit communications of affect expressed in parallel with verbal communications. It is continuously monitored for misattunements in the therapist-patient bond. For insecurely attached patients, such ruptures signal a repetition of relational trauma and intolerable affect.

Shame is induced by the therapist's misattunement and disconnection, which is communicated implicitly. I am referring to the inevitable therapist misattunements in clinical-life-as-lived. Each time our attention wanes or is averted, each time our agenda intrudes, each time we are not responding contingently, it is communicated, and the patient reacts to it.

Insecure internal working models are activated in anticipation of shame. Insecurely attached patients are likely to begin treatment with their attachment system activated. Safety in the therapeutic relationship may be, most fundamentally, trust that one will not be shamed. We gain patients' trust by attuning to them, by not misattuning too often, and by reattuning quickly and reliably enough when the therapeutic attachment bond has been ruptured.

Schore (1994, 2012) proposes that, at the heart of the therapeutic relationship, there are moments of attunement, misattunement, and reattunement. Therapists' misattunements and failure to repair the rupture are often due to their own dysregulation-dissociation. When a therapist becomes dysregulated, it further dysregulates the patient. When both therapist and patient find themselves in dysregulated-dissociated self-states, intersubjectivity collapses. Such mutually dissociated interactions are often the leading edge of an enactment of a larger scale.

Clinical misattunements elicit hypoarousal and emotional distancing in avoidant personalities. Recall Kenneth, the avoidant infant depicted in Chapter 1. As an adult, when dysregulated, his thinking is likely to be diminished, his experience detached, his attention disposed away from the source of stress, his affect numbed and unprocessed. Coping passively, he may accommodate the therapist and go through the motions of therapy, but he is thinly engaged, dulled, and unlikely to digest what is being said.

Misattunements elicit hyperarousal in preoccupied personalities. As an adult patient, Barbara is likely to actively reengage with the therapist in ways ranging from caretaking, including mirroring the therapist, to picking a fight. In this state she is vulnerable to hypermentalizing, with considerable misattribution and distortion. Although she may be emotionally expressive and tightly engaged with the therapist, she is in a fragmented, dissociated self-state and unable to integrate what she is experiencing.

So, that is the theory of pathogenesis—the relational traumas of insecure attachment. But, as Marion Solomon does not tire of saying at her groundbreaking Lifespan Learning Conferences, "What do we do Monday morning back in our offices?"

Part IV

Theory of Therapeutic Actions

Therapeutic Processes and
the Emergence of the Self

CHAPTER 12

Therapeutic Aims

Restoration of Self-Development

REGULATION THEORY AND interpersonal neurobiology (Schore, 1994, 2003a, 2003b, 2012; Siegel, 1999) are in their early stages of development. Models applying them are being developed in a widening array of therapeutic modalities.[73] Psychodynamic psychotherapists, body therapists, expressive art therapists, and trauma therapists are finding a theoretical home in interpersonal neurobiology and are integrating regulation theory into their approaches. (see, e.g., Ogden & Fisher, 2014). Interpersonal neurobiology and regulation theory provide theoretical support for new forms of couples therapy, individual therapy, and the treatment of addiction.[74] Schore and Newton (2012)

---

73 Regulation theory and interpersonal neurobiology are also influencing theory and research in a widening array of disciplines, for example, ecology and transspecies psychology (Bradshaw, 2009; Bradshaw & Schore, 2007), moral psychology (Narvaez, 2008, 2014), the neurobiology of trauma and dissociation (Lanius et al., 2010a), religious fundamentalism (Hill, 2010), the neurobiology of personality disorders (Meares, 2012; Meares, Schore, & Melkonian, 2011), and family law (McIntinosh et al., 2011).

74 On regulation theory as applied to couples therapy, see Solomon and Tatkin (2011) and Stan Tatkin's psychobiological approach to couples therapy at http://stantatkin.com/; for individual therapy, see Fosha (2003, 2009a, 2009b, 2013), Fosha, Paivio, Gleiser, and Ford (2009), and the AEDP Institute's approach to

apply them to the assessment of the mother-infant attachment relationship. Siegel (2007, 2010) bases his understanding of the therapeutic action of mindfulness in interpersonal neurobiology. Relational psychotherapists and psychoanalysts are increasingly influenced by regulation theory and interpersonal neurobiology (Bromberg, 2011; Ginot, 2012; Goldner, 2014; Knox, 2011; Maroda, 2012; Marks-Tarlow, 2012; Wilkinson, 2010). Schore (2012) has proposed that regulation theory represents a paradigm shift for psychoanalysis.

Therapeutic Approaches: Top-Down, Bottom-Up, Brain-to-Brain

Interpersonal neurobiology conceives of the organism as a whole and regards the brain, mind, and body as reciprocally related subsystems. Regulation-integration versus dysregulation-dissociation is system-wide.

One can approach the organism through any of its subsystems. Top-down treatments of regulatory deficiencies employ reflective functioning and engage the conscious mind through left-brain to left-brain communications mediated by words. Bottom-up therapies act to regulate affect through the body. Regulation theory prescribes a direct engagement of the right brain. That is, therapeutic actions are mediated by implicit communications of affect between the right brains of therapist and patient. Implicit communications, it should be remembered, are touch at a distance and regulation theory may in this sense be considered a bottom up approach. Actually, regulation theory accesses the body through the autonomic nervous system.

Implicit communication is mediated by the limbic system in the right

accelerated experiential dynamic psychotherapy at http://www.aedpinstitute. org/; for treatment of addiction, see the website of the Center for Healthy Sex, founded by Alexandra Katehakis, at http://centerforhealthysex.com.

brain. Implicit memories determining the operations of the primary affect-regulating system are stored in the right orbitofrontal cortex and its cortical and subcortical connections. Implicit cognitions that guide us through relational interactions are also products of the right brain. That is, the internal working model, comprising perceptual and representational schemas for assessing relational life, and implicit memories that script intrapsychic and interpersonal affect-regulating procedures, are mediated by the right brain.

Regulation theory focuses therapeutic action on the right brain through an emphasis on implicit therapeutic processes. Implicit communications of affect directly engage the limbic-autonomic structures responsible for the implicit, primary, automatic regulation of affect.

In this chapter I discuss the aims of affect regulation therapy. In Chapters 13 and 14 I discuss therapeutic processes and describe their implementation. As we progress, keep in mind that regulation theory provides a principle-based treatment. Affect regulation therapy must be adjusted to the emotional capacities of each patient according to the emotional capacities of each therapist. (See Schore, 2003b, Appendix.)

First-Order Versus Second-Order Change

Eagle and Wolitzky (2009) distinguish between first-order and second-order change:

> A distinction between, on the one hand, therapeutic changes in self-reflective capacity (as well as in related areas such as insight, self-awareness, and self-knowledge) and, on the other hand, changes in the very tendencies, states, and affects that one is reflecting on. Consider, for example, in the context of attachment theory, the distinction between, on the one hand, one's implicit and "automatic" expectation (as well as accompanying feelings) of rejection on the part of one's attachment figure and,

on the other hand, one's reflection on that implicit and "automatic" expectation. (p. 360)

The authors provide the example of a patient who is attracted to the "wrong men"—men who are rejecting and unable to commit to a relationship. When the patient recognizes this pattern and, despite continued attraction, stops pursuing such men, second-order change has occurred. When she is no longer attracted to the wrong men, there has been first-order change. In other words, first-order change is change at the implicit, automatic level.

Psychotherapy directly effecting secondary change would include mentalizing the patient's affect and self- and object representations when attracted to the wrong men, as well as what she imagines they are thinking and feeling about her. Change is carried out by engaging the conscious, reflective, verbal processes of the secondary affect-regulating system. The goal is for the explicit to become implicit.

Experience has taught that primary, implicit processes are slow to change using exclusively top-down, secondary, explicit processes. Eagle and Wolitzky (2009) note that "even in successful treatment, some individuals may continue to have an 'automatic' expectation of, say, rejection, but, through an increased ability to reflect on and evaluate this automatic expectation, are better able to modulate the strong negative effects and maladaptive behaviors that, in the past, have accompanied the implicit and 'automatic' expectations" (p. 360).

Schore (2012, p. 202) cites a 2007 paper by Greenberg: "It is the building of implicit or automatic emotion regulation capacities that is important for enduring change, especially for highly fragile personality disordered clients" (p. 416). He also cites Carter (1999) "Our conscious control over emotions is weak, and feelings often push out thinking whereas thinking fights mainly a losing battle to banish emotions. . . . The connections from the emotional systems to the cognitive systems are stronger than the connections that run the other way" (p. 201).

We can imagine the patient in a hyperaroused-dissociated self-state when attracted to the wrong men. Her attraction seems to have a life of its own, undeterred by memories, knowledge, and self-experience available when regulated. Such a dissociated self-state would be organized around dissociated affect and encase its own segmented memories and sense of self, and be accompanied by an altered state of consciousness. Regulation theory suggests that the focus of treatment should be on the regulation of the dissociated affect. This would allow the self–affect–wrong man schema to be processed and integrated. Its therapeutic aims, however, are more ambitious.

Regulation theory targets not only particular dissociated affects but also the neurobiological system responsible for the processes that regulate affects in general. It proposes implicit therapeutic actions that engage and change the implicit affect-regulating processes themselves. One might say that regulation theory aims at first-order change of the first order. A focus on first-order change brings therapists face to face with the primacy of the right brain. Affect is processed first in the right brain and then in the left. The effects of relational trauma interfere with the primary processing of affect.

The Right Brain as Locus of Trauma and Target of Therapeutic Action

Schore (2012) diagrams the flow of information processing (see Figure 12.1). Affective information coming up from the body and in through the senses is first processed in the limbic system in the right brain, first subcortically and unconsciously and then cortically and preconsciously. It is then transferred through the corpus callosum over to the left hemisphere for conscious processing, and then back to the right orbitofrontal cortex, where it receives a final, implicit integration into autobiographical memory. First-order problems arise when affect cannot undergo primary processing in the right brain.

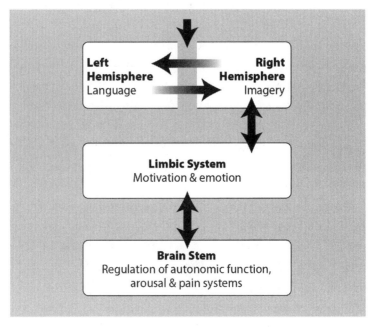

Figure 12–1.

Schore (1994, 2012) proposes that the insecure internal working model is composed of networks of implicit memories of relational trauma and the intrapsychic and interpersonal strategies for coping with them. This includes imprints of dissociated fear, shame, and disgust that lie at the core of the traumatic memories—residue of chronic unrepaired ruptures of the attachment bond. The procedures of the insecure internal working model include, perhaps as a defense against the traumatic, unbearable affects, the dissociation of the right brain. As a consequence, negative affect does not receive primary processing. This occurs each time the insecure attachment system is activated and has far reaching effects. Primary affect regulation must occur for there to be effective, secondary, left-brain mentalizing in the midst of live affect.

Therapeutic Aims

Schore's regulation theory (1994, 2003a, 2003b, 2012) argues that relational trauma results in deficient regulation of the intensity of affect states and difficulty shifting from dysregulated to regulated states, and, ultimately, in underregulated, overregulated, or unregulated personality disorders. It leaves a shadow of social anxiety,[75] pervasive shame, and chronic dissociation—a growth-inhibiting internal environment that results in arrested development of the self.

The overarching aim of affect regulation therapy is to restore the capacity for the development of the self. The therapist treating insecure attachment aims for first-order change by repairing deficiencies in the primary affect-regulating system. The goal is to enhance patients' capacity to regulate affect and allow development to resume. There must be a buildup of tolerance for fear and shame associated with the relational trauma. The affect-regulating procedures of the insecure internal working model, based in expectations of misattunement and shame, must be supplanted by procedures established by therapeutic affect-regulating experiences that engender trust, a valued sense of self, and positive expectations. The primary affect-regulating system must be reorganized.

Affect Tolerance, Resiliency, and Relational Trauma Sequelae

Deficits in the primary affect-regulating system result in impaired shame and pride regulation. Continued development requires that shame be experienced as a signal affect to be assessed for self-correction. Pride must be processed for maintaining self-esteem and inte-

---

75 Anxiety is anticipated danger. Fear is experienced in the presence of danger.

grated into a positive sense of self. Deficient affect regulation results in dissociation at low levels of stress that impedes development. Chronic dissociation interferes with experiencing the present and blocks implicit and explicit learning.

The repair of the primary affect-regulating system increases affect tolerance and thereby enables the processing of shame and pride, and decreases vulnerability to dissociation. Increased access to affect provides core data for subjective and intersubjective functioning. Rendering intolerable affects tolerable makes them accessible for mentalization and enables the expansion of the affect array and complex blends of categorical affects. Increasing stress tolerance allows conflicting affects to be held together in working memory and experienced simultaneously. Splitting is replaced by growth inducing conflict.

Disorders of affect regulation are marked by the intensity, frequency, and duration of negative affect states. By increasing emotional resiliency, more time is spent in regulated, positive affect states in which physioemotional and socioemotional information can be processed with reasonable accuracy, response flexibility is optimized, and exploration and learning are maximized.

To review, first-order change requires strengthening the capacity to regulate affect. This includes improved stress tolerance, which increases the capacity to process shame, diminishes vulnerability to dissociation, improves overall socioemotional functioning, and establishes the capacity for continued development.

This is all easier said than done. The insecure internal working models that our patients bring into therapy generate negative expectations, misperceptions of self and others, hypersensitivity and reactivity to misattunement, chronic dissociated states of consciousness, dissociated content, and defensive object relations. These manifest as transference in the *implicit* therapeutic relationship and interfere with therapeutic processes.

Establishing a Secure Internal Working Model

Internal working models consist of networks of implicit memories encoding affective-cognitive-behavioral strategies for self-regulation while maintaining the attachment relationship. A cognitive function filters perceptions and provides prefabricated representations and intuitions (implicit cognitions) used for assessing and navigating the relational environment. At the core of the working model is the primary affect-regulating system supporting strategies of active or passive coping.

Affect regulation therapy aims to develop a secure internal working model that supersedes the insecure model. It assembles around experiences with the therapist that develop a generalized imprint of a dysregulated self regulated by an attuned object and that establish a valued sense of self, positive expectations of others, and confidence necessary for exploration.

An insecure internal working model develops as an adaptation to relational trauma. At its core is an imprint of the trauma encoded as dysregulated self shamed by a misattuned object and attendant negative expectations of attachment relationships. It is the internalization of a growth-inhibiting attachment relationship. Surrounding this core are procedures that guard against re-experiencing the trauma. This includes procedures for preempting and enduring misattunement and shame. These are experienced in dissociative states of consciousness that act as a buffer against overwhelming fear and intolerable shame.

First-order change involves supplanting the implicit affective-cognitive-behavioral processes (implicit memories) of the insecure internal working model with those of a growth-facilitating secure internal working model. Affect regulation therapy works to change the insecure internal working model by providing affect-regulating experiences that establish adaptive affect-regulating procedures.

Let's now look at the neurobiological changes to the primary affect-regulating system. This is the locus of first-order change.

The Reorganization of the Primary Affect-Regulating System

The right orbitofrontal cortex performs final integration of socio-emotional information about the relational environment with body-based affective information about the internal environment. It mediates survival functions and is the decision point for passive or active responses to the internal and external environments. It functions at the apex the limbic system and is able to inhibit fear and other body-based motivations (sex, hunger, etc.) mediated by the subcortical components. It performs the executive function for the automatic functioning of the organism.

However, neurotoxic conditions induced by relational trauma result in a thinning of connections between the right orbitofrontal cortex and the subcortical components. As a result, the inhibiting capacity of the right orbitofrontal cortex is diminished.

The repair of the primary affect-regulating system involves building stronger connections between the right orbitofrontal cortex and the subcortical components of the limbic system. The right orbitofrontal cortex, the "thinking part of the emotional brain," is then better able to inhibit subcortical processes. The system is better able to remain organized under stress. The enhanced capacity of the limbic system diminishes chronic dissociation, facilitates implicit learning, and improves appraisal competence and socioemotional functioning in general.

Therapeutic maturation of the limbic-autonomic structures into a more flexible and stable system includes establishing a new store of implicit memories. Therapeutic experiences of empathic, competent, and consistent affect regulation are encoded as dysregulated self regulated by an attuned object.

Secure patient-therapist experiences, encoded as implicit memories, become the dominant operating instructions of the primary affect-regulating system and the core of an earned secure internal working model. They generate a valued sense of self, positive expectations, and a (flexible) disposition toward trust. This displaces the insecure internal working model that developed as a defensive strategy to cope with traumatic attachment experiences and fear of further rejection or abandonment.

Repair of the Implicit Self

Trauma to the primary affect-regulating system impairs the capacity to maintain a secure, integrated, positive sense of self across affect states. The preoccupied bias toward hyperaroused dysregulation gives rise to an exploded, fragmented sense of self. The avoidant endures hypoaroused dysregulation that generates an imploded sense of self—an experience of no-self.

There is, I think, no more widely felt or deeply appreciated result of therapy than the capacity to maintain a vital, coherent, positively toned sense of self. It is the essence of earned security and self-mastery. Ongoing positive implicit self-experience and the established capacity for continued development are markers of the repair of the primary affect-regulating system. They are brought about by emotional experiences cocreated in the implicit therapeutic relationship.

CHAPTER 13

Therapeutic Actions

Implicit and Explicit

HOW DO WE change the maladaptive affect-regulating and relational patterns of insecure internal working models? How do we expand emotional resiliency and affect tolerance? How do we reduce proneness to dissociation and establish the capacity to process shame so that emotional development may resume?

Schore (1994, 2003b, 2012) proposes that we must engage the right brain where affect is first processed. We communicate via two parallel channels: implicit communications of affect are streamed between right brains; explicit verbal communications flow between left brains. It is the implicit communications that matter for efficient changes to regulatory capacities. They engage the psychobiological structures/processes of the primary affect-regulating system.

Recall the route of neurological processing of emotional information. Body-based affective information traveling up through the brainstem and socioemotional information flowing in from the external environment are first processed implicitly in the right brain. The information is then made available to the left brain for secondary, verbal processing. It is then routed back to the right brain for a final holistic integration and consolidation into autobiographical memory.

When affective intensity exceeds tolerances for hyper- or hypoarousal, the right brain disorganizes and affect cannot be processed. The secondary processes of the left brain are without essential information.

Dissociated memories of relational trauma are stored in the limbic system. They become the basis of the insecure internal working model developed to preempt and cope with fear and narcissistic injury. This strategy and the accompanying dissociated fear and shame are communicated implicitly. As therapists we must attend with our right brains to gather crucial information about our own and our patients' inner states; i.e. be tuned into physiological experiences, implicit communications and implicit cognitions.

The left brain processes what has happened and what will happen but not what is happening. It strives for certainty and control by organizing the world into known, abstract categories represented by words. The right brain processes and puts us in the present rather than a step removed from it with words. It accepts things as they are and regards objects as unique rather than reducing them to the limitations imposed by verbal conceptual categories. It tolerates ambiguity (McGilchrist, 2010).

The right brain assembles cognitive gestalts that come to us as intuitions, metaphors, and run-of-the-mill implicit knowings crucial for assessing and responding to clinical life as lived. It processes emotional information, recognizes others as subjects, and provides a direct emotional snapshot of patients as they are at a given moment.[76] It provides us and our patients with our subjective reactions to one another. By engaging our patients' right brains with ours, we establish a direct, in-the-moment, psychobiological connection. Our explicit and implicit preoccupation with the affect states of patients resonates with the early

---

76 Freud advocated free-floating attention, and the British psychoanalyst Wilfred Bion advised achieving a state of reverie and listening without desire—both of these approaches engage right brain states of bodymind.

attachment relationship and activates their internal working models. Our emotional transactions with patients engage the same processes that originally shaped the neurobiological structures that subserve the primary affect regulating system.

Of course, we do more than engage in right-brain to right-brain, here-and-now emotional communications. Although the bulk of what follows is devoted to implicit therapeutic processes, I also discuss top-down interventions, including psychoeducation, observations of attachment patterns, and the mentalization of affect states.[77] Along the way I elaborate differences in working with avoidant and preoccupied patients and what is involved in being therapeutic with each.

I say *being* therapeutic because the way we actually are is continuously expressed. Involuntary implicit communications reveal, consciously or unconsciously, whether we are regulated or dysregulated, whether we have received and accurately assessed patients' emotional communications, our gut reactions, and so forth. As much as we at moments may wish, we cannot hide. The good news is that we can be ourselves in affect regulation therapy. Indeed, we have no choice. We are emotionally engaged or not, responding contingently or not, attuned or not. The relationship that matters in affect regulation therapy is between implicit selves. [78] That said, let's begin with top-down therapeutic processes.

---

77 In practice, though not discussed here, I have also learned from sensorimotor psychotherapy (Ogden et al., 2006; Ogden & Fisher, 2015) to read and help patients recognize dissociated affects expressed through the body. (I have not been trained in techniques that work with the body to regulate dissociated affect and ameliorate their effects or else I would use those techniques as well.) I have also occasionally suggested mindfulness practice and eye movement desensitization and reprocessing (EMDR) when appropriate. Several of my students are finding both sensorimotor therapy, neurofeedback and EMDR to be useful adjunctive techniques with some patients.

78 Schore (2012) writes, "At the most fundamental level the intersubjective work of psychotherapy is not defined by what the clinician does for the patient

Explicit Therapeutic Processes

Top-down interventions use verbal cognition and reflective processes to effect changes in the internal working model and in the capacity to regulate affect. This includes observations, psychoeducation, and the mentalization of affect states. Avoidant and preoccupied personalities tend to find these interventions useful in different ways.

For example, avoidant patients usually have limited experience with emotion and need an introduction. A left-brain cognitive approach such as observations of affect experienced outside of therapy may provide a safe way to dip their toes in the water. Avoidant personalities fear emotional arousal and direct emotional contact. They are helped by knowing first and feeling second, helped to know what they are looking for and allowed to approach it privately. This is a delicate balance: one must be concerned that treatment with avoidant patients is not reduced to emotionless, left-brain intellectualization, yet therapists must also be mindful that even the verbalization of affect may dysregulate them. Adding to the problem is that avoidant patients tend to be ashamed of their lack of feeling. I no longer ask avoidant patients what they are feeling as the question tends to shame them.

Preoccupied patients, on the other hand, seem universally to be drawn to and helped by observations of their affective experience. They are reassured by cognitive recognition and relieved by the regulation that the cognitive grasp of affect provides. Clarifying and distinguishing among their affects helps them to organize their internal states and to make sense of them and provides a measure of relief from the affective onslaught and confusion they experience. At the same time, one

---

or says to the patient (left brain focus). Rather, the key mechanism is *how to be with the patient* especially during affectively stressful moments when the patient's implicit core self is dis-integrating in real time (right brain focus)" (p. 103; italics original).

must be concerned with their limited capacity for self-objectification. Simply the implicit experience of being observed objectively can frustrate their mirroring needs and shame preoccupied personalities.

EARLY IN TREATMENT I make psychoeducational interventions that will helpful for future work. For example, I introduce such concepts as regulation and dissociation. I may say things like "when you are in such and such state," underscoring that one is different in different states, that one's sense of self and way of relating to others are state dependent. Patients' understanding that they are not always "that way" helps alleviate shame about the way they feel and act in an undesirable state. When exploring their experience of being in a dissociated state, I may also explain to patients that we enter dissociated states when dysregulated and that they become dissociated at low levels of stress.

Exploration of the internal working model is a key top-down project in the early stages of treatment. This includes determining patients' arousal bias in response to stress, their overdependence on auto- or dyadic regulation, and the origins and strategies of their object relations. Avoidant patients are helped by understanding that they turn their attention away from sources of stress; preoccupied patients benefit from knowing they are hypervigilant for signs of abandonment and often misinterpret them. Understanding that one's way of being in relationships is an adaptation to an early caretaking environment and that emotional deficits are the result of relational trauma helps to generate self-compassion and reduce shame.

Finally, as affect tolerance increases and affect is increasingly available as conscious information about one's own and others' subjectivity, the mentalization of affect states becomes a crucial top-down intervention (see Chapter 6). This often begins with making implicitly expressed affect explicit and goes on to entail elaboration and refinement of affective experience. There is not only a buildup of emotional vocabulary but also an appreciation of conflicting affect, blends of affects, and emotional dynamics such as the bypassing of shame with anger.

The mentalization of affect states includes discussing patients' subjective experiences of being dissociated from affect. This can help them recognize when they are dissociated, although that is more easily discussed than done. Reflective functioning is impaired or completely deactivated when we are dysregulated, and we are often aware of dissociated states only in retrospect. Nevertheless, I have found that an elucidation of what it is like to be hypersensitized, hyperactivated, and scrambled or in an emotionally numbed, hypoactivated state of consciousness is helpful for autoregulation and useful for letting partners know what is happening to them when they are dysregulated-dissociated.

Let's now shift our focus to therapeutic actions in the implicit realm.

Implicit Therapeutic Processes

Strengthening affect tolerance and increasing emotional resilience are fundamental aims of affect regulation therapy. Toward these ends, implicit therapeutic action occurs at the boundaries of patients' tolerance for hyper- and hypoarousal. The fundamental role of the therapist is to facilitate the regulation of the patient's affect and maintain optimal states of arousal for therapeutic progress. We monitor and adjust patients' levels of arousal when they are on the verge of dysregulation. When they become dysregulated, especially when we have induced it through our own misattunement, we move quickly to reconnect and bring them back to a regulated state. We also establish the conditions for exploration. These include safety, as well as states of positive arousal that fuel exploration and offset fear. We do this while providing interpersonal space for patients to find their own way.

Kierkegaard's beautiful description, given in Chapter 7, of the implicit processes involved in a growth-facilitating exploratory episode can now be appreciated more fully. To refresh your memory:

> The loving mother teaches her child to walk alone. She is far enough from him so that she cannot actually support him, but she holds out her arms to him. She imitates his movements, and if he totters, she swiftly bends as if to seize him, so that the child might believe that he is not walking alone . . . and yet, she does more. Her face beckons like a reward, an encouragement. Thus, the child walks alone with his eyes fixed on his mother's face, not on the difficulties in his way. He supports himself by the arms that do not hold him and constantly strives towards the refuge in his mother's embrace, little supposing that in the very same moment that he is emphasizing his need for her, he is proving that he can do without her, because he is walking alone. (Sroufe 1979, p. 462)

No words are exchanged—they would only interfere.

Imagine that instead of a baby walking for the first time, it is a patient processing, for the first time, intolerable memories, shameful parts of the self, or forbidden ideas about others. As therapist you are regulating not shaky first steps but a patient's teetering affect state, keeping the patient regulated and able to process novel material. Mostly, you are up- or downregulating the patient, nonverbally helping to maintain self-regulation in a way that does not intrude. "Simply" being attuned accomplishes this.

Kierkegaard's exploration-supporting mother is fully immersed in the experience of the infant. She shares his shifting states in order to know them firsthand and responds intuitively and spontaneously to adjust them. She not only provides the infant with a sense of safety but also encourages his derring-do by resonating with and amplifying his excitement. The boundaries are being pushed, but the infant remains regulated—sometimes wobbly, but in possession of himself enough and expecting success. Oh, that every moment of psychotherapy could be like this!

For the remainder of this chapter and in the next, I summarize and illustrate Schore's theory of therapeutic action (1994, chap. 33, 2003b, chaps. 1–3, 2007, 2012, chaps. 3 and 5). The fundamental therapeutic actions are affect-regulating transactions occurring in the split-second world of the therapeutic relationship.[79] Concerning this implicit domain, the Boston Change Process Study Group (2002) concludes that

> this is the level at which emotional procedures or implicit relational knowings are established and reorganized throughout life. Moreover, a great deal of the information that both analyst and patient gather about each other and their relationship derives from the implicit domain. Unless this is acknowledged, much of what transpires in an analysis will be missed. It therefore requires our most careful scrutiny in attempting to understand therapeutic action at this level. . . . Through it, the past is carried along, engagement is regulated and meaning generated. (p. 1060)

The targets of implicit therapeutic actions are the limbic-autonomic affect-regulating structures located in the right brain. Affect regula-

---

79 In a groundbreaking series of books and articles, infant researchers and psychoanalysts have proposed that events occurring in the split-second world of the patient-therapist relationship are fundamental to therapeutic change (Beebe & Lachman, 2002; Boston Change Process Study Group, 2010; Stern, 2004). Regulation theory argues that these processes are mediated by the right brain and that, specifically, it is the affect-regulating events that are fundamental to efficient first-order change.

tion therapy strives to reorganize the primary affect-regulating system by participating in the kind of affect-regulating interactions that shaped it initially and continue to influence it throughout the life span.

Engaging the Right Brain

Deficiencies in affect regulation are first and foremost deficiencies in the primary processing of emotional information. To change the affect-regulating structures of the patient's right brain, we need to engage them with the output of our right brain. The implicit therapeutic relationship is mediated by implicit communications of affect and captured in real time with implicit cognitions.

Left-brain, secondary processing (linear, conscious, verbal) is dominant during moderate levels of arousal. It is used for processing known information and navigating predictable events. Right-brain primary processing (holistic, nonconscious, nonverbal) is dominant at heightened levels of arousal, activated when processing novel events and stressful emotional information.

Recall that the right brain accepts the world as it is, whereas the left brain fits it into known categories. Schutz (2005) writes that "Right-brain problem solving generates a matrix of alternative solutions, as contrasted with the left brain's single solution of best fit" (cited in Schore, 2007). Right-brain holistic processing generates metaphor, intuition, and sudden insights, key processes for apprehending the complexities of the socioemotional events of psychotherapy.

Right-brain processing is dominant not only in dysregulated states of hyper- and hypoarousal, and not only when skirting the boundaries of dysregulation, but also in heightened states of positive regulated arousal such as in play, in creative pursuits, and when vitalized by attunement. Such states of positive arousal are not only pleasurable but also set optimal metabolic conditions for neurological growth.

Concerning the importance of working at the boundaries of

affect tolerance, Schore (2006) quotes Joseph LeDoux's 2002 book *Synaptic Self*:

> Because emotion systems coordinate learning, the broader the range of emotions that [an individual] experiences the broader will be the emotional range of the self that develops. . . . And because more brain systems are typically active during emotional than during nonemotional states, and the intensity of arousal is greater, the opportunity for coordinated learning across brain systems is greater during emotional states. By coordinating parallel plasticity throughout the brain, emotional states promote the development and unification of the self. (p. 322)

Exploring uncharted therapeutic territory and skirting the edges of affect tolerance generate fear. It must be offset by heightened, positive arousal that generates hopeful curiosity and fuels exploration of our inner world. Like a child taking its first steps, therapeutic processes occur in the midst of alternating fear and hope.

Transference, Countertransference, and the Therapeutic Alliance

A positive therapeutic alliance represents a growth-facilitating environment that includes a background of safety and a foreground of interest in exploring novel experiences; "safe but not too safe" (Bromberg, 2006) for us.

Allan Schore and his wife, Judith Schore, write that "the psychobiologically attuned, intuitive clinician, from the first point of contact, is learning the nonverbal moment-to-moment rhythmic structures of the client's internal states, and is relatively flexibly and fluidly modifying her own behavior to synchronize with that structure, thereby co-creating with the client a growth-facilitating context for the organization of the therapeutic alliance" (Schore, 201s2, p. 42). The therapist who attunes to the internal states of the patient is reading them via implicit communications and spontaneously adjusting to their ebbs and flows. Therapists must be both emotionally flexible and emotionally robust to establish a growth-facilitating environment. Their emotional capacity is a key factor in how much can be accomplished.

Maintaining a therapeutic stance of curiosity (Lichtenberg, 2005) and of not knowing (Fonagy et al., 2002) requires that therapists tolerate stressful states of ambiguity and exercise restraint from filling in the blanks for themselves or their patients. Allowing attention to float freely and entering states of reverie require that one be regulated. The psychotherapist must be able to tolerate hypo- and hyperaroused negative affects, including shame and disgust, anger and fear. And when the therapist does become dysregulated or simply misattunes, he or she must be resilient enough to repair the rupture.

Beginning with Bowlby (1973), attachment theorists have understood transferences and countertransferences to be the playing out of internal working models that act as impediments to therapeutic progress. This raises concerns about the effects of different patient-therapist attachment patterns on the process and outcome of psychotherapy (see, e.g., Eagle & Wolitzky, 2009; Fonagy, Gergely, & Target, 1999; Mikulincer & Shaver, 2007; Slade, 1999; Tolmacz, 2009; Wallin, 2007). The emotional undertow of avoidant attachment and the overflow of preoccupied attachment make very different demands and interact with the emotional vulnerabilities of avoidant and preoccupied therapists.

Insecure internal working models provide ways of being in a relationship based in expectations of shame-inducing intrusive or dismissive interactions. They manifest in the *implicit* transference-countertransference relationship. Dissociated states of consciousness are activated and serve as a buffer against the painfulness of anticipated shame. An avoidant transference involves moving away from attachment to the therapist and being in an emotionally distanced, hypoaroused-dissociated state of bodymind. A preoccupied transference manifests as a hyperaroused-dissociated state, ambivalently preoccupied with attachment to the therapist.

Just as we know our patients' inner states via implicit communications of affect, our dysregulation and misattunement are inevitably conveyed to the patient. As therapists we must become alert to our own dysregulation-dissociation, which may be revealed in subtle somatic "tells." I often first notice my own dysregulation as a slight tension in the muscles on the sides of my mouth or under my eyes, or in the back of my neck.

Insecure patient-therapist dyads may have congruent (avoidant-avoidant or preoccupied-preoccupied) or incongruent (avoidant-preoccupied) attachment patterns. Each has advantages and pitfalls. Congruent dyads have advantages of firsthand knowledge of the problems. However, problems are likely when the therapists' own insecure attachment pattern remains ego-syntonic, and especially when their arousal patterns and vulnerability to dissociation in response to stress interfere. For example, preoccupied therapists may fail to recognize a preoccupied patient's incapacity to tolerate hypoarousal and shame or may accept hyperreactivity to abandonment or enmeshed object relations as normal. Emotional flare-ups may be too frequent to maintain a therapeutic alliance. Avoidant therapists may be overly comfortable with their avoidant patients' narrow range of affect, the thinness of their attachment, and the avoidance of attachment themes. The avoidant dyad is vulnerable to emotional collapse and a lack of therapeutic vitality.

The incongruent dyad is relatively free from ego-syntonic problems but may be subject to particularly thorny and stressful dynamics. The avoidant therapist may feel disgust toward a preoccupied patient's emotionality and overt dependency needs. The preoccu-pied therapist may become narcissistically injured and angry at the avoidant patient's rejection of his or her caretaking. The incongruent dyad's opposite emotional biases present an obstacle to maintaining therapeutic emotional availability. For example, the avoidant thera-pist, frightened by and unable to tolerate hyperarousal, is vulnerable to becoming hypoaroused-dissociated in the face of a preoccupied patient's strong expression of affect. Such emotional abandonment is intolerable for preoccupied patients. The preoccupied therapist, unable to tolerate hypoarousal, may become hyperaroused and intrusive in response to an avoidant patient's chronic downregulation, denial of attachment needs, and emotional and relational distance. Such emo-tional forcefulness is intolerable for avoidant patients. Therapists' own relational traumas must be resolved to tolerate the stresses of psycho-therapy with insecurely attached patients.

In Chapter 14 I discuss Schore's ideas about vitalizing attunement and interactive regulation as the two fundamental implicit therapeutic processes. They establish the growth-facilitating environment of the therapeutic relationship and are the basic therapeutic actions altering the primary affect-regulating system. We saw both at work in Kierkeg-aard's depiction of the ideal exploration-supporting mother, who regulates interactively from a distance and shares a resonant state of positive arousal with the infant. Interactive regulation and vitalizing attunement establish the therapist's nurturing intentions and emo-tional competency. They generate a sense of "us-ness" that supports therapeutic trust.

CHAPTER 14

Interactive Regulation, Vitalizing Attunement, and the Emergence of the Self

THERAPEUTIC CHANGE CAN occur dramatically, as a result of powerful therapeutic events, or quietly and incrementally, as a result of ongoing, run-of-the-mill therapeutic actions. Schore (1994, 2003a, 2003b, 2012) emphasizes *interactive regulation* and *vitalizing attunement* as fundamental therapeutic processes. They are crucial to both sudden and gradual therapeutic change. In what follows I first illustrate and discuss Schore's ideas about the interactive regulation of dissociated affect in therapeutic enactments. I then illustrate and discuss the role of sustained states of vitalizing attunement in the emergence of the self.

Interactive Regulation of Dissociated Affect: Therapeutic Enactments (and Denactments)

There is a tendency to think of affect regulation as only calming. However, therapists must be able to both upregulate hypoaroused patients into vitalized states and downregulate patients from hyperaroused affect states. And, it is not only after patients become dysregulated that we regulate them—the empathically attuned therapist is continuously monitoring patients and modulating affective intensity to keep them from becoming dysregulated.[80]

Let's examine an example of interactive regulation in the split-second world of everyday life to view the subtlety of the emotional transactions, how they are foundational for the implicit relationship, and how much happens in what we experience as a "moment." Stern (2004) has demonstrated that putting moments of implicit events under a microscope reveals a "world in a grain of sand."[81] Assume you and I are in college, interested in one another and talking for the first time. Looking for something to talk about and hoping to connect positively with you, I open with my enthusiasm for a movie. Unfortunately, you do not share my enthusiasm for it, and in the next sequence of events, I become deflated (rejected/shamed), and you become dismayed and move to repair the damage.

The words I say are "Have you seen *Terrific Movie*." Caught off guard, you say "I just saw it" in a tone that reveals your lack of enthusiasm. Indeed, it is written on your face, and I react to it even before you start to speak. You pick up my reaction and in the next moment

---

80 Psychotherapists have always and quite naturally monitored and regulated patients' affect as a means to a therapeutic end, helping them tolerate and elaborate emotional experience. Beginning with Winnocott's writing about the "holding environment" (1972) and most recently in Slochower's (1996) elaboration of the idea, regulation has gained increasing prominence as an end in and of itself: a process to be internalized. Schore's contribution is to explain it psychobiologically, understand it in terms of implicit processes, and theorize about its effects on the reorganization of the primary affect-regulating system.

81 Daniel Stern, in *The Present Moment in Psychotherapy and Everyday Life* (2004), proposes "present moments" as units for analyzing implicit events and as a portal into the implicit realm. He argues that what we think of as the present is actually the result of our attempt to make sense of the continuous flow of experience. We chunk the flow into discrete manageable episodes that actually take from 1 to 10 seconds. Each chunk is full of information about what just happened, what is happening, and what is expected to happen next. This is an extraordinary book that reveals present moments to be the "dream of the implicit realm"

your face changes again, and you initiate a repair: "Something must be wrong with me. I'm the only person I know who didn't love it." Again, before you utter a word, I sense your distress, your intention to help out, and your wish to reconnect. I am buoyed, you are relieved, and we are back on track searching for connection. Our future together (at least for the next moment) has become hopeful. This takes maybe 2.5 seconds—the communications of my enthusiasm and wish for connection, your flat response and misattunement, my rejection, shame, and deflation, your distress at shaming me and your reparative intention. It is actually been somewhat of an intimate experience: each of us reading and responding to the other's inner states and vulnerabilities.

Of course, things need not have gone so well. This time my shame was manageable, you were able to tolerate it, your repair of the rupture was successful, and we were able to move on hopefully. If I had been more intensely dysregulated, your job would have been more difficult. Perhaps my shame would have dysregulated you, and as a result of your intolerance for shame, you would have been in no shape to respond so competently—empathizing with me and responding contingently toward our shared goal.

In this not-so-good scenario we would both find ourselves in dissociated self-states. Both of our right brains would have disorganized, and thus we would be without the ability to process socioemotional information and without the capacity to understand the complexities of what was happening in each other or to process our own emotional reactions. We would be experiencing dissociated states of consciousness. We would be more or less automated. The rupture would not have been repaired. Our future together would not look so good. Note that the stage was set by my narcissistic vulnerability and that the success or failure of our encounter hinged on your emotional capacity to contain and respond helpfully to my dissociated shame.

Let's do a "stop motion" review of the reparative moment: I was buoyed by your efforts, lifted out of my shame state, and enabled to return to the fray. You in turn were encouraged by my positive response. We are still stressed by the novelty and narcissistic risks of our meeting, but we are regulated. We have been reassured of our intentions and have learned about each other's emotional capacities. Most fundamentally, we have experienced mutually induced states of positive arousal that moved us toward each other and opened us to taking more risks. All this occurred in our implicit relationship via implicit communications.

Things are no different in the patient-therapist relationship. Alongside the words, there is a parallel stream of implicit communications expressing and determining the affect states of the participants and the nature of their relationship. Positive and negative transferences and countertransferences are expressed and built up through implicit communications. Split-second ruptures are repaired or not, depending on the real-time emotional capacities of the therapist. The therapeutic alliance benefits or suffers according to the successes and failures of the affect-regulating interactions taking place in the implicit patient-therapist relationship.

There are ongoing, and underappreciated, incremental therapeutic moments when the patient becomes dysregulated and we remain regulated and return them to a regulated state. Likewise, there is a buildup of therapeutic action as we help patients stay regulated when they are on the brink of dysregulation. The former engrain resiliency; the latter expand affect tolerance. Let's see what happens when therapist and patient both become dissociated and how such actions can be either therapeutic moments or iatrogenic repetitions of relational trauma.

Enactments and Denactments

Enactments have come to be understood at the explicit level as a playing out of dissociated parts of the patient and therapist—transference-countertransference events that resonate with some unresolved aspect of each participant's past. The mechanism mediating enactments is understood to be projective identification in which both patient and therapist have the experience that they are being made to feel and do things by the other.[82] Each is unaware of their complicity in the problem. If left unresolved, enactments impede therapeutic progress and undermine the therapeutic alliance. Resolutions of enactments reveal a rich vein of dissociated material and can mark turning points in the therapeutic relationship.

Enactments have been understood to take place during a session or over the course of weeks or even an entire treatment. Once discovered, they are reflected on and explored: What happened? What did it mean to the patient and (if the therapist is so inclined) to the therapist? What does it say about the relationship and the patient's sense of self in that relationship? What are the origins? And so forth.

Although reflection on an enactment is often necessary and usually helpful, analyzing past experience with words engages the left-brain processes of the secondary affect-regulating system. Efficient treatment of the primary affect-regulating system requires experiences that activate the right brain. This provides direct access to the implicit processes of the internal working model. New affect regulating *experiences* must be provided. To understand them, we need to look into the implicit realm.

Schore's understanding of enactments focuses on the split-second transmissions of dysregulated-dissociated affect (Schore, 2003b, chap. 3, 2012, chap. 5; Bromberg, 2010). It reveals what is at stake in an enactment: Is the therapist able to tolerate the expressed affect and regulate the patient? What are the effects of such transactions on the

---

82 See Schore (2003b, chap. 3) for an important understanding of defensive projective identification as the expression of dissociated affect rather than the insertion of objects.

therapeutic relationship? What are the effects of such experiences on the internal working model and on the primary affect-regulating system at its core?

From the perspective of regulation theory, the most interesting aspects of enactments are those that resonate with relational trauma. Recall that this involves a dysregulated self who, while seeking attachment, is further dysregulated and shamed by a misattuned attachment figure. In treatment this occurs when a patient becomes dysregulated and expresses affect that dysregulates the therapist, who cannot then connect with and regulate the patient. Note that, although both members of the dyad are dysregulated-dissociated, such events may involve hyper- or hypoarousal   depending on the response to stress of each participant.

Such collisions may represent repetitions of relational trauma in which the attachment bond is ruptured and left unrepaired. What happens next determines whether the experience is iatrogenic or therapeutic. For the enactment to be therapeutic, the therapist must self-organize and reconnect with and regulate the patient.

It is not generally recognized that enactments may be either hyper- or hypoaroused. The latter are common with avoidant patients and often occur when the therapist succumbs to the undertow of a patient's hypoaroused state. Both patient and therapist enter into downregulated dissociated states. The implicit therapeutic relationship, lacking in the vitality engendered by exchanged affects, becomes deadening. Patient and therapist become dulled and deactivated. These hypoaroused, transference-countertransference interactions might best be under stood as *denactments*.

Most of the literature on enactments discusses hyperaroused enactments, perhaps because denactments are boring, and depictions of them would be as well. Nothing much is happening, and that is the point. In what follows I, too, describe a hyperaroused enactment.

However, it is crucial to keep in mind that prolonged shared states of hypoaroused dissociation are reenactments of avoidant relational trauma. In a hyperaroused enactment, the dyad must downregulate; in a hypoaroused denactment, life must be breathed into the intersubjective field.

Therapeutic Enactments

The stage is set for an enactment when the patient becomes dysregulated and expresses dissociated affect. The enactment begins if the therapist cannot receive the patient's projected affect and stay regulated. Now both participants are dysregulated-dissociated. They are automated, in altered states of consciousness, and enacting defensive, encapsulated ways of being with others. Their affect is dissociated and cannot be processed. Subjectivity and intersubjectivity have collapsed, and the enactment is off and running.

In a therapeutic enactment, the therapist is initially dysregulated by the patient but catches herself, partially rights herself, attunes to the patient, and facilitates the regulation of the patient's dissociated affect. Therapeutic enactments are enactments that get nipped in the bud. They are corrective emotional experiences. Let's look at an example of a hyperaroused enactment. I first provide the precipitating events, and then offer three different endings: devolving into an iatrogenic enactment, working at the level of second-order therapeutic change, and effecting first-order change through therapeutic enactment.

Barbara (preoccupied), a middle-age, no-nonsense academic, has been in therapy for about two years dealing with a fraught marriage and the loss of her "impossible" mother. Shortly into a session she looks at an incoming call on her cell phone. It is her son calling at an unusual time. "Jeezuus Christ. I know what this is about." It was the end of the school year, and he was in a panic. Barbara is instantly revved up and launches into a diatribe about her son's irresponsibility and lack of standards. "It's not a mystery why he couldn't get into a decent school. He never learns. It's ridiculous. No matter how many times. . . I never learn either. He asks for help and every time I give it there's a fight. He makes me crazy." In the midst of this rant there are a series of seemingly verbatim snippets of things that she has said to him and he to her. They were interjected very rapidly, squirting out from her inner world. Her son's voice is whiney. Hers is laced with contempt, infusing lines like "Plan ahead anybody?" "It's not rocket science," and a sarcastic "Duhuh"—all said with a mocking face. All this is lightening fast.

I found myself drawn into the recalled interactions with her and her son, watching her humiliate him. She told the story in a way that implied that I was on her side in all this, not only sympathetic with her frustration but also sharing and enjoying her sarcasm and contempt. I had heard Barbara on the topic of her son before and was struggling to stay regulated from the moment she started, but this last piece undid me. I was not about to be included in her withering treatment of him. The next thing I knew, I started to make an observation, which was actually a thinly veiled criticism of her narcissistic relationship to her son. I did not even make a cursory attempt to offer empathy for how stressful this must have been for her.

She saw it coming. Before I got the first word out, her arms went straight out in front of her with her palms facing me, her back pressed against the chair. She began to talk over me. Having none of this interruption, I dug in my heels and continued to say what I wanted to say but more forcefully. Barbara did the same, and we spoke simultaneously. The battle went on for no more than two seconds. We were both dysregulated-dissociated—reduced to parts of ourselves.

Let's stop there and imagine three different endings. In the first scenario Barbara and I get through our battle of the wills. I do or do not make my point about her relationship to her son, but in either case, we move on, and the incident goes into the accounting of our relationship on the negative side of the ledger. Barbara's relational trauma has been repeated. She has been shamed by an intrusive, misattuned object. There has been a rupture without repair. Trust and the therapeutic alliance have been undermined. Therapeutic opportunities have been missed.

In the second scenario we get through our skirmish, calm down, and soldier on to discuss Barbara's difficulties with her son. At some point I note that I think it important to discuss the incident. The discussion gets into what each of us experienced: the role that shame played both in her relationship with her son and in our interaction—her shame about him and her shaming of him, my identification with her son and inability to tolerate her anger or his shame, my misattunement and my agenda intruding, her correctly reading my intention to shame her, her anger at me for shaming her, her difficulty tolerating her shame and disgust toward her son, the origins of this in her relationship with her own demanding mother, how this resonates with her own relational trauma, and so on.

It was a good therapeutic talk. Our relationship was repaired, indeed improved. We had seized the opportunity to explore Barbara's preoccupied attachment dynamics, dissociated parts of herself, and difficulties regulating affect. Her left-brain, secondary affect-regulating system was employed to good purpose and improved. All enactments should be resolved so well. She learned a lot that would be helpful as long as she can tolerate her own shame and the disgust and anger she feels toward her son for how poorly he reflects on her. That, of course, may be a tall order.

The third scenario portrays what Schore calls a therapeutic enactment. In this case the therapeutic action engages and directly effects right-brain affect-regulating processes. The therapeutic action begins at the point when Barbara and I both find ourselves in dissociated self-states. In therapeutic enactments the therapist becomes dysregulated but regains equilibrium and is able to reattune to the patient. The therapist's emotional attunement—a shared state that couples the therapist psychophysiologically to the patient—has the effect of regulating the patient. In this scenario I am able to recover from my dysregulation, tolerate Barbara's contempt for her son, pull myself out of the enactment, attune to her shame and anger at her son, and reflect it back to her at a level of intensity she can tolerate. My attunement plays the central role in interactive regulation and enables Barbara to process her contempt toward her son. Most important, Barbara had the experience of becoming reregulated and tolerating and processing what had been dysregulated-dissociated shame and anger.

The sequence of events in a therapeutic enactment is this: dysregulated therapist autoregulates and catches herself in the act of an enactment and, in doing so, brings the patient along with her from a dysregulated-dissociated to a regulated-integrated self-state. In my experience, such moments of re-regulation are experienced as sudden state shifts. They include an unexpected, eye-opening revelation of the dissociated affect. It seems to hover in midair, there for both patient and therapist to feel and see clearly. It provides a moment of insight in which time seems to stop. Thoughts associated with the dissociated affect are now accessible to consciousness. They are first formulated as right-brain-mediated gestalts—insights that dawn on the patient in the midst of live, regulated affect.

Schore (2012) writes:

> As a result of such modulation, the patient's affectively charged but now regulated right brain experience can then be communicated to the left brain for further processing. This effect, which must follow a right brain then left brain temporal

sequence, allows for the development of linguistic symbols to represent the *meaning* of an experience *while one is feeling and perceiving the emotion generated by the experience.* The objective left hemisphere can now coprocess subjective right brain communications, and this allows for a linkage of the nonverbal implicit and verbal explicit domains. (p. 202; italics in original)

Most of us have had such experiences in or outside of therapy. For example, you might say to a friend, in a matter-of-fact way, that you were hurt that so-and-so did not include you in whatever. You say it, but flippantly, and do not really know about it—there's no felt sense of it; the shame is dissociated. Now, in the telling, because of your friend's reaction, you experience and process the hurt. What was that reaction of your friend that facilitated your processing of the hurt for the first time?

Schore argues that it was your friend's attunement with your hurt. That is, your friend was not dysregulated by your dysregulation and was able to process and experience your shame. It is reflected back to you at a level of intensity you are able to tolerate. Additionally the attunement creates a positively toned, shared, uplifting affective resonance that offsets shame and makes the dissociated affect bearable and available for assessment. At the same time, the resonance amplifies and prolongs the affective experience, drawing attention to it and making it vivid.

There are important cognitive and emotional aspects to the experience of suddenly shifting from a dysregulated-dissociated into a regulated-integrated self-state and becoming conscious of dissociated affect. The dissociated experience is left reverberating in working memory while an integrated sense of things takes hold.[83] The patient

---

83 Bromberg (1998) conceptualizes this as standing in the spaces between self-states.

gets a panoramic snapshot of what the dissociated self-state and dissociated object relationship involved—how everything was different. Conflicting versions come together and beg for resolution.

Recall that relational trauma leaves an imprint of dissociated implicit memories encoding the experience of dysregulated self shamed by a misattuned object. It is the basis for the strategy of the insecure internal working model—a set of affective-cognitive-behavioral procedures that function to anticipate and cope with expected misattunements and shame. The therapeutic enactment provided Barbara with powerful, novel experiences of dysregulated self *regulated* by an *attuned* object. The negative expectations around which her insecure internal working model was organized were upended. Her cognitive schemas, which filter perceptions and organize implicit knowings, were stymied by experiences that could not be assimilated. They must be reformulated to accommodate the new experience.

Barbara also had a powerful experience of resilience: of becoming dysregulated-dissociated and returning to a regulated state, and of *her* doing it. The experience of modulating the intensity of her own arousal can serve as the basis for a more confident sense of self and expected self-mastery. This experience may have shifted Barbara's internal working model toward increased use of autoregulation and less reliance on the dyadic model. At the same time there was a powerful experience of dysregulated self *regulated by an attuned object*. Here again, the expectations of the insecure internal working model are disrupted. The attachment pattern may begin to organize around positive expectations of a trusted, emotionally competent object. Finally, Barbara and I have had a moment of heightened intimacy and nurturance supporting a secure attachment bond. Her object relations may begin to change from moving against to moving toward attachment figures.

Schore argues that a similar disorganization and reorganization take place among the neural networks mediating the affect-regulating procedures. He also proposes that the experience engenders a more robust connection between the cortical and subcortical components of the limbic system. The right orbitofrontal cortex is thus better able to perform its executive regulatory function, allowing for greater affect tolerance and resiliency.

Vitalizing Attunement and the Emergence of the Self

As we have just seen, attunement plays a central role in the interactive regulation of dissociated affect. The therapist sampled the patient's dysregulated affect and reflected it back to the patient at a moderate level of intensity, which regulated the patient and brought her into a shared state of regulated attunement. I now discuss what Schore calls vitalizing attunement—sustained states of attunement that act as a catalyst for the emergence of a coherent, positively toned sense of self.

Schore (2003b) proposes that, when attuned, patient and therapist enter into a shared state of "co-synchronized biorhythms": "The crescendos and decrescendos of the therapist's affect state must be in *resonance* with similar states of crescendos and decrescendos of the patient" (p. 48; italics in original). This mutual, rhythmic synchronization establishes a psychobiological coupling and sets up a resonance that has a positively toned, intrinsically organizing and regulating effect.

Schore (2003b) further proposes that vitalizing attunement establishes an ideal growth-enhancing environment. The resonance generates a "positively charged curiosity" (p. 40) that energizes voluntary encounters with stressful material in the exploration of inner states and the socioemotional environment. At the neurological level, the heightened state of positive arousal generated by resonance is an ideal metabolic condition for neural growth. I would add that, with resonance, therapist and patient both experience immersive states of consciousness marked by clarity, intense interest, expansiveness, and pleasure that blends with and offsets the fear and distress.

Even shame-ridden states are made bearable by the therapeutic effects of vitalizing attunement. In addition to the comfort and reassurance provided by the "us-ness" of attunement, its vitalizing effects transform shame into a hope-infused "good pain"—a tolerable state of pain from which we sense we will benefit.

At the same time that attuned resonance makes dissociated affect vivid and energizes exploration, the psychobiological coupling maximizes interactive regulation and enables the therapist to buoy the avoidant and calm the preoccupied as they approach material infused with negative affect. The synchonization of affect states not only provides essential data for interactive regulation but also generates compassion in the therapist whose nurturing intentions are experienced by the patient.

Sustained states of vitalizing attunement result from a voluntary surrender to and immersion in the patient's flow of affective experiencing. Breaks and returns to the shared state are ongoing for the therapeutic dyad. They constitute rupture-repair sequences that bolster affective resilience and deepen trust and the therapeutic alliance. Vitalizing attunement creates a compelling sense of recognition, acceptance, safety, and well-being in patients (Schore, 2003a), who feel felt and are felt. Both patient and therapist sense it and sense that the other senses it. There is a shared delight and pride in vitalizing attunement—a loving intimacy that is at the heart of the secure attachment bond and is the lifeblood of the implicit therapeutic alliance. Gradually, because of consistent experiences of vitalizing attunement and interactive regulation, the obstacles to development are sufficiently diminished and a coherent, vitalized, positive sense of self emerges.

The Emergence of the Self

Stern (1986) notes the "strong clinical impression" of qualitative shifts in infants' sense of self over the two years of life. He posits that the earliest sense of self is organized around a "sense of emergence," a sense of developing, which is followed by a "sense of subjectivity." Similar transformations occur in the course of successful psychotherapy when there has been a developmental arrest: first a sense of restored development and hopefulness, and then the emergence of the self as a subject that endures across self-states. The restored sense of development begins with the lessoning of shame and dissociation. It provides a hopeful excitement that infuses the therapeutic relationship. The emergence of the sense of subjectivity is revealed as the patient becomes increasing agentic and autonomous in the therapy sessions.

At some point patients begin to work differently. They are not simply telling things to and expecting things of the therapist. Rather, they begin a free-associative process of voluntarily letting the mind go where it goes, think what it thinks, feel what it feels.[84] Both hemispheres of the brain are participating, the right informing the left with the emotional information it needs. The right brain is able to stand up to negative affect states without disorganizing or, if it does, to recover efficiently. Conflict can be resolved and used for development. Thoughts never formulated begin to take shape and are organized into a coherent narrative.

Patients increasingly explore uncharted territory, processing novel material while skirting the edges of their affect tolerances. Sessions are marked by sustained states of vitalizing attunement of increasing length. Patients begin to use sessions to develop themselves by

---

84 See Grossmark (2012) for a similar understanding of the therapeutic process.

themselves in the context of the therapeutic relationship. Therapists increasingly find themselves going along for an invigorating ride.

Patients begin to show signs of a secure self—positively toned and increasingly capable of autonomous thinking and agentic action. The therapist moves to a state of receptive resonance, available for inter-active regulation as needed, and occasionally making observations or asking questions that extend patients' exploration of their inner and outer worlds. I increasingly find myself in relaxed-alert states of almost pure curiosity, trusting that patients will find their way. If I do intervene I might ask, addressing their subjectivity directly, "What's your take on that?" or "What do you want to have happen?" Alterna-tively, I might address their intersubjectivity and ask, "Did you have a sense of what he was experiencing?" But mostly, when sessions take this turn, I am not saying much. Affect tolerance and resiliency have improved, and shame and dissociation have been sufficiently over-come for a sense of self-mastery to take hold. Patients have begun to "come into their own" and are increasingly "on their own." The emer-gence of the self as a subject is the beginning of the end of therapy and the best part.

The experience of this process differs for avoidant and preoccupied patients. Avoidant development stopped in the early phase of the criti-cal period in the development of the primary affect-regulating system, at the point when the subjective self first begins to form (Stern, 1986). Affective experience was so diminished that the development of sub-jectivity barely got off the ground. The preoccupied infant's subjective self got off the ground but never cohered. Its fragmentation was the result of underregulated affect that came in torrents and disabled inte-grative processes. There was also a mixture of attunement and intru-siveness that generated inconsistent self-experience.

Successful therapy enables avoidant patients to first encounter their subjectivity. It provides an exhilarating sense of the *self coming to life* and of increasing complexity, depth, and connection to others who can now be experienced as subjects. Objects, too, come to life. In contrast, preoccupied personalities have always encountered subjective parts of the self and others. Their experience of self-formation is of the *self coming together*—of being made whole. Objects, too, become whole. Preoccupied patients become integrated and increasingly at peace with themselves and others.

The pride and joy stemming from restored development were expressed by an avoidant patient who had successfully explored stressful territory toward the end of a session. He had had a couple of sessions like this in a row. As he passed me on the way out he looked at me with a smile and winked—I had never seen this cocky side of him. Another patient commented on the process of therapy. Gathering his things at the end of his last session, he thanked me for a successful treatment and then added, "The funny thing is that you never seemed to be doing anything." We shook hands laughing and that was that.

BIBLIOGRAPHY

Agrawal, H. R., Gunderson, J., Holmes, B. M., & Lyons-Ruth, K. (2004). Attachment studies with borderline patients: A review. *Harvard Review of Psychiatry, 12*(2), 94–104.

Ainsworth, M. D. S., Blehar, M. D., Waters, E., & Wall, S. (1978). *Patterns of attachment: A psychological study of the strange situation.* Hillsdale, NJ: Erlbaum.

Allen, J., & Fonagy, P. (Eds.). (2006). *Handbook of mentalization-based treatment.* Chichester, UK: Wiley.

Allen, J., Fonagy, P., & Bateman, A. (2008). *Mentalizing in clinical practice.* Arlington, VA: American Psychiatric Publishing.

Atkinson, L., & Zucker, K. J. (Eds.). (1997). *Attachment and psychopathology.* New York, NY: Guilford Press.

Bach, S. (1985). *Narcissistic states and the therapeutic process.* New York, NY: Jason Aronson.

Bateman, A., & Fonagy, P. (2004). *Psychotherapy for borderline personality disorder: Mentalization based treatment.* Oxford, UK: Oxford University Press.

Beebe, B. (2000). Co-constructing mother-infant distress: The microsychrony of maternal impingement and infant avoidance in the face-to-face encounter. *Psychoanalytic Inquiry, 20,* 412–440.

Beebe, B., & Lachman, F. (2002). *Infant research and adult treatment: Co-constructing interactions*. Hillsdale, NJ: Analytic Press.

Beebe, B., Lachmann, F. M., Markese, S., Buch, K. A., Bahrick, L. E., Chen, H., . . . Andrews, H. (2012). On the origins of disorganized attachment and internal working models: Paper II. An empirical microanalysis of 4-month mother-infant interaction. *Psychoanalytic Dialogues, 22*, 352–374.

Benjamin, J. (1990). Recognition and destruction: An outline of intersubjectivity. In S. A. Mitchell & L. Aron (Eds.), *Relational psychoanalysis: The emergence of a tradition* (pp. 193–200). Hillsdale, NJ: Analytic Press.

Bokhorst, C. L., Bakermans-Kranenburg, M. J., Fearon, R. M., van Ijzendoorn, M. H., Fonagy, P., & Schuengel, C. (2003). The importance of shared environment in mother-infant attachment security: A behavioral genetic study. *Child Development, 74*(6), 1769–1782.

Bollas, C. (1987). *The shadow of the object: Psychoanalysis of the unthought known*. New York, NY: Columbia University Press.

Boston Change Process Study Group. (2002). Explicating the Implicit, *International Journal of Psychoanalysis, 83*, 1051–1062.

Boston Change Process Study Group. (2010). *Change in psychotherapy*. New York, NY: Norton.

Bowlby, J. (1969). *Attachment and loss*, Vol. 1: *Attachment*. New York, NY: Basic Books.

Bowlby, J. (1973). *Attachment and loss*, Vol. 2: *Separation*. New York, NY: Basic Books.

Bowlby, J. (1977). The making and breaking of affectional bonds: I. Aetiology and psychopathology in the light of attachment theory. *British Journal of Psychiatry, 130*, 201–210.

Bradley, R., & Westen, D. (2005). The psychodynamics of borderline personality disorder: A view from developmental psychopathology. *Development and Psychopathology, 17*, 927–957.

Bradshaw, G. (2009). *Elephants on the edge: What animals teach us about humanity*. New Haven, CT: Yale University Press.

Bradshaw, G. A., & Schore, A. N. (2007). How elephants are opening doors: Developmental neuroethology, attachment and social context. *Ethology, 113*, 426–436.

Bremner, J. D. (1999). Acute and chronic responses to psychological trauma: Where do we go from here? *American Journal of Psychiatry, 156*, 349–351.

Bretherton, I. (2005). In pursuit of the internal working model construct and its relevance to attachment relationships. In K. E. Grossmann, K. Grossmann, & E. Waters (Eds.), *Attachment from infancy to adulthood: The major longitudinal studies* (pp. 13-47). New York, NY: Guilford Press.

Bretherton, I., & Munholland, K. A. (1999). Internal working models in attachment relationships: A construct revisited. In J. Cassidy & P. Shaver (Eds.), *Handbook of attachment: Theory, research, and clinical applications* (pp. 89-114). New York, NJ: Guilford Press.

Briere, J., & Armstrong, J. (2007). Psychological assessment of post-traumatic dissociation. In V. Vermetten, M. J. Dorahy, & D. Spiegel (Eds.), *Traumatic dissociation: Neurobiology and treatment* (pp. 259-274). Arlington, VA: American Psychiatric Publishing.

Bromberg, P. (1998). *Standing in the spaces: Essays on clinical process, trauma, and dissociation*. Hillsdale, NJ: Analytic Press.

Bromberg, P. (2006). *Awakening the dreamer: Clinical journeys*. Mahwah, NJ: Analytic Press.

Bromberg, P. (2011). *In the shadow of the tsunami and the growth of the relational mind*. New York, NY: Routledge.

Broucek, F.J. (1991). *Shame and the Self*. New York, Guilford Press.

Brown, R. J., & Trimble, M. R. (2000). Dissociative psychopathology, non-epileptic seizures, and neurology. *Journal Neurology, Neurosurgery, and Psychiatry, 69*, 295–291.

Brunet, A., Holowka, D. W., & Lawrence, J. R. (2001). Dissociation. In M. J. Aminof & R. B. Daroff (Eds.), *Encyclopedia of the neurological sciences* (pp. 25-27). Academic Press. San Diego.

Bureau, J., Martin, J., & Lyons-Ruth, K. (2010). Attachment dysregulation as hidden trauma in infancy: Early stress, maternal buffering and psychiatric morbidity in young adulthood. In R. Lanius, E. Vermetten, & C. Pain (Eds.), *The impact of early life trauma on health and disease: The hidden epidemic.* New York, NY: Cambridge University Press.

Busch, F. (Ed.). 2008. *Mentalization: Theoretical considerations, research findings, and clinical implications.*

Carlson, V., Cicchetti, D., Barnett, D., & Braunwald, K. (1989). Disorganized/disoriented attachment relationships in maltreated infants. *Developmental Psychology, 25*(4), 525–531.

Cassidy, J., & Shaver, P. (Eds.). (1999). *Handbook of attachment: Theory, research, and clinical applications.* New York, NY: Guilford Press.

Chafetz, R., & Bromberg, P. (2004). Talking with "me" and "not-me": A dialogue. *Contemporary Psychoanalysis, 40,* 409–464.

Cicchetti, D. (2010). Resilience under conditions of extreme stress: A multilevel perspective. *World Psychiatry, 9*(3), 145–154.

Cicchetti, D., & Toth, S. (1995). A developmental psychopathology perspective on child abuse and neglect. *Journal of the American Academy of Child & Adolescent Psychiatry, 34*(5), 541–565.

Cobb, R., & Davila, J. (2009). Internal working models and change. In J. H. Obegi & E. Berant (Eds.), *Attachment theory and research in clinical work with adults.* New York, NY: Guilford Press.

Collins, N., & Read, S. J. (1990). Adult attachment, working models and relationship quality in dating couples. *Journal of Personality and Social Psychology, 59,* 633–644.

Corrigan, F. (2014). The clinical sequelae of dysfunctional defense responses: A dissociative amnesia, pain and somatization, emotional motor memory, and interoceptive loops. In U. Lanius, S. Paulsen, & F. Corrigan (Eds.), *Neurobiology and treatment of traumatic dissociation: Toward and embodied self.* New York, NY: Springer.

Courtois, C. and Ford, J. D. (2012). *Treatment of Complex Trauma: a Sequenced, Relationship-based Approach.* New York, NY. Guilford Press.

Courtois, C. and Ford, J.D., (2014). *Treating Complex Traumatic Stress Disorders (Adults): Scientific Foundations the Therapeutic Models.* New York, NY. Guilford Press.

Damasio. A. R. (1994). *Descartes' error.* New York, NY: Grosset/ Putnam.

Darwin, C. (1965). *The expression of the emotions in man and animals.* Chicago: University of Chicago Press. (Original work published 1872)

Dell, P. (2009a). The phenomena of pathological dissociation. In P. Dell & J. O'Neil (Eds.), *Dissociation and the dissociative disorders: DSM-V and beyond.* New York, NY: Routledge.

Dell, P. (2009b). Understanding dissociation. In P. Dell & J. O'Neil (Eds.), *Dissociation and the dissociative disorders: DSM-V and beyond* (pp. 709-826). New York, NY: Routledge.

Demos, V. (1986). Crying in early infancy: An illustration of he motivational function of affect. In T. B. Brazelton & M. W. Yogman (Eds.), *Affective development in infancy.* Norwood, NJ: Ablex.

Dickenson, K. A., & Pincus, A. J. (1998). Interpersonal analysis of grandiose and vulnerable narcissism. *Journal of Personality Disorders, 17,* 108–207.

Dozier, M., Stoval, K. C., & Albus, K. (1999). Attachment and psychopathology in adulthood. In J. Cassidy & P. Shaver (Eds.), *Handbook of attachment: Theory, research, and clinical applications.* New York, NY: Guilford Press.

Eagle, M., & Wolitzky, D. L. (2009). The perspectives of attachment theory and psychoanalysis: Adult psychotherapy. In J. Obegi & E. Berant (Eds.), *Attachment theory and research in clinical work with adults.* New York, NY: Guilford Press.

Ekman, P., & Friesend, W. V. (1975). *Unmasking the face.* Los Altos, CA: Malor Books.

Fonagy, P. (1999). Attachment, the development of the self, and its pathology in personality disorders. In J. Derksen et al. (Eds.), *Treatment of personality disorders* Pp. 53–68). New York, NY: Plenum.

Fonagy, P., Gergely, G., Jurist, E., & Target, M. (2002). *Affect regulation, mentalization and the development of the self.* New York, NY: Other Press.

Fonagy, P., Gergely, G., & Target, M. (1999). Psychoanalytic constructs and attachment theory and research. In J. Cassidy & P. Shaver (Eds.), *Handbook of attachment: Theory, research and clinical applications* (pp. 183–811). New York, NY: Guilford Press.

Fonagy, P., Steele, H., & Steele, M. (1991). Maternal representations of attachment during pregnancy predict the organization of infant-mother attachment at one year of age. *Child Development, 62,* 891–905.

Fonagy, P., & Target, M. (2005). Bridging the transmission gap: An end to an important mystery of attachment research? *Attachment and Human Development, 7,* 333–343.

Fonagy, P., & Target, M. 2006. The mentalization-focused approach to self pathology. *Journal of Personality Disorders, 20*(6), 544–576.

Ford, J. D. (1999). Disorders of extreme stress following war-zone military trauma: Associated features of posttraumatic stress disorder or co-morbid but distinct syndromes? *Journal of Consulting and Clinical Psychology, 67,* 3–12.

Fosha, D. (2003). Dyadic regulation and experiential work with emotion and relatedness in trauma and disordered attachment. In M. F.

Solomon & D. J. Siegel (Eds.), *Healing trauma: Attachment, trauma, the brain and the mind* (pp. 221–281). New York, NY: Norton.

Fosha D. (2009a). Emotion and recognition at work: Energy, vitality, pleasure, truth, desire and the emergent phenomenology of transformational experience. In D. Fosha, D. J. Siegel, & M. F. Solomon (Eds.), *The healing power of emotion: Affective neuroscience, development, clinical practice* (pp. 172–203). New York, NY: Norton.

Fosha, D. (2009b). Healing attachment trauma with attachment (. . . and then some!). In M. Kerman (Ed.), *Clinical pearls of wisdom: Twenty-one leading therapists offer their key insights* (pp. 43–56). New York, NY: Norton.

Fosha, D. (2013). Turbocharging the affects of healing and redressing the evolutionary tilt. In D. J. Siegel & M. F. Solomon (Eds.), *Healing moments in psychotherapy* (pp. 129–168). New York, NY: Norton.

Fosha, D., Paivio, S. C., Gleiser, K., & Ford, J. (2009). Experiential and emotion-focused therapy. In C. Courtois & J. D. Ford (Eds.), *Complex traumatic stress disorders: An evidence-based clinician's guide* (pp. 286–311). New York, NY: Guilford Press.

Fox, N., & Hane, A. (2008). Studying the biology of human attachment. In J. Cassidy & P. Shaver (Eds.), *Handbook of attachment: Theory, research and clinical applications* (pp. 811–829). New York, NY: Guilford Press.

Freud, S. (1957). Mourning and melancholia. In J. Strachey (Ed.), *The complete edition of the psychological works of Sigmund Freud* (Vol. 14, pp. 243–258). London: Hogarth Press.

Gabbard, G. O. (1989). Two subtypes of narcissistic personality disorder. *Bulletin of he Menninger Clinic, 53*, 527–532.

Gazzaniga, M. S. (1989). Organization of the human brain. *Science, 245*, 947–952.

Gazzaniga, M. S., & LeDoux, J. E. (1978). *The integrated mind*. New York, NY: Plenum Press.

George, C, Kaplan, N, & Main, M. (1985). Adult Attachment Interview. Unpublished manuscript, University of California, Berkeley.

Ginot, E. (2012). Self-narratives and dysregulated affective states: The neuropsychological links between self-narratives, attachment, affect and cognition. *Psychoanalytic Psychology, 29*, 59–80.

Goldner, G. (2014). Romantic Bonds, Binds, and Ruptures: Couples on the Brink. Psychoanaltyical Dialogues, Vol. 24. Pp. 420-418

Golemen, D. (2006). *Emotional intelligence.* New York, NY: Random House.

Golemen, D. (2007). *Social intelligence.* New York, NY: Random House.

Grice, H. P. (1975). Logic and conversation. In P. Coole & J. L. Moran (Eds.), *Syntax and semantics III: Speech acts*, pp. 41–5.

Grossman, K. E., Grossman, K., & Zimmerman, P. (1999). A wider view of attachment and exploration. Stability and change during the years of immaturity. In J. Cassidy & P. Shaver (Eds.), *Handbook of attachment: Theory, research, and clinical applications.* New York, NY: Guilford Press.

Grossmark, R. (2012). The flow of enactment engagement. *Contemporary Psychoanalysis, 19*(3), 287–300.

Herman, J. (1997). *Trauma and Recovery: The Aftermath of Violence— from Domestic Abuse to Political Terror.* Guildord, New York.

Herman, J. (2007) *Shattered Shame States and Their Repair.* Presented as the John Bowlby Memorial Lecture at the 2007 John Bowlby Memorial Conference, London, England.

Hesse, E. (1996). Discourse, memory and the Adult Attachment Interview: A note with emphasis on the emerging cannot classify category. *Infant Mental Health Journal, 17,* 4–11.

Hesse, E. (1999). The Adult Attachment Interview: Historical and current perspectives. In J. Cassidy & P. Shaver (Eds.), *Handbook of attachment: Theory, research, and clinical applications.* New York, NY: Guilford Press.

Hesse, E., & Main, M. M. (1999). Second-generation effects of unresolved trauma in nonmaltreating parents: Dissociated, frightened, and threatening parental behavior. *Psychoanalytic Inquiry, 19*, 481–540.

Hill, D. (2010). Fundamentalist faith states: Regulation theory as a framework for the psychology of religious fundamentalism. In C. Strozier, D. Terman, & J. Jones (Eds.), *The fundamentalist mind set.* New York, NY: Oxford University Press.

Hinde, R. (2006). Ethology and attachment theory. In K. Grossman, K. Grossman, & E. Waters (Eds.), *Attachment from infancy to adulthood: The major longitudinal studies* (pp. 1-13). New York, NY: Guilford Press.

Holmes, J. (2003). Borderline personality disorder and the search for meaning: An attachment perspective. *Australia–New Zealand Journal Psychiatry, 37,* 524–531.

Holmes, J. (2006). Mentalizing from a psychoanalytic perspective: What's new? In J. G. Allen & P. Fonagy (Eds.), *Handbook of mentalization-based therapy* (pp. 31–49). Chichester, UK: Wiley,

Howell, E. (2005). *The dissociative mind.* Hillsdale, NJ: Analytic Press.

Howell, E., & Blizard, R. (2009). Chronic relational trauma disorders: A new diagnostic scheme for borderline personality disorder and the spectrum of dissociative disorders. In P. Dell & J. O'Neil (Eds.), *Dissociation and the dissociative disorders: DSM-V and beyond* (pp. 495-511). New York, NY: Routledge.

Janet, P. (1904). L'amnésie et la dissociation des souvenirs par l'émotion. *Journal de Psychologie, 1,* 417–453.

Jurist, E. (2005). Mentalized affectivity. *Psychoanalytic Psychology, 22,* 426–444.

Jurist, E. (2008). Minds and yours: New directions for mentalization theory. In E. Jurist, A. Slade, & S. Bergner (Eds.), *Mind to mind: Infant research, neuroscience, and psychoanalysis* (pp. 88-114). New York, NY: Other Press.

Jurist, E., & Meehan, K. (2009). Attachment, mentalization, and reflective functioning. In J. H. Obegi & E. Berant (Eds.), *Attachment theory and research in clinical work with adults.* New York, NY: Guilford Press.

Karen, R. (1994). *Becoming attached.* New York, NY: Warner Books.

Kaufman, G. (1992). *Shame: The power of caring.* Rochester, VT: Schenkman Books.

Kernberg, O. (1975). *Borderline conditions and pathological narcissism.* New York, NY: Jason Aronson.

Knox, J. (2011). *Self agency in psychotherapy: Attachment, autonomy and intimacy.*

Kohut, H. (1971). *The analysis of the self.* New York, NY: International University Press.

Kohut, H. (1977). *The restoration of the self.* Madison, WI: International Universities Press.

Lanius, R. A., Bluhm, R., Lanius, U., & Pain, C. (2006). A review of neuroimaging studies in PTSD: Heterogeneity of response to symptom provocation. *Journal of Psychiatric Research, 40,* 709–729.

Lanius, R. A., Vermetten, E. Loewenstein, R. J., Brand, B. Schmahl, C., Bremner, J. D., & Spiegel, D. (2010a). Emotion modulation in PTSD: Clinical and neurobiological evidence for a dissociative subtype. *American Journal of Psychiatry, 167*(6): 640–647.

Lanius, R., Vermetten, E., & Pain, C. (Eds.). (2010b). *The impact of early life trauma on health and disease: The hidden epidemic.* New York, NY: Cambridge University Press.

Lanius, R. A., Williamson, P. C., Bluhm, R. L., Densmore, M., Boksman, K., Neufeld, R., . . . Menon, R. S. (2005). Functional connectivity of dissociative responses in posttraumatic stress disorder: A functional magnetic resonance imaging investigation. *Biological Psychiatry, 57,* 873–884.

Lanius, R. A., Williamson, P. C., Boksman, K., Densmore, M., Gupta, M., Neufeld, R., . . . Menon, R. S. (2002). Brain activation during script-driven imagery induced dissociative responses in PTSD: A functional magnetic resonance imaging investigation. *Biological Psychiatry, 52*, 305–311.

Levine, P. (1997). *Waking the tiger: Healing trauma.* Berkeley, CA: North Atlantic Books.

Levy, K. (2005). The implications of attachment theory and research for understanding borderline personality disorder. *Development and Psychopathology, 17*, 959–986.

Lewis, H. B. (1987a). Introduction: Shame—the "sleeper" in psychopathology. In H. B. Lewis (Ed.), *The role of shame in symptom formation.* NJ: Erlbaum.

Lewis, H. B. (1987b). Shame and the narcissistic personality. In Nathanson, D. (1987). *The Many Faces of Shame.* New York: The Guilford Press.

Lewis, M., & Todd, R. (2007). The self-regulating brain: Cortical-subcortical feedback and the development of intelligent action. *Cognitive Development, 22*, 406–430.

Lichenstein Phelps, J. Belsky, J., & Crnic, K. (1998). Earned security, daily stress, and parenting: A comparison of five alternative models. *Development and Psychopathology, 10*, 21–38.

Lichtenberg, J. (2005). *Craft and spirit: A guide to the exploratory psychotherapies.* Hillsdale, NJ: Analytic Press.

Liotti, G. (1992). Disorganized/disoriented attachment in the etiology of the dissociative disorders. *Dissociation, 5*, 196–204.

Liotti, G. (2000). Disorganized attachment, models of borderline states and evolutionary psychotherapy. In K. G. Bailey & P. Gilbert (Eds.), *Genes on the couch: Explorations in evolutionary psychotherapy* (pp. 232–256). New York, NY: Brunner-Routledge.

Liotti, G. (2004). Trauma, dissociation, and disorganized attachment: Three strands of a single braid. *Psychotherapy: Theory, Research, Practice, Training, 41*, 472–486.

Lopez, F. (2009). Clinical correlates of adult attachment organization. In J. H. Obegi & E. Berant (Eds.), *Attachment theory and research in clinical work with adults* (pp. 94-120). New York, NY: Guilford Press.

Lyons-Ruth, K., & Jacobvitz, D. (1999). Attachment disorganization: Unresolved loss, relational violence, and lapses in behavioral and attentional strategies. In J. Cassidy & P. Shaver (Eds.), *Handbook of attachment: Theory, research, and clinical applications* (pp. 520-554). New York, NY: Guilford Press.

Lyons-Ruth, K., Melnick, S., Bronfman, E., Sherry, S., & Llanas, L. (2003). Hostile-helpless relational models and disorganized attachment patterns between parents and their young children: Review of research and implications for clinical work. In L. Atkinson & K. Zucker (Eds.), *Clinical applications of attachment.* New York, NY: Guilford Press.

Mahler, M. (1979). *Separation-individuation.* Northvale, NJ: Jason Aronson.

Mahler, M., Pine, F., & Bergman, A. (1975). *The psychological birth of the human infant.* New York, NY: Basic Books.

Main, M. (1991). Metacognitive knowledge, metacognitive monitoring, and singular vs. multiple (incoherent) model of attachment. In C. Parkes, J. Stevenson-Hinde, & P. Maris (Eds.), *Attachment across the life cycle* (pp. 127-160). London: Routledge.

Main, M. (1995). Attachment: Overview, with implications for clinical work. In S. Goldberg, R. Muir, & J. Kerr (Eds.), *Attachment theory: Social, developmental, and clinical perspectives* (pp. 407-474). Hillsdale, NJ: Analytic Press.

Main, M. (1996). Introduction to the special section of attachment and psychopathology: 2. Overview of the field of attachment. *Journal of Consulting and Clinical Psychology, 64,* 237-243.

Main, M., & Goldwyn, R. (1998). *Adult attachment scoring and clas-*

sification systems (2nd ed.). Unpublished manuscript, University of California at Berkeley.

Main, M., Hesse, E., & Kaplan, N. (2005). Predictability of attachment behavior and representational processes at 1, 6, and 19 years of age. In K. E. Grossmann, K. Grossmann, & E. Waters (Eds.), *Attachment from infancy to adulthood: The major longitudinal studies* (pp. 245-304). New York, NY: Guilford Press.

Main, M., Kaplan, N., & Cassidy, J. (1985). Security in infancy, childhood and adulthood: A move to the level of representation. In I. Bretherton & E. Waters (Eds.), *Growing points of attachment theory and research*. Chicago: University of Chicago Press.

Main, M., & Solomon, J. (1986). Discovery of an insecure-disorganized/disoriented attachment pattern. In T. B. Brazelton & M. W. Yogman (Eds.), *Affective development in infancy*. Norwood, NJ: Ablex.

Marks-Tarlow, T. (2011). Merging and emerging: A nonlinear portrait of intersubjectivity during psychotherapy. *Psychoanalytic Dialogues, 21*(1), 110–127.

Marks-Tarlow, T. (2012). *Clinical intuition in psychotherapy: The neurobiology of embodied response*. New York, NY: Norton Press.

Maroda, K. (2012). *Psychodynamic techniques: Working with emotion in the therapeutic relationship*. New York, NY: Guilford Press.

McGilchrist, I. (2010). *The master and his emissary: The divided brain and the making of the western world*. New Haven, CT: Yale University Press.

Meares, R. (2012). *A dissociation model of borderline personality disorder*. New York, NY: Norton.

Meares, R., Schore, A., & Melkonian, D. (2011). Is borderline personality a particularly right hemispheric disorder? A study of P3a using single trial analysis. *Australian and New Zealand Journal of Psychiatry, 45*, 131–139.

Mikulincer, M., & Shaver, P. (2007). *Attachment in adulthood*. New York, NY: Guilford Press.

Mikulincer, M., Shaver, P., Cassidy, J., & Berant, E. (2009). Attachment-related defensive processes. In J. H. Obegi & E. Berant (Eds.), *Attachment theory and research in clinical work with adults* (pp. 293-327). New York, NY: Guilford Press.

Miller, A. (1997). *The drama of the gifted child: The search for the true self*. New York, NY: Basic Books.

Narvaez, D. (2008). Triune ethics: The neurobiological roots of our multiple moralities. *New Ideas in Psychology, 26*, 95–119.

Narvaez, D. (2014). Neurobiology and the development of human morality: Evolution, culture, and wisdom. New York, NY: Norton.

Nathanson, D. (Ed.). (1987a). *The many faces of shame*. New York, NY: Guilford Press.

Nathanson, D. (1987b). The shame/pride axis. In H. B. Lewis (Ed.), *The role of shame in symptom formation*. NJ: Erlbaum.

Nathanson, D. (1992). *Shame and pride: Affect, sex, and birth of the self*. New York, NY: Norton.

Obegi, J. H., & Berant, E. (Eds.). (2009). *Attachment theory and research in clinical work with adults*. New York, NY: Guilford Press.

O'Connor, T. G., & Croft, D. (2001). A twin study of attachment in preschool children. *Child Development, 72*(5), 1501–1511.

O'Connor, T. G., Croft, D., & Steele, H. (2000). The contributions of behavioural genetic studies to attachment theory. *Attachment and Human Development, 2*(1), 107–122.

Ogawa, J. R., Sroufe, L. A., Weinfeld, N. S., Carlson, E. A., & Egeland, B. (1997). Development and the fragmented self: Longitudinal study of dissociative symptomatology in a nonclinical sample. *Development and Psychopathology, 9*, 855–880.

Ogden, P., & Fisher, J. (2015). *Sensorimotor psychotherapy: Interventions for trauma and attachment*. New York, NY: Norton.

Ogden, P., Minton, K. (2000). Sensorimotor psychotherapy: one method for processing traumatic memory. Traumatology. Vol VI, 3(3), 1-20.

Ogden, P., Minton, K., & Pain, C. (2006). *Trauma and the body: A sensorimotor approach to psychotherapy.* New York, NY: Norton.

Pietromonaco, P. R., & Barrett, L. F. (2000). The internal working models concept: What do we really know about the self in relation to others? *Review of General Psychology, 4*(2), 155–175.

Porges, S. (2011). *The polyvagal theory: Neurophysiological foundations of emotions, attachment, communication, and self-regulation.* New York, NY: Norton.

Putnam, F. W. (1997). *Dissociation in children and adolescents: A developmental perspective.* New York, NY: Guilford Press.

Russ, E., Shedler, J., Bradley R., & Westen, D. (2008). Refining the concept of narcissistic personality disorder: Diagnostic criteria and subtypes. *American Journal of Psychiatry, 165*, 1473–1481.

Sander, L. (1992). Letter to the editor. Discussion of Evelyne Schwaber's "Countertransference: The analyst's retreat from the patient's vantage point." *International Journal of Psychoanalysis, 73*, 582–584.

Schmahl, C., Lanius, R. A., Pain, C., & Vermetten, E. (2010). Biological framework for traumatic dissociation related to early life trauma. In R. A. Lanius, E. Vermetten, & C. Pain (Eds.), *The impact of early life trauma on health and disease: The hidden epidemic.* New York, NY: Cambridge University Press.

Schore, A. N. (1994). *Affect regulation and the origin of the self: The neurobiology of emotional development.* New York, NY: Norton.

Schore, A. N. (2003a). *Affect regulation and disorders of the self.* New York, NY: Norton.

Schore, A. N. (2003b). *Affect regulation and the repair of the self.* New York, NY: Norton.

Schore, A. N. (2006). *Neurobiology and attachment theory in psychotherapy: psychotherapy for the twenty-first century.* Presented at Mt.

Sinai Medical Center at PsyBC conference, CD Rom. Retrieved , from http://www.psybc.com

Schore, A. N. (2007). *The interpersonal neurobiological origins of curiosity: An essential human activity.* Paper presented at the Genoa Science Festival.

Schore, A. N. (2009). Attachment trauma and the developing right brain: Origins of pathological dissociation. In P. Dell & J. O'Neil (Eds.), *Dissociation and the dissociative disorders: DSM-V and beyond.* New York, NY: Routledge.

Schore, A. N. (2010a). Part 3: Synopsis. In R. Lanius, E. Vermetten, & C. Pain (Eds.), *The impact of early life trauma on health and disease: The hidden epidemic.* New York, NY: Columbia Press.

Schore, A. N. (2010b). The right brain implicit self: A central mechanism of the psychotherapy change process. In J. Petrucelli (Ed.), *Knowing, not knowing and sort of knowing.* London: Karnac Books.

Schore, A. N. (2011). The right brain implicit self lies at the core of psychoanalysis. *Psychoanalytic Dialogues, 21,* 1–26.

Schore, A. N. (2012). *The science of the art of psychotherapy.* New York, NY: Norton.

Schore, A. N. (2013). Regulation theory and the early assessment of attachment and autistic spectrum disorders: A response to Voran's clinical case. *Journal of Infant, Child, and Adolescent Psychotherapy, 12*(3), 164–189.

Schore, A. N., & Newton, R. (2012). Using regulation theory to guide clinical assessments of mother-infant attachment relationships. In A. N. Schore, *The science of the art of psychotherapy.* New York, NY: Norton.

Schore, J. R., & Schore, A. N. (2008). Modern attachment theory: The central role of affect regulation in development and treatment. *Clinical Social Work Journal, 36,* 9–20.

Schutz, L.E. (2005). Broad perspective perceptual disorder of the right hemisphere. *Neuropsychology Review, 15,* 11-27.

Siegel, D. (1999). *The developing mind: How relationships and the brain interact to shape who we are.* New York, NY: Guilford.

Siegel, D. (2004). *Attachment, the brain and the developing mind.* Presentation delivered at Lifespan Learning Conference, Healing Trauma: Attachment, Trauma, the Brain and the Mind.

Siegel, D. (2007). *The mindful brain: Reflection and attunement in the cultivation of well-being.* New York, NY: Norton.

Siegel, D. (2010). *The mindful therapist: A clinician's guide to mindsight and neural integration.* New York, NY: Norton.

Sierra, M., & Berrios, G. E. (1998). Depersonalization: Neurobiological perspectives. *Biological Psychiatry, 44*(9), 898–908.

Sierra, M., Senior, C., Dalton, J., McDonough, M., Bond, A., Phillips, M. L., . . . David, A. S. (2002). Autonomic response in depersonalization disorder. *Archives of General Psychiatry, 59*(9), 833–838.

Slade, A. (1999). Attachment theory and research: Implications for the theory and practice of individual psychotherapy with adults. In J. Cassidy & P. Shaver (Eds.), *Handbook of attachment: Theory, Research, and Clinical Applications* (pp. 762–782). New York, NY: Guilford Press.

Slade, A. (2008). Mentalization as a frame for working with parents in child psychotherapy. In E. Jurist, A., Slade, & S. Bergner (Eds.), *Mind to mind: Infant research, neuroscience, and psychoanalysis.* New York, NY: Other Press. **P307-334**

Slade, A. (2012). *Minding the baby: attachment, fear, and mentalization.* Paper presented at the PsyBC conference The Most Compelling Work We Do: Treating Relational Trauma in Mother-Infant Dyads.

Slochower, J. (1996). *Holding and psychoanalysis.* New York, NY: Routledge.

Solomon, M., & Tatkin, S. (2011). *Love and war in intimate relationships.* New York, NY: Norton.

Spiegel, D., Loewenstein, R., Lewis-Fernandez, R., Sar, V., Simeon, D.,

Vermetten, E., . . . Dell, P. (2011). Dissociative disorders in DSM-5. *Depression and Anxiety, 28,* 824–852.

Sroufe, A. L. (1977). Attachment as an organizational construct. *Child Development, 48,* 1184–1199.

Sroufe, A. L. (1979). Socioemotional development. In J. Osofsky (Ed.), *Handbook of infant development.* New York, NY: Wiley.

Sroufe, A. L. (1996). *Emotional development: The organization of emotional life in the early years.* New York, NY: Cambridge University Press.

Sroufe, A. L., Egeland, B., & Carlson, E. A. (2005). *The development of the person.* New York, NY: Guilford Press.

Steel, M. (2012). *Finding the antidote to child maltreatment.* Paper presented at PsyBC conference The Most Compelling Work We Do: Treating Relational Trauma in Mother-Infant Dyads.

Steele, H., Steel, M., & Fonagy, P. (1996). Associations among attachment classifications in mothers, fathers and their infants: Evidence for a relationship-specific perspective. *Child Development, 67,* 541–555.

Steele, K., Dorahy, M. J., van der Hart, O., & Jenhuis, R. S. (2010). Dissociation versus alterations in consciousness: Related but different concepts. In P. Dell & J. O'Neil (Eds.), *Dissociation and the dissociative disorders: DSM-V and beyond.* New York, NY: Routledge.

Stern, D. B. (1997). *Unformulated experience: From dissociation to imagination in psychoanalysis.* Hillsdale, NJ: Analytic Press.

Stern, D. N. (1986). *The interpersonal world of the child.* New York, NY: Basic Books.

Stern, D. N. (2004). *The present moment in psychotherapy and everyday life.* New York, NY: Norton.

Thelen, E., & Smith, L. (1996). *A dynamic systems approach to the development of cognition and action.* Cambridge, MA: MIT Press.

Tolmacz, R. (2009). Transference and attachment. In J. H. Obegi & E.

Berant (Eds.), *Attachment theory and research in clinical work with adults*. New York, NY: Guilford Press.

Tomkins, S. (1962). *Affect imagery consciousness*, Vol. 1: *The positive affects*. London: Tavistock.

Tomkins, S. (1987). Shame. In D. L. Nathanson (Ed.), *The many faces of shame* (pp. 133–161). New York, NY: Guilford Press.

Trevarthen, C. (1979). Communication and cooperation in early infancy: A description of primary intersubjectivity. In M. M. Bullows (Ed.), *Before speech: The beginning of interpersonal communication* (pp. 321-348). New York, NY: Cambridge University Press.

Trevarthen, C. (1993). The self born in intersubjectivity: The psychology of infant communicating. In U. Neisser (Ed.), *The perceived self: Ecological and interpersonal sources of self-knowledge* (pp. 121–173).

Tronick, E. (2007). *The neurobehavioral and social-emotional development of infants and children*. New York, NY: Norton.

Tronick, E. (2008). Multilevel meaning making and dyadic expansion of consciousness theory: The emotional and the polymorphic polysemic flow of meaning. In D. Fosha, D. Siegel, & M. Solomon (Eds.), *The healing power of emotion*. New York, NY: Norton.

Van der Kolk, B. H. (2005). Developmental trauma disorder: Towards a rational diagnosis for chronically traumatized children. *Psychiatric Annals, 35*(5), 401–408.

Van der Kolk, B. H., & Fisler, H. (1995). Dissociation and the fragmentary nature of traumatic memories: Overview and exploratory study. *Journal of Traumatic Stress, 8*(4), 505–525.

Van der Kolk, B. H., & Fisler, H., & Rita, E. (1994). Childhood abuse and neglect and loss of self-regulation. *Bulletin of the Menninger Clinic, 58*(2), 145–168.

Van der Kolk, B. A., Pelcovitz, D., Roth, S., Mandel, F., McFarlane, A., & Herman, J. (1996). Dissociation, somatization, and affect dysregulation: The complexity of adaptation to trauma. *American Journal of Psychiatry, 153*(Suppl.), 83–93.

van IJzendoorn, M. H. (1995). Adult attachment representations, parental responsiveness and infant attachment: A meta-analysis on the predictive validity of the Adult Attachment Interview. *Psychological Bulletin, 117,* 387–403.

Vermetten, V., Dorahy, M. J., & Spiegel, D. (2007). *Traumatic dissociation: Neurobiology and treatment.* Arlington, VA: American Psychiatric Publishing.

Wallin, D. (2007). *Attachment in psychotherapy.* New York, NY: Guilford Press.

Westen, D., Nakash, O., Thomas, C., & Bradley, R. (2006). Clinical assessment of attachment patterns and personality disorder in adolescents and adults. *Journal of Consulting and Clinical Psychology, 74*(6), 1065–1085.

Widiger, T. (2003). Personality disorder diagnosis. *World Psychiatry, 2*(3), 131–135.

Wilkinson, M. (2010). *Changing minds in therapy: Emotion, attachment, trauma, and neurobiology.* New York, NY: Norton Press.

Wink, P. (1991). Two faces of narcissism. *Journal of Personality and Social Psychology, 61,* 590–597.

Winnicott, D. W. (1958). The capacity to be alone. *International Journal of Psychoanalysis, 39,* 416–420.

Winnicott, D. W. (1965). *The maturational processes and the facilitating environment.* New York, NY: International Universities Press.

Winnicott, D. W. (1971). *Playing and reality.* London: Routledge.

Winnicott, D. W. (1972). *Holding and interpretation.* London: Hogarth Press.

Wurmser, L. (1987). Shame: The veiled companion to narcissism. In D. L. Nathanson (Ed.), *The many faces of shame.* New York, NY: Guilford Press.

Zanarini, M. C., Ruser, T., Frankenburg, F. R., & Hennen, J. (2000). The dissociative experiences of borderline patients. *Comparative Psychiatry, 41*(3), 223–227.

INDEX

Note: Page locators accompanied by *f* indicate figure, *t* indicate table, and *n* indicate footnote.

AAI. *see* Adult Attachment Interview (AAI)

absorption
  moderate states of, 160–61

active–submissive strategy
  in narcissistic personality disorders, 175–76

adaptation
  Darwinian principles of, 27
  to self-states, 31

adaptive capacity
  self-states and, 29

adaptive functioning, 2–3
  affect regulation in, 48

adaptive shame, 185

adaptive strategies, 87

adaptive value–positive approach, 135

adult attachment, 92–97

Adult Attachment Interview (AAI), 85, 181, 97*n*, 92–97, 92*n*

in attachment system activation, 93

of avoidant and preoccupied individuals, 138

coherent narrative in, 94–95

function of, 92–93

"metacognitive monitoring" during, 99

research using, 95–96

Strange Situation Procedure and, 96–97, 97*n*

adult personality patterns
  developing from infant attachment patterns, 87–88

affect(s), 5–6
  body-based, 74, 7–8
  categorical (secondary), 5, 106–7. *see also* categorical (secondary) affect
  defined, 6, 5, 27
  described, 1
  discrete, 106

affect(s) (*continued*)
    dissociated, 154, 46–47, 219–31
    distal implicit communication
        of, 79–80
    dyadic regulation of, 9–11
    dysregulated, 47, 45, 223–24
    dysregulation of, 28
    elaboration of, 108
    exchange of, 8–9
    explicit, 106
    felt, 109
    function of, 135, 107
    identification of, 108
    implicit communication of,
        7–9, 79–80
    interpersonal transmission
        of, 8
    mentalization of, 105–9
    naming of, 107–8, 108*n*
    negative, 118
    observed, 6
    overwhelmed by, 178
    primary, 5–6, 106–7
    regulated. *see also* affect
        regulation
    regulation of, 47, 1–12. *see also*
        affect regulation
affect arousal
    types of, 25
affect-regulating system(s)
    function of, 27
    primary, 49–67, 65*f*. *see also*
        primary affect-regulating
        system

    secondary, 98–111. *see also*
        secondary affect-regulating
        system
    self-states as assemblages of,
        37–46
affect regulation
    in adaptive functioning, 48
    attachment relationship and,
        15–26
    capacities for, 4
    classical attachment theory in
        development of, 85–97. *see
        also* classical attachment
        theory
    deficits in, 214, 155
    described, 1, 38–39
    development of, 83–131
    disordered, 135–53. *see also*
        disordered affect regulation
    effects of, 28
    in infants, 9–11
    primary, 200–1
    procedures used for, 25, 26*t*
    in survival, 2
*Affect Regulation and the Origin
    of the Self,* 2*n*
affect-regulation disorders
    described, 202
affect-regulation theory
    described, ix
affect-regulation therapy
    goals of, 2, 201–5
affect regulation–dysregulation,
    2, 3*f*

affect resilience, 2–4
affect states
 lack of responsiveness to others
  in, 178
affect tolerance, 2, 146, 140
 in regulation theory, 201–2
 strengthening of, 211–18
affective dysregulation, 55–56
affective reunions
 psychobiology of, 114
affective subsystems
 comprising self-states, 37–46
Ainsworth, M.D.S., 85, 87, 92, 96,
  112, 15–16
alexithymia
 in avoidant personality, 178
altered states of consciousness
 in dissociated self-states, 36–37
 of dissociative phenomena, 155
 moderate, 161–62
 severe hyperaroused
  dissociation and, 159
ambivalent infants, 24
ambivalent-resistant attachment
 pattern, 21
amygdala, 56–58, 55f
 development of, 142n
 fear responses of, 58
 hippocampus relationship
  with, 60
 overregulated, 60
 oversensitive, 60
anger
 narcissism and, 178–79

outbursts of, 178–79
 preoccupied trauma and, 147
ANS. see autonomic nervous
  system (ANS)
anterior cingulate, 56, 57, 59, 55f
anxiety
 defined, 201n
 social, 173
anxious/ambivalent attachment
 pattern, 25, 17
 characteristics of, 25, 26t
arousal
 affect, 25
 parasympathetic, 146, 121–26
 sympathetic, 178–79, 114–20
 types of, 155–56, 156f
arousal levels
 range of, 2, 3f
arousal patterns
 insecure, 138–39
assimilation
 left brain in, 72
assimilative function
 of internal working model,
  90–91
attachment
 adult, 92–97
 avoidant, 145, 176–79
 disorganized, 23, 179–81,
  33n. see also disorganized
  attachment
 insecure, 17–25, 135–53. see
  also insecure attachment
 "internal working model of," 87

attachment (*continued*)
preoccupied, 22, 174–76
secure. *see* secure attachment
types of, 15–26. *see also*
specific types, e.g., avoidant
attachment
attachment pattern(s)
characteristics of, 25, 26*t*
implications of, 168
infant, 87–88
parenting roles in, 95–96
types of, 15–26. *see also*
specific types, e.g., avoidant
attachment
attachment relationship(s)
affect regulation and, 15–26
internal working model in
mediating, 89–90
secure, 140
attachment system
AAI in activating, 93
aim of, 86
attachment theory, 16
attachment transferences, 77–78
attachment trauma, 187
attention
consciousness determined by,
25
described, 38
focal, 58
forms of, 38–39
free-floating, 207*n*
function of, 39

attentional system, 38–39
attunement, 9
described, 120
"psychobiological synchrony"
of, 120
vitalizing, 120, 231–32
autobiographical memories, 76–77
automaticity
in dissociated self-states, 35–36
of dissociative phenomena, 155
autonomic nervous system (ANS),
6, 61–66, 65*f*
components of, 62
in disorganized attachment,
151–52
dual circuits connecting to
limbic system, 64–66, 65*f*
early relational trauma effects
on, 140–41, 141*n*
functions of, 63, 62
in homeostatic states, 63
limbic system connected to,
64–66, 65*f*
in moderate dissociation, 167
in modern attachment theory,
126–29
parasympathetic aspect of, 62
in psychobiology of secure
attachment, 172–73
in regulation theory, 196
sympathetic aspect of, 62
as target of implicit therapeutic
actions, 213–14

avoidance
  hypoarousal related to, 138
avoidance of conflict
  narcissistic personality
    disorders and, 177
avoidant attachment, 20, 25, 17, 145
  characteristics of, 25, 26t
  psychobiology of, 176–79
avoidant child, 24–25
avoidant-dismissive attachment
  pattern, 20
avoidant infant(s), 24
  described, 143–46
  shame of, 145
avoidant narcissism, 174–76
avoidant patients
  therapeutic actions for, 209
avoidant personality(ies), 170–71
  alexithymia in, 178
  male vs. female, 170
avoidant therapists, 217–18
avoidant transference, 217
avoidant trauma
  psychobiology of, 143–46
  results of, 156
avoidant–avoidant marriages,
  177
avoidant–avoidant therapeutic
  dyads, 177
avoidant–dismissive dyad,
  143–46
Axis 1 psychiatric disorders, 168
  vulnerability to, 169

Becoming Attached, 85n
Beebe, B., 151
behavior(s)
  contradictory, 22–23
Bergman, A., 114
bias(es)
  parasympathetic, 145
Bion, W., 207n
biorhythm(s)
  "co-synchronized," 231
Blizzard, R., 30
body-based affect, 74, 7–8
body-based experience
  naming of, 107–8, 108n
bodymind
  theory of, 13–82
Bollas, C., 73
borderline personality disorder
  (BPD)
  characteristics of, 4, 179
  hyper-and hypoaroused, 169
  mentalization in, 100
  psychobiology of disorganized
    attachment and, 179–81
  splitting in, 42
Boston Change Process Study
  Group, 213, 213n
bottom-up therapies, 196
Bowlby, J., 96, 168, 117, 216,
  15–18, 85–92, 20–22, 86n,
  112n, ix
BPD. see borderline personality
  disorder (BPD)

Bradley, R., 180
brain(s)
    as complex system, 50–52
    "coo" of, 59
    described, 50–52
    integration of, 69–70
    left. *see* left brain
    modes of, 50
    modules of, 50
    as open system, 52
    "red phone" of, 57–58
    right. *see* right brain
    structures of, 53
    subsystems of, 50
    systems of, 50
    vertical organization of, 54
brainstem, 53
Broca's area for expressive
    language, 70*n*
Bromberg, P., 160, 229*n*
Broucek, F.J., 189, 183

cannabinoid(s)
    in severe hyperaroused
        dissociation, 159
"cannot classify" attachment
    pattern, 24, 17
caregiver(s)
    disorganized, 150–52
    preoccupied, 24, 146–50
Carter, 198
categorical (secondary) affect,
    5–6, 106–7

defined, 5
    hyperaroused, 5
    hypoaroused, 5
    types of, 5
cerebral cortex, 54, 53
chalkboard of the mind, 76
chronic dissociation, 154–67
    in developmental arrest, 155
Cicchetti, D., 4*n*
classical attachment theory, 85–97
    adult attachment and, 92–97
    affect regulation development
        and, 85–97
    internal working model and,
        85–91
"co-synchronized biorhythms," 231
cognition
    verbal, 209
cognitive subsystems
    comprising self-states, 37–46
    flashbacks in, 45–46
cognitive systems
    self-states as assemblages of,
        37–46
coherent narrative(s), 99–100
    in AAI, 94–95
    Grice's maxims in measuring,
        94–95
cold shaming, 145
communication
    of affect, 7–9
    implicit. *see* implicit
        communication

compartmentalization
  in dissociated self-states, 36
compartmentalization of content
  of dissociative phenomena,
    155
complex system(s)
  brain as, 50–52
  described, 50–52
  deterioration of, 51
  self-organization of, 51
  shifting states by, 51
  therapeutic actions effects on,
    52
"complex" trauma, 187, 136
complexity theory, 50–51
  principles of, 51
  shifting states in, 51
conflict
  avoidance of, 177
congruent dyads, 217–18
conscious representations, 41
consciousness
  altered states of. *see* altered
    states of consciousness
  attention in determination of,
    25
  focal attention for, 58
  threshold for, 70
content
  compartmentalization of, 155
contradictory behaviors, 22–23
"coo"
  of brain, 59

coping
  narcissistic personality
    disorders and, 177
  resigned/passive, 177
corpus callosum, 68, 69f
cortisol, 141
countertransference, 215–18
curiosity
  of therapist, 216
cycling
  reciprocal, 63

Damasio, A.R., 6, 6n
Darwin, C., 5, 106, 184, 5n
Darwinian principles of
    adaptation, 27
declarative memory, 76–77
deficient reflective
    functioning
  BPD and, 179
Dell, P., 34
Demos, V., 118
denactment(s), 224–25
depersonalization
  in freeze states, 158
derealization
  in freeze states, 158
despair
  narcissistic personality
    disorders and, 177
detachment
  moderate *vs.* severe, 162
  sense of, 36–37

development
   of affect regulation, 83–131
   of amygdala, 142n
   of primary affect-regulating
      system, 112–31. see also
      primary affect-regulating
      system development
   theory of, 83–131
developmental arrest
   chronic dissociation in, 155
developmental psychiatric
      disorders
   dissociated shame and, 183
"developmental" trauma, 187, 136
Diagnostic and Statistical Manual
      of Mental Disorders, 5th
      edition (DSM-V)
   on dissociative disorders, 34
discrete affect(s), 106
disgust
   display of, 122, 122n
   narcissistic personality
      disorders and, 177
dismissive attachment pattern, 20
disordered affect regulation
   developmental origins of, 135–53
   relational trauma resulting in,
      137–39
disorganized attachment, 23,
      150–52, 33n
   ANS in, 151–52
   BPD and, 179–81
   psychobiology of, 179–81
disorganized caregivers, 150–52

disorganized/disoriented
      attachment pattern, 22, 23,
      25, 17
   characteristics of, 25, 26t
disorganized parents, 150–52
disorganized trauma
   psychobiology of, 150–52
   results of, 156
dissociated affect
   defined, 154
   interactive regulation of,
      219–31. see also interactive
      regulation, of dissociated
      affect
   primary affect-regulating
      system and, 46–47
dissociated memories, 42
   of relational trauma, 207
dissociated self-states
   altered states of consciousness
      in, 36–37
   automaticity in, 35–36
   characteristics of, 32–37
   compartmentalization in, 36
   moderately, 160
   partially vs. fully, 30
dissociated shame
   causes of, 183
   in clinical situations, 188–89
   developmental psychiatric
      disorders related to, 183
   emotions associated with, 189
   manifestations of, 188–89
   narcissism and, 188–89

dissociation, 23
  chronic, 154–67
  defined, 32, 156, 157n
  described, 32–33
  developmental origins of, 155
  insecure attachment and, 156, 156f
  moderate. see moderate dissociation
  pathological, 33–34
  peritraumatic, 33, 158
  of primary affect-regulating system, 154
  severe, 157–59. see also severe dissociation
  somatoform, 34
  "subclinical," 157
  subjective experience of, 162
  "subsyndromal," 157
  trauma-based, 42
dissociative disorders
  defined, 34
  DSM-V and ICD-10 on, 34
dissociative identity disorder, 30n
  alters of, 33–34
dissociative phenomena
  characteristics of, 32, 155, 35–37
  described, 155–56
  forms of, 33, 33n
  hyper- vs. hypoaroused, 34, 155
  moderate, 155, 162–63
  severe, 155
  spectrum of severity of, 157

distancing
  narcissistic personality disorders and, 177
dorsal vagal system, 63
  activation of, 158–59
  freeze states in, 181, 158–159
DSM-V. see Diagnostic and Statistical Manual of Mental Disorders, 5th edition (DSM-V)
dyadic regulation
  of affect, 9–11
dysregulated affect, 47, 45
  effects of, 28
dysregulated-dissociated self-states, 32
  subjective experience in, 29–30
dysregulated state
  described, 1–2
dysregulated–dissociated affect
  split-second transmissions of, 223–24
dysregulation
  affective, 55–56
  emotional, 180
  hypoaroused, 137
  rupture–repair sequences of, 127
dysregulation–dissociation
  at low levels of stress, 155
  of therapist, 217

Eagle, M., 197–98
early memory, 77–78
"earned security" studies, 96

egocentrism
  narcissistic personality
    disorders and, 173
Ekman, P., 184, 5n
elaboration
  described, 108
EMDR. *see* eye movement
    desensitization and
    reprocessing (EMDR)
emotion(s)
  shame-related, 189
  "sleeper," 123
emotional connection
  need for, 118–19
emotional detachment
  moderate, 161–62
emotional dysregulation
  defined, 180
emotional information
  deficiencies in processing, 214
"emotional refueling," 114
emotional resilience, 140
  increasing, 211–18
empathy
  deficient, 173
enactment(s), 222–24
  therapeutic, 225–31
endogenous opioids
  in freeze states, 158
  narcissistic personality
    disorders effects of, 178
  overexposure to, 141
endorphin(s)
  overexposure to, 141

episodic memories, 76–77
ethology
  defined, 86n
experience(s)
  reliving, 159
  right brain in integration of,
    71–72
explicit affect(s), 106
explicit memory(ies)
  defined, 76
  described, 76–77
  implicit memory *vs.*, 76–78, 82t
explicit processes
  implicit processes *vs.*, 82t
  left brain in, 68
  mediation of, 70–71
  therapeutic, 209–11
explicit processing
  attributes of, 71–76, 75f
expressive language
  Broca's area for, 70n
exteroceptive information, 40
eye contact
  in implicit communication,
    114–15
eye movement desensitization and
    reprocessing (EMDR), 208n

face-to-face play
  mother–infant, 114–20
fear
  defined, 201n
"feigned death," 158
felt affect, 109

"felt" security, 86
fight-flight-freeze reactions, 86
fight-or-flight reactions, 58
first-order change
  described, 203
  in regulation theory, 197–99
flashback(s), 43
  in cognitive self-state
    subsystems, 45–46
  real-seeming, 159
fluidity (lack of constancy) of
  self- and object
  representation
  BPD and, 179
focal attention
  for consciousness, 58
Fonagy, P., 97, 100, 179, 44n, ix
free-floating attention, 207n
freeze response, 62–63
freeze states
  depersonalization and
    derealization in, 158
  dorsal vagal, 181
  severe hypoaroused
    dissociation and, 158
Freud, S., 27, 90, 74, 73, 185,
  68–69, 41n, 73n, 207n, ix
Friesend, W.V., 184
full mentalization, 44n
  in mentalizing processes
    development, 105–9

gaze aversion, 178
Goldwyn, R., 95

grandiosity
  narcissistic personality
    disorders and, 173
Greenberg, 198
Grice, H.P., 94
growth-enhancing experience
  affect attunement in, 9
  vitalizing attunement in,
    231–32
guilt
  described, 184–86
  onset of, 184
  shame vs., 124, 183–86

"having mind in mind," 101
Hawthorne, N., 186
hedonic tone
  function of, 135
hemispheric dominance
  as influence on personality,
    170–71
Herman, J., 183, 184, 136
hippocampus, 56, 59–61, 55f
  amygdala relationship with,
    60
"holding" environment, 220n
homeostatic states
  ANS in, 63
Horney, K., 25n
Howell, E., 30
HPA. see hypothalamic-pituitary-
  adrenal (HPA) axis
hyper-aroused dissociative
  phenomena, 34, 155

hyperarousal, 58
attuned, 115
in BPD, 169
of dissociative phenomena, 155
enactments and, 224
in moderate dissociation,
160–61
in narcissistic personality
disorders, 169, 173–76
preoccupied trauma and,
146–50
in severe dissociation, 159
hyperaroused dissociation
moderate, 163–67
severe, 159
hyperindependence
narcissistic personality
disorders and, 177
hyperreactivity, 58
hypervigilance, 58, 60, 22
hypo-aroused dissociative
phenomena, 34
hypoarousal, 137
avoidance and, 138
in BPD, 169
of dissociative phenomena, 155
enactments and, 224
in moderate dissociation,
160–61
in narcissistic personality
disorders, 169
negative, 144–45
in severe dissociation, 158–59

hypoaroused-dissociated self-
states, 31
hypoaroused dissociation
moderate, 164–67
severe, 158–59
hypoaroused dysregulation, 137
hypothalamic-pituitary-adrenal
(HPA) axis, 7, 61–66, 65f
early relational trauma effects
on, 140–41, 141n
functions of, 64
limbic system in, 63
in modern attachment theory,
127
in physiological changes
through release of hormones,
64

ICD-10
on dissociative disorders, 34
"ideal types"
deviation from, 170–71
implicit cognitive, 78–79, 82t
implicit communication, 206,
79–81, 196–97, 82t
of affect, 7–9
distal, 79–80
eye contact in, 114–15
involuntary, 208
implicit memory(ies), 197
described, 77–78
explicit memory vs., 76–78, 82t
of rupture–repair sequences

of dysregulation and
reregulation, 127
implicit processes
explicit processes vs., 82t
mediation of, 70–71
right brain in, 68–82
implicit processing
attributes of, 71–76, 75f
implicit self(ves), 80–81, 82t
described, 80
repair of, 205
implicit self-states, 81
implicit therapeutic processes,
211–18
targets of, 213–14
implicit transference-
countertransference
relationship, 216–17
incongruent dyads, 217–18
infant(s)
affect regulation in, 9–11
ambivalent, 24
avoidant, 24, 143–46
infant attachment patterns
adult personality patterns
developing from, 87–88
infant–mother dyads, 114–20
information
emotional, 214
exteroceptive, 40
interoceptive, 40
physioemotional, 64
socioemotional, 64

information processing
right brain in, 206–8, 69–71
insecure arousal patterns
limitations imposed by, 138–39
insecure attachment, 17–25
dissociation and, 156, 156f
emotional transactions of, 139
organized, 173–79
personality disorders and,
169–73
stress response patterns of, 138
structured pattern of, 155–56
traumas of, 135–53. see also
relational trauma(s)
insecure internal working model,
216–17
as adaptation to chronic
misattunement–shame, 187
composition of, 200
development of, 203
in shame anticipation, 190
insecure patient–therapist dyads,
217
insecure personalities
dissociated shame and, 189
insight, 78–79
insula, 59, 56
insular cortex, 59
integration
failure of, 42
integration of past, future, and
present experience
right brain in, 71

intensity
function of, 135
intention(s)
interpretation of others', 103
intentional
defined, 101
interactive regulation
case example, 220
of dissociated affect, 219–31
"interiorized actions," 87
internal working model(s), 85–91
assimilative function of,
90–91
of attachment, 87
attachment figure in, 88–89
autonomic response in, 139
described, 87–88
evaluation and prediction
components of, 88–89
as idea of work in progress, 91
insecure. *see* insecure internal
working model
in mediating attachment
relationships, 89–90
secure, 126, 203–4
ways of being in relationships,
87–88
interoceptive information, 40
interpersonal neurobiology
described, 196
uses of, 195–96, 195*n*
interpretation(s)
left brain in, 72

intersubjectivity
"primary," 80
intrusive memories, 159
intuition, 78–79
isolationism
narcissistic personality
disorders and, 177

Janet, P., 42
joy
paucity of, 145

Karen, R., 85*n*
Kaufman, G., 183.184
Kernberg, O., 107*n*
Kierkegaard, 119, 218, 117, 211–13
known
unthought, 73
Kohut, H., 185
Konrad, 87*n*
language
expressive, 70*n*
receptive, 70*n*
Lanius, R.A., 34, 156, 156*n*–57*n*
LeDoux, J., 215, 6*n*
left brain
engaging of, 214
information processed by,
70–71
secondary processing by, 214
left-brain dominance
personality disorders and,
170–71

left-brain explicit processes, 68
right-brain implicit processes
vs., 82t
left-brain processing, 214, 71–76,
75f
assimilative quality of, 72
secondary, 74, 214, 75f
speed of, 72–73
Levy, K., 179
Lewis, H.B., 183, 185, 123–24
Lewis, M., 111
Lifespan Learning Conferences, 191
limbic system, 53–61
amygdala of, 57–58
anterior cingulate of, 59
connection to ANS, 64
"coo" of, 59
described, 53
dual circuits connecting to
ANS, 64–66, 65f
early relational trauma effects
on, 140–41, 141n
function of, 7
functions of, 53–55
hierarchical component
organization of, 57
hippocampus of, 59–61
in HPA axis, 63
insula of, 59
integration of, 55–56, 56f
location of, 55–56, 56f, 55f
in modern attachment theory,
126–27

orbitofrontal cortex of, 56, 57,
55f
postnatal growth spurt of,
53–54
in primary affect-regulating
system development, 113–14
self-states of, 55
subcortical structures of, 57
as target of implicit therapeutic
actions, 213–14
thinking part of, 57
Liotti, G., 179, 157
Lorenz, K., 87n, 86n

Mahler, M., 114
Main, M., 92, 85, 112, 98–100
marriage(s)
avoidant–avoidant, 177
McGilchrist, I., 72, 74, 68
"me-but-not-me," 162
memory(ies). see also specific
types
autobiographical, 76–77
declarative, 76–77
dissociated, 42, 207
early, 77–78
episodic, 76–77
explicit, 76–78, 82t
implicit, 197, 127, 76–78, 82t
intrusive, 159
narrative, 77
phobia of, 42
procedural, 77–78

memory(ies) (*continued*)
recording and retrieval of,
59–61
semantic, 76–77
working, 76
memory system, 42–44
mentalization, 98–111. *see also*
secondary affect-regulating
system
of affect, 209, 105–9
in borderline personality
disorder, 100
defined, 98, 101, 109*n*
described, 98, 100–1
full, 105–9, 44*n*
measure of, 101*n*
mind reading in, 100–1
in secure attachment
development, 101–2
mentalization-based therapy,
105*n*
mentalization of affect states
in top-down treatments, 209
mentalization theory, 11, 98*n*, ix
"mentalizing," 99, 99*n*
mentalizing capacities
emergence of, 130
mentalizing processes
development of, 102–5. *see*
also specific modes, e.g.,
teleological mode
mentalizing system
development of, 130–31

metacognition
in secure attachment, 93
"metacognitive monitoring"
during AAI, 99
mind reading
in mentalization, 100–1
mindfulness practice, 208*n*
"minding the baby," 102
misattunement(s)
insecure internal working
model as adaptation to, 187
shame and, 190–91
therapist's, 190
misattunement ruptures, 144
misattunement–dysregulation–
attunement–reregulation, 126
misattunement–shame–collapse–
repair, 125
moderate detachment
severe detachment *vs.*, 162
moderate dissociation, 157,
160–67
ANS in, 167
case example, 161
described, 160
hyperaroused, 163–67, 160–61
hypoaroused, 164–67
as relational trauma sequelae,
155
severe dissociation *vs.*, 162
symptoms of, 160–61
moderate dissociative phenomena
examples of, 155, 162–63

moderate emotional detachment,
161–62
moderate hypoaroused
dissociation, 164–67
moderate shaming, 144
regulation theory on, 185
modern attachment theory,
112–31. *see also* primary
affect-regulating system
development
ANS in, 126–29
development of capacity to
regulate parasympathetic
arousal in, 121–26
development of capacity to
regulate sympathetic arousal
in, 114–20
HPA axis in, 127
limbic system in, 126–27
neurobiology of secure
attachment in, 126–28
optimal neurological
development of, 128
module(s)
brain, 50
"moments of meeting," 116n
mother–infant dyads, 114–20
mother–infant face-to-face play,
114–20

narcissism
avoidant, 174–76
healthy, 185–86

as personification of shame,
188–89
preoccupied, 174, 176–79
narcissistic equilibrium
management of, 130
narcissistic personality disorders
active–submissive strategy in,
175–76
anger outbursts associated
with, 178–79
characteristics of, 173–79
deficiencies in regulation
underlying, 4
endogenous opioids effects on,
178
hyperaroused, 169, 173–76
hypoaroused, 169
organized insecure attachment
and, 173–79
psychobiology of, 174–79
self-states in, 30
shame and, 186, 175
types of, 173
narrative(s)
coherent, 94, 99–100
"truthful and collaborative," 95
narrative memories, 77
Nathanson, D., 185, 183
negative affect(s)
maternal responses to, 118
negative/avoid, 135
negative hypoarousal, 144–45
neural networks, 50

neurodevelopmental disorder
relational trauma as, 140–42
neuron(s), 50
excess, 141
Newton, R., 195–96
nightmare(s), 159
nonconscious, 73n
"not-me," 162
"not really," 162

"object equivalence," 44n
observation(s)
left brain in, 72
in top-down treatments, 209
observed affect, 6
opioid(s)
endogenous. see endogenous
opioids
orbitofrontal cortex, 56, 57, 204,
55f
function of, 61
location of, 56, 57, 61, 55f
organized insecure attachment
narcissistic personality
disorders and, 173–79
overdependence, 137–38

Panksepp, J., 6n
parasympathetic arousal
development of capacity to
regulate, 121–26
as stress response, 146
parasympathetic bias, 145

parasympathetic nervous system,
63, 62
described, 121, 121n
dorsal vagal components of,
158
parent(s)
disorganized, 150–52
parenting roles
in attachment patterns, 95–96
partially dissociated self-states, 30
pathogenesis
theory of, 133–91
pathological dissociation, 33–34
perceptual system, 40
peritraumatic dissociation, 33
in freeze states, 158
personality(ies)
attachment patterns
implications for, 168
avoidant, 178, 170–71
development of, 87–88
factors shaping, 170
hemispheric dominance effects
on, 170–71
insecure, 189
preoccupied, 170–71
uniqueness of, 170
personality disorders, 168–82
Axis 1 psychiatric disorders,
168
characteristics of, 170
deviations from ideal type in,
170–71

insecure attachment and, 169–73
narcissistic. *see* narcissistic
   personality disorders
pervasive dissociated shame,
   183–91
"phobia" of memories, 42
physioemotional information
   limbic system in processing
   and integrating, 64
Piaget, J., ix
Pine, F., 114
play
   mother–infant face-to-face,
   114–20
Porges, S., 63, 158, 8*n*
post-traumatic stress disorder
   (PTSD)
   severe dissociation of, 158
   shame associated with, 186–87
   types of, 157*n*
preconscious
   system, 73
"prementalizing," 44*n*
preoccupied attachment, 22
   psychobiology of, 174–76
preoccupied caregivers, 24, 146–50
preoccupied narcissism, 174,
   176–79
preoccupied patients
   therapeutic actions for, 209
preoccupied personalities,
   170–71
preoccupied therapists, 217–18

preoccupied transference, 217
preoccupied trauma
   anger with, 147
   hyperarousal with, 146–50
   psychobiology of, 146–50
   results of, 155–56
   shaming in, 148–49
"present moments," 220*n*
presymbolic representations, 41
"pretend," 44*n*
pretend mode
   in mentalizing processes
   development, 104
pride–shame axis
   regulation of, 130
primary affect, 5–6, 106–7
primary affect-regulating system
   ANS of, 61–66, 65*f*. *see also*
      autonomic nervous system
      (ANS)
   described, 49–50
   dissociated affect and, 46–47
   dissociation of, 154
   function of, 49–50
   HPA axis of, 61–66, 65*f*. *see
      also* hypothalamic-pituitary-
      adrenal (HPA) axis
   limbic system of, 53–61. *see
      also* limbic system
   neurobiological structures
      comprising, 52–67. *see also*
      specific components, e.g.,
      limbic system

primary affect-regulating system
(*continued*)
neurobiology of, 49–67, 65*f*
reorganization of, 204–5
repair of, 204–5
secondary affect-regulating
system *vs.*, 109–11
primary affect-regulating system
development, 112–31. *see also*
modern attachment theory;
primary affect-regulating
system
of capacity to regulate
parasympathetic arousal,
121–26
of capacity to regulate
sympathetic arousal, 114–20
limbic system in, 113–14
neurobiology of secure
attachment in, 126–28
optimal neurological, 128
phases of, 113
primary affect regulation, 200–1
"primary intersubjectivity," 80
procedural memory, 77–78
psychiatric disorders
Axis 1, 168–69
developmental, 183
psychic equivalence mode
in mentalizing processes
development, 104
"psychobiological synchrony"
of attunement, 120

"psychobiology of affective
reunions," 114
psychoeducation
in top-down treatments, 209
psychoform symptoms, 34
psychoneurobiological theory
of development of self-
regulation, 112
psychopathology
attachment patterns
implications for, 168
psychotherapy
pitfalls associated with, ix–x
PTSD. *see* post-traumatic stress
disorder (PTSD)

"real-but-not-really," 162
real-seeming flashbacks, 159
receptive language
Wernicke's area for, 70*n*
reciprocal cycling, 63
"red phone" of brain, 57–58
reflective functioning, 99, 99*n*,
101*n*
deficient, 179
described, 45
reflective processes
in top-down treatments, 209
reflective system, 44–45
regulated affect. *see also* affect(s);
affect regulation
described, 47
regulated-integrated self-states, 32

regulation
  of affect, 1–12. *see also* affect
    regulation
  deficiencies in, 4
  dyadic, 9–11
  interactive, 219–31. *see also*
    interactive regulation
  in shame, 185
regulation theory, 2, 11, 112,
    27–28, 195–205
  affect tolerance in, 201–2
  ANS in, 196
  background of, 195–96,
    195*n*–96*n*
  described, 201, 170
  enactments from perspective
    of, 224
  first-order change in, 197–99
  on moderate shaming, 185
  relational trauma sequelae in,
    201–2
  resiliency in, 201–2
  right brain as locus of trauma
    and target of therapeutic
    action in, 199–201, 200*f*
  right brain engagement in,
    196–97
  second-order change in, 197–99
  self-state perspective of, 29
  targets of, 199
  therapeutic aims of, 201–5
  therapeutic approaches in, 196–97
  uses of, 195–96, 195*n*

relational trauma(s), 133–91. *see
    also specific types*
  avoidant trauma, 143–46
  defined, 154, 136
  described, 154, 187, 136
  disordered affect regulation
    related to, 137–39
  disorganized trauma, 150–52
  dissociated memories of, 207
  effects of, 140–42
  mechanism of, 142–43
  as neurodevelopmental
    disorder, 140–42
  preoccupied trauma, 146–50
  psychobiology of, 140
  results of, 154
  sequelae of, 154–67. *see also*
    relational trauma sequelae
  types of, 137–39
relational trauma sequelae, 154–
    91. *see also specific types*
  characteristics of, 181
  moderate dissociation, 155
  personality disorders,
    168–82
  pervasive dissociated shame,
    183–91
  in regulation theory, 201–2
relationship(s)
  attachment, 89–90, 15–26
  internal working model in
    mediating, 89–90
  ways of being in, 87–88

reliving experiences, 159
representation(s)
    conscious, 41
    defined, 103
    described, 41
    presymbolic, 41
    symbolic, 41
representational system, 41–42
reregulation
    rupture–repair sequences of, 127
resigned/passive coping
    narcissistic personality
        disorders and, 177
resilience
    affect, 2–4
    defined, 4
    emotional, 140, 211–18
    in regulation theory, 201–2
responsiveness to others
    lack of, 178
reunion(s)
    affective, 114
right brain, 68–82
    engaging of, 214–15
    implicit processes in, 68–82
    implicit processes mediated by,
        76–81, 82t
    information processing by,
        206–8, 69–71
    as locus of trauma and target of
        therapeutic action, 199–201,
        200f
    primary processing by, 214

    in regulation theory, 196–97
    in transitional experiencing
        mediation, 72
right-brain dominance
    personality disorders and,
        170–71
right-brain implicit processes,
    68–82, 82t
    left-brain explicit processes vs.,
        82t
right-brain processing, 71–76,
    214–15, 75f
    cortical, 74, 75f
    deficits in, 75–76
    holistic, 71
    primary, 214
    speed of, 71–73
    subcortical, 74, 75f
rupture–repair sequences
    of dysregulation and
        reregulation
    implicit memories of, 127
Russ, E., 173

"safe but not too safe," 215
safe haven function, 86
Sander, L., 116n
Scarlet Letter, 186
Schore, A.N., 9, 2, 80, 78, 34, 74,
    49, 57, 97, 231, 187, 223, 186,
    184, 218, 183, 215, 120, 213,
    181, 174, 169, 206, 144, 167,
    190, 68–69, 136–37, 177–79,

123–28, 112–16, 139–41,
149–55, 227–29, 2n, 158–59,
195–96, 34n, 25n, 198–201,
115n, 107n, 220n, 121n,
142n, 208n–9n, 85n–87n, ix
Schutz, L.E., 214
second-order change
in regulation theory, 197–99
secondary affect. *see* categorical
(secondary) affect
secondary affect-regulating
system, 98–111. *see also*
mentalization
described, 98
primary affect-regulating
system *vs.*, 109–11
secure attachment, 83–131
mentalization in development
of, 101–2
metacognition in, 93
neurobiology of, 126–28
psychobiology of, 172–73
secure attachment pattern, 17–18
characteristics of, 25, 26t
secure attachment relationship
beneficial effects of, 140
secure-autonomous, 18
secure base function, 86
secure internal working model
establishing, 203–4
misattunement–dysregulation–
attunement–reregulation at
core of, 126

securely attached attachment
pattern, 25
securely attached child, 24
security
"felt," 86
self(ves)
emergence of, 193–235
implicit, 205, 80–81, 82t
multiple, 31
in shame, 184–85
subjective sense of, 80
vitalizing attunement in
emergence of, 231–32
self-development
restoration of, 195–205
self-formation, 233–35
self-in-the-world
model of, 86n
self-regulation
development of, 112
self-state(s), 27–48
adaptation to, 31
adaptive capacity and subjective
experience of, 29–32
affective and cognitive
subsystems comprising,
37–46
attentional system in, 38–39
described, 28
dissociated. *see* dissociated
self-states
dysregulated-dissociated, 32,
29–30

self-state(s) (*continued*)
flashbacks in, 45–46
fully dissociated, 30
hypoaroused-dissociated, 31
implicit, 81
integrated, 29
of limbic system, 55
memory system in, 42–44
narcissistic personalities and,
30
partially dissociated, 30
perceptual system in, 40
reflective system in, 44–45
regulated-integrated, 27–48
representational system in,
41–42
state shifting in, 31
types of, 29
self–affect–object, 107*n*
semantic memory, 76–77
"sense of emergence," 233–35
severe detachment
moderate detachment *vs.*, 162
severe dissociation, 157–59
hyperaroused, 159
hypoaroused, 158–59
moderate dissociation *vs.*, 162
of PTSD, 158, 157*n*
symptoms of, 157
shame. *see also* shaming
adaptive, 185
anticipation of, 190
of avoidant infant, 145

capacity to process adaptively,
123–24
described, 184–86, 123–25
display of, 124–25, 124*n*
dissociated. *see* dissociated
shame
emotions associated with, 189
facial expression with, 184
factors ending, 184
guilt *vs.*, 124, 183–86
insecure internal working
model as adaptation to, 190,
187
misattunements and,
190–91
moderate, 125–26
narcissistic personality
disorders and, 177, 186, 175
onset of, 184
origination of, 124–25
pathogenic power of, 186–88
pervasive dissociated, 183–91
pervasive influence of, 186–88
preoccupied trauma and, 148–49
prototypical experience of, 125
PTSD–related, 186–87
regulating and processing of, 185
regulation theory on, 185
self-involvement of, 184–85
tolerance for, 185
in transference-
countertransference, 189–91
"shame family of emotions," 189

shaming. *see also* shame
    cold, 145
    moderate, 185, 144
    in preoccupied trauma, 148–49
Siegel, D., 9, 53, 51, 196
Slade, A., 102, 100
"sleeper" emotion, 123
Slochower, J., 220*n*
social anxiety
    narcissistic personality
       disorders and, 173
social engagement system, 63
socioemotional information
    limbic system in processing
       and integrating, 64
Solomon, M., 191
somatoform dissociation
    defined, 34
"sort-of-going-on-being," 162
splitting, 42
    BPD and, 179
Sroufe, A.L., 117
state shifting, 31
Stern, D.N., 80, 73, 233, 220, 220*n*
still-face experiment, 116–17, 116*n*
stoicism
    narcissistic personality
       disorders and, 177
Strange Situation Procedure, 16,
    31, 34, 39, 49, 92, 66, 77, 85,
    86, 168, 137, 138, 165, 181,
    95–96, 60–61, 177–78
    AAI and, 96–97, 97*n*

stress
    dysregulation–dissociation at
       low levels of, 155
    maladaptive responses to,
       138–39
stress response pattern(s)
    of insecure attachment, 138
    parasympathetic arousal, 146
stress system, 7, 63–64
structure insecure attachment
    patterns, 24
"subclinical" dissociation, 157
subjective experience
    in dysregulated-dissociated
       self-states, 29–30
"subsyndromal" dissociation, 157
symbolic representations, 41
sympathetic arousal
    development of capacity to
       regulate, 114–20
    regulation of, 118–19
    stifling of, 178–79
sympathetic nervous system, 62
Synaptic Self, 215
synthesis
    right brain in, 71
system preconscious, 73

teleological mode
    in mentalizing processes
       development, 103
temperament
    inborn *vs.* learned, 170

The Master and His Emissary, 74
The Present Moment in Psychotherapy and Everyday Life, 220n
theory(ies). *see also specific types*
    affect-regulation, ix
    attachment, 16
    of bodymind, 13–82
    classical attachment, 85–97
    complexity, 50–51
    of development, 83–131
    mentalization, 98n
    modern attachment, 112–31. *see also* modern attachment theory
    of pathogenesis, 133–91
    psychoneurobiological, 112
    regulation. *see* regulation theory
    of therapeutic actions, 193–235
therapeutic actions, 206–18
    complex systems effects of, 52
    countertransference, 215–18
    explicit therapeutic processes, 209–11
    implicit therapeutic processes, 211–18
    right brain as target of, 199–201, 200f
    theory of, 193–235
    therapeutic alliance, 215–18
    transference, 215–18

therapeutic aims
    of regulation theory, 201–5
therapeutic alliance, 215–18
therapeutic approaches, 196–97
therapeutic dyads
    avoidant–avoidant, 177
therapeutic enactment(s), 225–31
    case example, 230, 225–28
therapeutic processes
    explicit, 209–11
    implicit, 211–18
therapist(s)
    avoidant, 217–18
    curiosity of, 216
    misattunement of, 190
    preoccupied, 217–18
thought
    unformulated, 73
Timbergen, N., 87n, 86n
Todd, R., 111
tolerance
    affect, 2, 146, 140, 201–2, 211–18
    for shame, 185
Tomkins, S., 183
tone
    hedonic, 135
top-down treatments, 196
    described, 209
trance-like states, 23
transference, 77–78, 215–18
    attachment, 77–78

avoidant, 217

preoccupied, 217

"transference resistance," 90

transference–countertransference

implicit, 216–17

shame in, 189–91

transference–countertransference

events, 222–23

transitional experiencing

right brain in mediation of, 72

"transmission gap," 97, 97n

trauma(s)

attachment, 187

avoidant, 156, 143–46

"complex," 187, 136

"developmental," 187, 136

disorganized, 156, 150–52

of insecure attachment,

135–53. see also relational

trauma(s)

preoccupied, 155–56, 146–50.

see also preoccupied trauma

relational, 133–91. see also

specific types and relational

trauma(s)

right brain as locus of, 199–201,

200f

trauma-based dissociation, 42

Trevarthen, C., 80

Tronick, E., 115n

"truthful and collaborative"

narratives, 95

unformulated thought, 73

University of Virginia, 16

unthought known, 73

vagal system

dorsal, 63

ventral, 63

vagus nerve, 63

Van der Kolk, B.A., 136

ventral vagal system, 63

verbal cognition

in top-down treatments, 209

vitalizing attunement, 120

emergence of self by, 231–32

in growth-enhancing

environment, 231–32

Volz, 78

von Cramon, 78

Wenicke's area for receptive

language, 70n

Westen, D., 180

"windows of tolerance," 2, 3f

Winnicott, D.W., 80, 18, 220n

Wolitzky, D.L., 197–98

working memory, 76

Wurmser, L., 189

*The Neuroscience of Human Relationships: Attachment
and the Developing Social Brain*

Louis Cozolino

The Neuroscience of Psychotherapy: Healing the Social Brain

Louis Cozolino

*From Axons to Identity: Neurological Explorations
of the Nature of the Self*

Todd E. Feinberg

*Loving with the Brain in Mind: Neurobiology and
Couple Therapy*

Mona DeKoven Fishbane

*Body Sense: The Science and Practice of Embodied
Self-Awareness*

Alan Fogel

*The Healing Power of Emotion: Affective Neuroscience,
Development & Clinical Practice*

Diana Fosha, Daniel J. Siegel, Marion Solomon

*Healing the Traumatized Self: Consciousness,
Neuroscience, Treatment*

Paul Frewen, Ruth Lanius

*The Neuropsychology of the Unconscious:
Integrating Brain and Mind in Psychotherapy*

Efrat Ginot

The Impact of Attachment

Susan Hart

*Brain-Based Parenting: The Neuroscience of
Caregiving for Healthy Attachment*

Daniel A. Hughes, Jonathan Baylin

*Self-Agency in Psychotherapy: Attachment, Autonomy,
and Intimacy*

Jean Knox

*Infant/Child Mental Health, Early Intervention, and
Relationship-Based Therapies: A Neurorelational Framework
for Interdisciplinary Practice*

Connie Lillas, Janiece Turnbull

*Clinical Intuition in Psychotherapy:
The Neurobiology of Embodied Response*

Terry Marks-Tarlow

*Awakening Clinical Intuition:
An Experiential Workbook for Psychotherapists*

Terry Marks-Tarlow

A Dissociation Model of Borderline Personality Disorder

Russell Meares

*Borderline Personality Disorder and the
Conversational Model: A Clinician's Manual*

Russell Meares

*Neurobiology Essentials for Clinicians:
What Every Therapist Needs to Know*

Arlene Montgomery

Trauma and the Body: A Sensorimotor Approach to Psychotherapy

Pat Ogden, Kekuni Minton, Clare Pain

The Archaeology of Mind: Neuroevolutionary Origins of Human Emotions

Jaak Panksepp, Lucy Biven

The Polyvagal Theory: Neurophysiological Foundations of Emotions, Attachment, Communication, and Self-regulation

Stephen W. Porges

Affect Dysregulation and Disorders of the Self

Allan N. Schore

Affect Regulation and the Repair of the Self

Allan N. Schore

The Science of the Art of Psychotherapy

Allan N. Schore

The Mindful Brain: Reflection and Attunement in the Cultivation of Well-Being

Daniel J. Siegel

Pocket Guide to Interpersonal Neurobiology: An Integrative Handbook of the Mind

Daniel J. Siegel

Healing Moments in Psychotherapy

Daniel J. Siegel, Marion Solomon

Healing Trauma: Attachment, Mind, Body and Brain

Daniel J. Siegel, Marion Solomon

Love and War in Intimate Relationships: Connection, Disconnection, and Mutual Regulation in Couple Therapy

Marion Solomon, Stan Tatkin

The Present Moment in Psychotherapy and Everyday Life

Daniel N. Stern

The Neurobehavioral and Social-Emotional Development of Infants and Children

Ed Tronick

The Haunted Self: Structural Dissociation and the Treatment of Chronic Traumatization

Onno Van Der Hart, Ellert R. S. Nijenhuis, Kathy Steele

Changing Minds in Therapy: Emotion, Attachment, Trauma, and Neurobiology

Margaret Wilkinson

For complete book details, and to order online, please visit the Series webpage at
wwnorton.com/psych/IPNBSeries